D1334382

Foundations of
the Law of Tort

Foundations of
the Law of Tort

Second edition

Glanville Williams, QC, LLD, FBA

Honorary and Emeritus Fellow of Jesus College, Cambridge; Honorary
Bencher of the Middle Temple; formerly Professor of Public Law and
Quain Professor of Jurisprudence in the University of London; and Rouse
Ball Professor of English Law in the University of Cambridge

B. A. Hepple, MA, LLB

of Gray's Inn, Barrister; Professor of English Law in the University of
London at University College

London
Butterworths
1984

England	Butterworth & Co (Publishers) Ltd, 88 Kingsway, LONDON WC2B 6AB
Australia	Butterworths Pty Ltd, SYDNEY, MELBOURNE, BRISBANE, ADELAIDE and PERTH
Canada	Butterworth & Co (Canada) Ltd, TORONTO Butterworth & Co (Western Canada) Ltd, VANCOUVER
New Zealand	Butterworths of New Zealand Ltd, WELLINGTON
Singapore	Butterworth & Co (Asia) Pte Ltd, SINGAPORE
South Africa	Butterworth Publishers (Pty) Ltd, DURBAN
USA	Butterworth Legal Publishers, ST PAUL, Minnesota Butterworth Legal Publishers, SEATTLE, Washington; BOSTON, Massachusetts; and AUSTIN, Texas D & S Publishers, CLEARWATER, Florida

© Butterworth & Co (Publishers) Ltd 1984

British Library Cataloguing in Publication Data

Williams, Glanville
Foundations of the law of tort.—2nd ed.
1. Torts—England
I. Title   II. Hepple, B.A.
344.2063   KD1949
ISBN hardcover 0 406 68386 7
softcover 0 406 68387 5

Typeset by Cotswold Typesetting Ltd, Gloucester
Printed by Billings Bookplan, Worcester

Preface

We hope that this edition, like its predecessor, may prove useful to three classes of reader: the beginner who wants to know something about the scope, purposes and basic concepts of the subject he is about to study, in the context of other compensation systems such as social security and insurance; the student who has progressed some way but who wishes to test rules critically in the light of the purposes of the law; and those ordinary members of the public who would like some understanding of the legal framework in which matters such as the reform of the law relating to personal injuries are being debated. There is also a foreign audience: the first edition was translated into Italian (by Pietro Perlingieri) and Japanese (by Makitaro Hotta).

It is now eight years since the first edition and in that time there have been major developments in case law, an expansion of empirical research into the operation of compensation systems, and a great ferment of ideas, on both sides of the Atlantic, about the theory and future of tort law. This has led us to revise the text extensively, and to replace the former chapter 6 with two new chapters, one dealing more adequately than before with the relationship between tort and social security and the other with some of the underlying issues which face reformers, including the proper balance between corrective and distributive justice, the achievement of economic efficiency and social welfare, the redistribution of the costs of accidents, the relationship with regulatory policies, and whether there is a residual role for tort law. The complexity of the issues is no reason to avoid them, but students may wish to postpone detailed reading of the final chapter until towards the end of their tort course.

Chapters 5, 6 and 7 are the work of the second-named author; the earlier chapters represent the joint work of the authors, but much the greater part of the work of updating has been performed by the second-named author.

February 1984   G.L.W.
                                                               B.A.H.

Acknowledgments

We are extremely grateful to our reviewers and to Peter Glazebrook for comments on the first edition, all of which we have attempted to take into account. For this edition Harold Luntz kindly provided us with information on current developments in Australia, and Ian Dennis directed attention to some changes in civil procedure.

We also wish to thank Reuben Hasson, Gillian Howard, Derek Morgan and Cento Veljanowski for the time and trouble they each took to read all or part of chapters 6 and 7, and for their helpful remarks, and guidance to sources.

We wish to acknowledge the Guardian Royal Exchange Assurance Group's assistance with information on current liability insurance practice; and the copyright holder's permission to quote the lines from Anthony Shaffer's *Sleuth* (published by Calder and Boyars) on p 143.

Contents

Preface   v
Acknowledgments   vii
Table of statutes   xiii
List of cases   xvii
Abbreviations   xxiii

1   The scope and function of tort   1
The meaning of tort   1
The overlap between tort and crime   2
The action for damages and other civil remedies   7
Extra-judicial remedies   10
Tort and breach of contract   13
Tort and equitable wrongs   20
Tort and restitution   22
Claims for statutory compensation   24
Summary of the definition of tort   27
The aims of the law of tort   27

2   The ghost story   31
Old rules as to the forms of action   31
The abolition of the forms of action   32
The influence of the forms of action on legal categories   38
Their surviving importance in pleading   39
The action of trespass   42
The action upon the case   45
The element of fault in trespass   49
The burden of proof   53

3   Damage   56
Damage and injury   56
Nominal damages and the forms of action   57
General and special damage   66
Injunctions   68
Aims of damages: the award of exemplary damages   73
Compensation for personal injury   78
The effect of death on claims in tort   86
Glossary   88

4   Fault   90
The forms of fault: intention, recklessness and inadvertent
      negligence   91
Negligence as an independent tort   95
The duty of care   96
Principle and policy   101
Negligence as a conflict of values   111
The standard of the reasonable person   114
Negligence and strict statutory duties   116
Negligence and nuisance   123
Hazards and strict liability   127
Vicarious liability   132
An evaluation of the fault principle   135

5   Insurance   143
Social justification   143
Intentional torts an exception   145
Limits of liability insurance   149
Types of liability insurance   150
Compulsory insurance   152
Third-party rights   154
Failure to insure   157
The Motor Insurers' Bureau   158
The gaps that remain   160
The effect of liability insurance on the law of tort   163
The effect of insurance on the bringing of actions   166
Evaluation   168

6   Social security   171
The growth of social security   172
Developments since Beveridge   177
Industrial injuries   180
Sickness and disability   183
Overlap with tort damages   186

7   Theory and the future   191
Paths of reform   191
Corrective and distributive justice   197
Economic efficiency   203
Social welfare   206
Redistributing the costs of accidents   209
The regulatory approach   214
Residual role of the law of tort   216

Appendix. Further reading   221

Index   225

Table of statutes

References in the Table to *Statutes* are to Halsbury's Statutes of England (Third Edition) showing the volume and page at which the annotated text of the Act will be found.

PAGE

Accident Compensation Act
1974 (New Zealand) . . . 191
Administration of Justice Act
1969 . . . . . . 35, 37
Administration of Justice Act
1982 (52 *Statutes* 653, 789) . 85,
87, 196
s 1(1) 84
4(2) 86
5 189
6 80
Animals Act 1971 (41 *Statutes*
84)
s 1(1) 129, 130
2 130
4 129
5(3) 12
7 129
(1), (2) 12
9(3) 13
11 . . . . . . 12, 129
British Telecommunications
Act 1981 (51 *Statutes* 1794)
s 23(1) 20
Carriage by Air Act 1961 (2
Statutes 604)
Sch 1 141

PAGE

Chancery Amendment Act 1858
(Lord Cairns's Act) (25 *Statutes*
703) 70
Civil Aviation Act 1982 (52
Statutes 28)
s 76 113
Civil Evidence Act 1968 (12
Statutes 910)
s 11 4
Coal Mines Act 1911
s 102(8) 119
Common Law Procedure Act
1852 . . . . . . 32, 49
Congenital Disabilities (Civil
Liability) Act 1976 (46
Statutes 1837) 216
s 1(2) 207
Control of Pollution Act 1974: 215
Criminal Law Act 1977 (47
Statutes 142)
s 6, 7 12
Crown Proceedings Act 1947 (8
Statutes 844)
s 2 20

Dangerous Wild Animals Act
1976 (46 *Statutes* 130) . . 153

PAGE

Defamation Act 1952 (19 *Statutes* 34)
s 11 145
Employers' Liability Act 1880:   173
Employers' Liability (Compulsory Insurance) Act 1969 (40 *Statutes* 553) . . . 149, 152
Employers' Liability (Defective Equipment) Act 1969 (40 *Statutes* 551)
s 1(2) 141
Employment Act 1980 (50(2) *Statutes* 2630)
s 17 73
Employment Act 1982 (52 *Statutes* 1914, 1955)
s 15–17 . . . . . . 20, 73
18, 19 73
Energy Act 1983
s 27 150
Factories Act 1961 (13 *Statutes* 400) 121
s 14(1) 118, 120
28 119
29(1) 119
Fatal Accidents Act 1846 (23 *Statutes* 780) 87
Fatal Accidents Act 1976 (46 *Statutes* 1115) . . . 86, 189
s 1A 85, 87
2(3) 87
3(5) 87
4 189
Federal Social Security Act 1935 (USA) 172
Forfeiture Act 1982 (52 *Statutes* 524) 147
s 2(4) 148
Guard Dogs Act 1975 (45 *Statutes* 27) 12
Health and Safety at Work etc. Act 1974 (44 *Statutes* 1083) . 122, 214
s 47(1) 116
71(1) 116

PAGE

Housing Act 1980 (50(1) *Statutes* 1191)
s 69(1) 12
Housing (Homeless Persons) Act 1977 (47 *Statutes* 34) . 9
Law Reform (Contributory Negligence) Act 1945 (23 *Statutes* 189) 142
Law Reform (Miscellaneous Provisions) Act 1934 (13 *Statutes* 115) . . . 35, 37, 86
s 1(2) 76, 87
Law Reform (Personal Injuries) Act 1948 (35 *Statutes* 548)
s 1(3) 141
2(1) 188
(4) 189
Limitation Act 1980 (50(1) *Statutes* 1253)
s 2, 5 . . . . . . 19, 40
8(1) 19
11(1) 19, 40
Manchester Ship Canal Act 1897:   24
Mineral Workings (Offshore Installations) Act 1971 (41 *Statutes* 940)
s 11 116
Mines and Quarries Act 1954 (22 *Statutes* 279)
s 48 118
157 119
National Insurance Act 1911 . 176
Norris La Guardia Act 1932 . 72
Nuclear Installations Act 1965 (37 *Statutes* 430) . . . 215
s 16(1) 150
Nuclear Installations Act 1969 (37 *Statutes*, 466) . . . 215
Offences against the Person Act 1861 (8 *Statutes* 147)
s 45 4
Offices, Shops and Railway Premises Act 1963 (13 *Statutes* 584) 121

PAGE

Pneumoconiosis etc. (Workers'
Compensation) Act 1979 (49
Statutes 956) 184
Policyholders Protection Act
1975 (45 *Statutes* 784) . . 157
Post Office Act 1969 (25 *Statutes*
470)
s 29(1) 20
Powers of Criminal Courts Act
1973 (43 *Statutes* 288)
s 38 6
Protection from Eviction Act
1977 (47 *Statutes* 661) . . 12
Public Health Act 1936 (26
Statutes 189) 103
Race Relations Act 1976 (46
Statutes 389) 65, 217
s 57(1), (4) 218
Representation of the People
Act 1983
s 63, 64 63
Reserve and Auxiliary Forces
(Protection of Civil Interests)
Act 1951 (29 *Statutes* 708)
s 13(2) 75
Riding Establishments Act 1964
(2 *Statutes* 275) 153
Riding Establishments Act 1970
(40 *Statutes* 181) 153
Road Traffic Act 1930 (28
Statutes 146) 154
Road Traffic Act 1934 (28
Statutes 176) 153, 154
Road Traffic Act 1972 (42
Statutes 1633)
s 145 152
(4) 155
148 148
(1) . . . 148, 154, 155
(3) 141
(4) 153
149 . . . . 148, 155, 159
(2), (3) 155

PAGE

Road Traffic Act 1972—*contd*
s 150 157
Road Traffic Act 1974 (44
Statutes 1339)
s 20 160
Sex Discrimination Act 1975
(45 *Statutes* 221) 217
s 66(1), (4) 218
Social Security Act 1938 (New
Zealand) 172
Social Security and Housing
Benefits Act 1982 . . 181, 185
Solicitors Act 1974 (44 *Statutes*
1478)
s 37 153
Statute Law Revision Act 1883
(32 *Statutes* 429) 70
Suicide Act 1961 (8 *Statutes* 519)
s 1 147
Supreme Court Act 1981 (51
Statutes 590)
s 32A 80
Supreme Court of Judicature
Act 1873 . . . . 20, 32, 68
Third Parties (Rights Against
Insurers) Act 1930 (3 *Statutes*
175)
s 1 156
Torts (Interference with Goods)
Act 1977 (47 *Statutes* 1340)
s 2(1) 42
Trade Union and Labour
Relations Act 1974 (44
Statutes 1766)
s 13 73
17(1), (2) 73
Unfair Contract Terms Act
1977 (47 *Statutes* 84)
s 2 141
Vaccine Damage Payments Act
1979 (49 *Statutes* 1081) . 184, 202
Workmen's Compensation Act
1897 174

List of cases

PAGE

Ackworth v Kempe (1778) . 164
Adams v Andrews (1964) . . 160
Albert v Motor Insurers' Bureau
  (1972) 161
Anglia Television Ltd v Reed
  (1972) 16
Anns v Merton London
  Borough Council (1978) . 101,
    103, 108
Archer v Brown (1983) . . 76
Arenson v Casson Beckman
  Rutley & Co (1977) . . . 99
Armory v Delamirie (1721) . 74
Ashby v White (1703) . . 61, 63,
    64, 65
Ashton v Turner (1981) . . 99
A-G v Canter (1939) . . . 9
A-G v PYA Quarries Ltd
  (1957) 9
A-G for Dominion of Canada v
  Ritchie Contracting and
  Supply Co Ltd (1919) . . 69
Austin v Dowling (1870) . . 47
Bain v Fothergill (1874) . . 16
Balsamo v Medici (1983) . . 16
Batty v Metropolitan Property
  Realisations Ltd (1978) . . 14
Best v Samuel Fox & Co Ltd
  (1952) 41
Beswick v Beswick (1968) . . 161
Bolton v Stone (1951) . . . 125

PAGE

Bourhill v Young (1943) . . 105
Bowker v Rose (1978) . . . 189
Brown v National Coal Board
  (1962) 118
Browning v War Office
  (1963) 188
Buchanan v Motor Insurers'
  Bureau (1955) 162
Byrne v Boadle (1863) . . . 115
C and P Haulage v Middleton
  (1983) 16
Calliope, The (1891) . . . 33
Caltex Oil (Australia) Pty Ltd v
  Dredge Willemstad (1976) . 109
Cassell & Co Ltd v Broome
  (1972) 74, 76, 79
Cassidy v Ministry of Health
  (1951) 134
Close v Steel Co of Wales Ltd
  (1962) 120
Cocks v Thanet District
  Council (1982) 10
Cole v Turner (1705) . . . 59
Constantine v Imperial Hotels
  Ltd (1944) 65
Cookson v Knowles (1979) . 81
Corfield v Groves (1950) . . 160
Coward v Baddeley (1859) . 59
Cox v Phillips Industries Ltd
  (1976) 17

PAGE

Cunningham v Harrison
(1973) 83
Daly v General Steam
Navigation Co Ltd (1980) . 83
Davy v Spelthorne BC (1983) . 9, 10
De la Bere v Pearson Ltd
(1908) 18
Denny v Supplies and Transport
Co Ltd (1950) 97
Dering v Uris (1964) . . . 59
Devonshire v Jenkins (1978) . 76
Deyong v Shenburn (1946) . 102
Dickenson v Watson (1682) . 51
Dicks v Brooks (1880) . . . 59
Dies v British and International
Mining and Finance Corpn
Ltd (1939) 33
Digby v General Accident Fire
and Life Assurance Corpn Ltd
(1943) 151
Donnelly v Joyce (1974) . . 83
Donoghue v Stevenson. *See*
M'Alister (or Donoghue) v
Stevenson
Drane v Evangelou (1978) . 38, 75
Dunlop v Woolahra Municipal
Council (1982) 63
Duport Steels Ltd v Sirs (1980): 73
Dutton v Bogner Regis UDC
(1972) 101
Edwards v Mallan (1908) . . 14
Edwards v West Herts Group
Hospital Management Com-
mittee (1957) 102
Entick v Carrington (1765) . 57
Esso Petroleum Co Ltd v
Mardon (1975) 100
Express Newspapers Ltd v
McShane (1980) 73
Fire and All Risks Insurance Co
Ltd v Powell (1966) . . 146, 148
Fletcher v Rylands (1866) . . 128
Fowler v Lanning (1959) . 52, 54
Francis v Cockrell (1870) . . 1
Gibbons v Pepper (1695) . . 44

PAGE

Glasgow Corpn v Muir
(1943) 114
Gorely v Codd (1967) . . . 50
Gourietv Union of Post Office
Workers (1978) 9
Gray v Barr (1971) . 146, 147, 148
Gregory v Piper (1829) . . 48
Griffiths v Earl of Dudley
(1881) 173
Groom v Crocker (1939) . . 167
Gurtner v Circuit (1968) . . 161
Hall Bros SS Co Ltd v Young
(1939) 25
Hardy v Motor Insurers' Bureau
(1964) 146
Hargreaves v Bretherton
(1959) 3
Harman v Crilly (1943) . . 163
Hartley (R S) Ltd v Provincial
Insurance Co Ltd (1957) . 156
Haseldine v Daw & Son
(1941) 93
Haseldine v Hosken (1933) . . 145
Haydon v Kent CC (1978) . . 104
Hedley Byrne & Co Ltd v Heller
& Partners Ltd (1964) . 18, 100
Henderson v Henry E Jenkins &
Sons (1970) 115
Heywood v Wellers (1976) . 17
Holmes v Mather (1875) . . 52
Home Office v Dorset Yacht Co
Ltd (1970) 99, 101
Houston v Buchanan 1940 SC
(HL) 17 158
Huckle v Money (1763) . . 75
Hulton v Hulton (1917) . . 8
Hunt v Dowman (1618) . . 60
Hunter v Chief Constable of
West Midlands Police (1982): 4
Irene's Success, The. *See*
Schiffahrt und Kohlen
GmbH v Chelsea Maritime
Ltd (1982) 111
James v British General
Insurance Co (1927) . . . 146

PAGE

Janvier v Sweeney (1919) . . 41
Jarvis v Swan Tours Ltd (1973): 17
Johnson v F E Callow
(Engineers) Ltd (1971) . . 120
Junior Books Ltd v Veitchi Co
Ltd (1983) . . 16, 108, 109, 111,
202, 219
Kennaway v Thompson
(1981) 71
Koufos Czarnikou (1969) . . 17
Langbrook Properties Ltd v
Surrey CC (1969) . . . 99
Launchbury v Morgans (1971) 163
Leeds Industrial Co-op Society
Ltd v Slack (1924) . . . 70
Letang v Cooper (1965) 33, 35, 40,
50, 58
Lim Poh Choo v Camden and
Islington Area Health
Authority (1980) 81
Lincoln v Hayman (1982) . . 189
Lister v Romford Ice and Cold
Storage Co Ltd (1957) . . 164
Livingstone v Rawyards Coal
Co (1880) 74
Lloyd v Grace Smith & Co
(1912) 164
Long v Hepworth (1968) . . 40
M'Alister (or Donoghue) v
Stevenson (1932) . 97, 100, 107,
108, 109, 199
McKay v Essex Area Health
Authority (1982) 207
McLoughlin v O'Brian (1982),
(1983) 85, 105, 106
Maharaj v A-G of Trinidad and
Tobago (No 2) (1979) . . 26
Malone v Metropolitan Police
Comr (1979) 64
Martin v Dean (1971) . . . 158
May v Burdett (1846) . . . 130
Metropolitan Police Comr v
Caldwell (1982) . . . 92
Midland Bank Trust Co Ltd v
Hett, Stubbs and Kemp
(1979) 14

PAGE

Miller v Jackson (1977) . 71, 125
Ministry of Housing and Local
Government v Sharp (1970). 109
Mitchell v Mulholland (No 2)
(1972) 81
Mitchil v Alestree (1676) . . 95
Monk v Warbey (1935). . 157, 158,
160
Morgans v Launchbury (1973) 134,
165
Morris v Ford Motor Co Ltd
(1973) 166
Morris v National Coal Board
(1963) 118
Mutual Life and Citizens'
Assurance Co Ltd v Evatt
(1971) 100
NWL Ltd v Woods (1979) . 73
Nabi v British Leyland (UK)
Ltd (1980) 189
National Coal Board v J E Evans
& Co (Cardiff) Ltd (1951) . 53
Nettleship v Weston (1971) . 114,
164
Newstead v London Express
Newspaper (1940) . . . 58
Nicholls v Ely Beet Sugar
Factory Ltd (1936) . . . 60
Nova Mink Ltd v Trans-Canada
Airlines (1951) 113
Oakley v Lyster (1931) . . . 32
O'Reilly v Mackman (1983) . 9, 10
Parry v Cleaver (1970) . . 187, 189
Parsons (H) (Livestock) Ltd v
Uttley Ingham & Co Ltd
(1978) 17
Phillips v Britannia Hygienic
Laundry (1923) 135
Pickett v British Rail
Engineering Ltd (1980) . . 82
Pirelli General Cable Works Ltd
v Oscar Faber & Partners
(1983) 20
Post Office v Norwich Union
Fire Insurance Society Ltd
(1967) 157, 163

PAGE

Price v Hilditch (1930) . . . 60
Pride of Derby and Derbyshire
  Angling Association Ltd v
  British Celanese Ltd (1953):   72,
                                 219
R v Chief National Insurance
  Comr, ex p Connor (1981) .   147
Randall v Motor Insurers'
  Bureau (1969) 162
Rapier v London Tramways Co
  (1893) 125, 126
Read v Coker (1853) . . . 58
Read v J Lyons & Co Ltd (1947): 126,
                                 131
Redland Bricks Ltd v Morris
  (1970) 68
Reynolds v Clarke (1725) . . 48
Reynolds v Police Comr
  (1982) 75
River Wear Comrs v Adamson
  (1877) 52
Rivoli Hats Ltd v Gooch
  (1953) 33
Roe v Minister of Health
  (1954) 140
Rondel v Worsley (1969) . . 100
Rookes v Barnard (1964) . . 74
Ross v Caunters (1980) 14, 16, 109
Rylands v Fletcher (1868) . 46, 51,
            93, 94, 128, 129, 131,
            132, 135, 198, 202, 213
SCM (UK) Ltd v Whittall &
  Son Ltd (1971) . . . 110, 164
Saif Ali v Sydney Mitchell & Co
  (1980) 100
Schiffahrt und Kohlen GmbH v
  Chelsea Maritime Ltd, The
  Irene's Success (1982) . . 111
Schwan, The (1892) . . . 52
Scott v Shepherd (1773) . . 44
Seager v Copydex Ltd (1967) . 21
Seager v Copydex Ltd (No 2)
  (1969) 22
Sedleigh-Denfield v O'Cal-
  laghan (1940) 124

PAGE

Sirros v Moore (1975) . . . 99
Slater v Swann (1730) . . . 59
Smith v Stone (1647) . . . 44
Sparrow v Fairey Aviation Co
  Ltd (1964) 120
Sparton Steel and Alloys Ltd v
  Martin & Co (Contractors)
  Ltd (1973) . . . 101, 110, 164
Stanley v Powell (1891) . 52, 53
Stonedale, The (No 1) (1956) . 25
Stratford (JT) & Son Ltd v
  Lindley (1965) 73
Stratford (JT) & Son Ltd v
  Lindley (No 2) (1969) . . 73
Summers (John) & Sons Ltd v
  Frost (1955) 118
Tattersall v Drysdale (1935) . 153
Thorne v University of London
  (1966) 103
Tinline v White Cross Insurance
  Association (1921) . . . 146
Turner v Ministry of Defence
  (1969) 188
Udale v Bloomsbury Area
  Health Authority (1983) . 207
Uddin v Associated Portland
  Cement Manufacturers
  (1965) 121
Union Oil Co v Oppen 501 F 2d
  558 (9th Cir, 1974) . . . 204
United Australia Ltd v Barclays
  Bank Ltd (1941) . . . 34, 37
Universe Tankships Inc of
  Monrovia v International
  Transport Workers' Feder-
  ation (1983) 22
Uren v John Fairfax & Sons
  (Pty) Ltd (1966) . . . 79
Vandepitte v Preferred
  Accident Insurance Corpn of
  New York (1933) . . . 154
Wagon Mound (No 2), The
  (1967) 124
Weaver v Ward (1616) . . . 51

PAGE

Weller & Co v Foot and Mouth
Disease Research Institute
(1966) 111
Wells v Cooper (1958) . . . 114
West (H) & Son Ltd v Shephard
(1964) 83
Westwood v Post Office
(1974) 121
White v London Transport
(1971) 161

PAGE

White v White (1950) . . . 141
Wilkinson v Downton (1897) . 41
Williams v Holland (1833) . 49
Williams v Humphrey (1975) . 50
Williams v Morland (1824) . 60
Williams v Peel River Land and
Mineral Co Ltd (1886) . . 60
Wise v Kaye (1962) 83
Yates v Whyte (1838) . . . 187

Abbreviations

Beveridge Report	Social Insurance and Allied Services, Cmd 6404 (1942)
Brit J Law and Soc	British Journal of Law and Society
CLJ	Cambridge Law Journal
Hepple and Matthews	B. A. Hepple and M. H. Matthews *Tort: Cases and Materials* (2nd edn, London, Butterworths, 1980)
Harv LR	Harvard Law Review
ILJ	Industrial Law Journal
LQR	Law Quarterly Review
J Leg Stud	Journal of Legal Studies
J Law and Econ	Journal of Law and Economics
J Soc Wel L	Journal of Social Welfare Law
Keeton & O'Connell	*Basic Protection for the Accident Victim. A Blueprint for Reforming Automobile Insurance* (Boston, 1965)
MLR	Modern Law Review
Oxf J Leg Stud	Oxford Journal of Legal Studies
Pearson Report	Royal Commission on Civil Liability and Compensation for Personal Injury. Chairman: Lord Pearson. Report 3 vols, Cmnd 7054 (1978)
Salmond and Heuston	R. F. V. Heuston and R. S. Chambers *Salmond and Heuston on the Law of Torts* (18th edn, London, Sweet & Maxwell, 1981)

Street	Harry Street *The Law of Torts* (7th edn, London, Butterworths, 1983)
U Chi LR	University of Chicago Law Review
U Tor LJ	University of Toronto Law Journal
Winfield and Jolowicz	W. V. H. Rogers *Winfield and Jolowicz on Tort* (11th edn, London, Sweet & Maxwell, 1979)
Winn Committee Report	Report of the Committee on Personal Injuries Litigation, Cmnd 3691
Woodhouse Report	Royal Commission of Inquiry. Report on Compensation for Personal Injury in New Zealand (1967)
Woodhouse-Meares Report	*Compensation and Rehabilitation in Australia* Report of the National Committee of Inquiry (1974)

1 The scope and function of tort

It was complaind that thou hadst done great tort
Unto an aged woman, poore and bare.

Spencer *Faerie Queene* II v 17

THE MEANING OF 'TORT'

There is no branch of English law the name of which
conveys so little meaning to the average layman as tort.
What is a tort? The word comes to us from the Norman-
French; etymologically, it signifies any wrong, and springs
from the Latin *tortus*, meaning 'twisted' or 'wrung'. And the
very word 'wrung' is merely another form of the word
'wrong'. In the loose and untechnical sense of 'wrong', the
word 'tort' was in quite general use; in that sense it is found
in literature as late as the eighteenth century, and of course it
is still so used in the French language. In England, however,
it is now purely technical. A tort is a wrong recognised by
law.[1]

---

1 So well established is the technical meaning of the word at the present day
that it is easy for us to forget how recent this meaning is. Although the
department of law that we now call 'tort' is ancient, and although the word
'tort' in the sense of wrong is ancient, the word was not generally used as a
term of art designating this department of law until the second half of the
nineteenth century. Blackstone had foreshadowed its use (*Commentaries*
iii 118), but the first treatise bearing the name 'Torts' was issued in 1859 by
Hilliard, an American author. The first English treatise under this name was
by Addison (1860). As late as 1870 a judge noticeably avoided using the word
'tort', and expressed the contract-tort dichotomy as 'contract-duty' (*Francis v
Cockrell* (1870) LR 5 QB 501 at 509).

But torts are not the only wrongs recognised by law. The reader will probably know the names of the major torts, such as negligence, nuisance, defamation, conversion, trespass to goods, trespass to the person (assault, etc) and trespass to land; but he may still need guidance on the distinction between torts and other legal wrongs. The great cleavage is between criminal wrongs, variously called *crimes* or *offences*, which may result in a prosecution and punishment, and *civil wrongs* which lead not to a criminal prosecution but to a civil proceeding for damages or other private redress. To explain in detail the distinctive features of the criminal prosecution is the task of the criminal lawyer: suffice it here to say that all legal proceedings that are not criminal are civil. Civil proceedings are the residuary class.

THE OVERLAP BETWEEN TORT AND CRIME

The distinction between torts and crimes is rendered slightly difficult by an area of overlap. We generally think of murder as a crime, because the criminal punishment is dramatic; but murder is at the same time a tort to the person killed and to his dependants. So also is manslaughter. Theft is a crime, but it is also the tort of conversion of property. As a crime, it can be prosecuted and punished. As a tort, it gives rise to an action for the value of the property stolen. It is broadly true to say that all crimes are torts if they amount to a physical interference with the plaintiff or his property, at least if they cause actual damage to him. But a crime is not generally a tort if, although potentially dangerous, it has not yet caused damage (dangerous driving where no injury has been inflicted, or attempted murder, where the victim fortunately remains unaffected by the abortive attempt). Also, a crime consisting in a violation of general public order is not a tort if no ascertainable individual is affected: an example is treason.[2]

Just as there are crimes that are not torts, so there are torts that are not crimes. The traditional example is trespass to land, which is a tort but is a crime only exceptionally, as when the trespass is committed with intent to commit one of certain criminal offences (eg to steal or rape), or is associated with other criminal or violent conduct. Parliament has been adding to the list of criminal trespasses, but still the simple trespass on a farmer's field is not a crime,[3] although it is a tort.

What underlies this distinction between crime and tort? The answer is that the object of the criminal law is broadly different from that of the civil law (of which the law of tort forms a part). The criminal law aims at controlling conduct, and this chiefly by threatening punishment if undesirable behaviour is indulged in. In modern times punishment does not occupy the whole of the picture, because criminal courts have other orders at their disposal, such as a probation order, a community service order, or (if the offender is a driver convicted of one of specified offences) an order disqualifying him from driving. But, whatever order is made by the court, the criminal law is principally directed towards influencing behaviour. In contrast, the aim of the law of tort is principally to compensate the victim of wrongdoing. The typical outcome of an action in tort is the award of damages to the plaintiff against the defendant, and these damages are intended to be roughly equivalent to the plaintiff's loss.

---

2 If treason caused actual harm to the State, as represented by the Crown, it might amount to a tort; but the question has never been argued. An action for damages will not lie at the suit of a person who has suffered damage as a result of perjury (a crime): *Hargreaves v Bretherton* [1959] 1 QB 45, [1958] 3 All ER 122.

3 Neither is an intrusion into Buckingham Palace, which led to a review of the *Law Relating to Trespass on Residential Premises* by the Home Office (1982), but the Government proposes to extend the criminal law in this respect.

When an act is a crime as well as a tort, both the criminal and the civil remedy may be pursued. The wrongdoer may both be prosecuted as a criminal and sued as a tortfeasor; he may both be punished and made to pay damages to his victim. Generally it does not matter which proceeding is brought first, although the court will usually stay a civil action while a prosecution is actually proceeding.

A few statutes provide that prosecutions under them shall bar a civil action. The most important of these is the Offences against the Person Act 1861, s 45, by which acquittal or conviction of assault and battery by a court of summary jurisdiction (a magistrates' court) bars a subsequent civil action. Certain qualifications upon the operation of this section need not be set out here.[4] Subject to these small statutory exceptions, the general principle is that prosecution for a crime, whether successful or unsuccessful, does not bar a subsequent civil action;[5] but a court has an inherent power to prevent the misuse of civil proceedings by those convicted of criminal offences.[6]

From the point of view of the victim of crime, however, the civil remedy may be worthless. Even if the criminal can

---

4 They are considered in detail by P. M. North in (1966) 29 MLR 16, who points out that the rule that bars later civil proceedings can be evaded by the simple expedient of suing first and making a charge later.

5 The criminal conviction may provide evidence that the offence was committed in the subsequent civil proceedings: see Civil Evidence Act 1968, s 11.

6 *Hunter v Chief Constable of West Midlands Police* [1982] AC 529, [1981] 3 All ER 727. There, the jury had convicted the 'Birmingham pub bombers', following the judge's direction to acquit them if they believed that their confessions were obtained by force, and the judge had admitted the confessions in evidence after an exhaustive investigation of allegations of force, one of the convicted men instituted civil proceedings for damages against the police alleging that they had beaten him up to make the confession: held, by the House of Lords, that in the absence of fresh evidence this was an abuse of the process of the court, the proper course being for the convicted man to appeal against the conviction to the Criminal Division of the Court of Appeal.

be identified and traced, he is likely to be in prison or bankrupt. With this in mind, the Government established a Criminal Injuries Compensation Scheme in 1964. This is administered by the Criminal Injuries Compensation Board which makes ex gratia payments to anyone who has sustained personal injury directly attributable to a crime of violence.[7] (The payment goes to his spouse or dependant if he has been killed.) A person who seeks compensation from the Board is not bound to pursue his civil remedy, but his compensation will be reduced by any sum he has received by way of damages in a civil court. He must undertake to repay the Board from any damages, settlement or compensation he may subsequently receive in respect of his injuries.[8] Compensation payable by the Board is also subject to reduction by any sum that the victim has received in pursuance of an order for compensation by a criminal court in respect of his injuries.

This last statement may strike the reader as curious, because we have said that it is the function of the law of tort and not the criminal law to provide compensation. However, for some years there have been Acts of Parliament allowing criminal courts, when convicting a person of a limited number of offences, to make compensation orders. In 1972 this power was extended to cover all offences of which a person is convicted and also any other offence that is taken into consideration for the purpose of determining

---

7 This excludes traffic offences, unless 'the injury is due to a deliberate attempt to run the victim down': Criminal Injuries Compensation Scheme, para 11. (Most victims of motoring offences, insofar as the conduct involved the commission of one or more torts, will have a claim against the Motor Insurers' Bureau if the motorist was uninsured or untraced: see Chap 5.) There are other exceptions: in particular, small claims are excluded. These are claims for less than £400 after deduction of social security benefits, and higher claims in the case of family violence; so that about half of all crimes of violence fall outside the scope of the Scheme.

8 Criminal Injuries Compensation Scheme, para 21.

sentence.[9] This type of criminal compensation order differs from an award of damages for tort. The criminal court can make its order only if the defendant is convicted of an offence; it must have regard to the means of the defendant; and it need not wait for a formal application for compensation by the victim. So compensation may be awarded where, in fact, no tort has been committed (since, as we have said, not all crimes are torts), and the victim will not be deprived of compensation simply because he lacks the courage or determination to pursue a civil remedy. If the victim is actually *paid* the amount awarded under a criminal compensation order, then the damages awarded in any subsequent civil proceedings will be reduced by that amount.[10]

Where does this leave the distinction between crime and tort? The Criminal Injuries Compensation Scheme provides a form of social security (although it is to be noted that the Scheme was established by the Government acting under the prerogative powers of the Crown and so can be withdrawn at any time). It leaves the law of crime and the law of tort intact. But criminal compensation orders are usually a simpler and more satisfactory means of compensating victims of crime than actions for damages for tort, so that they frequently supersede the civil action in practice.[11]

---

9 The power, in respect of both personal injuries and other 'loss or damage', is now exercisable under the Powers of Criminal Courts Act 1973. Nothing in the Act suggests that in assessing compensation the court should take into account previous awards of compensation where a person was convicted of a similar offence, but the position may be very different if those other offences were simply 'taken into consideration' on the earlier occasion. For comment see Harry Street in [1974] Crim LR 345.
10 Powers of Criminal Courts Act 1973, s 38.
11 But it should be remembered that the commission of the offence by the defendant must be proved beyond reasonable doubt before a criminal compensation order may be made. In a civil action the plaintiff need only prove his case on a balance of probabilities.

THE ACTION FOR DAMAGES AND OTHER CIVIL REMEDIES

A plaintiff who brings a civil action does so with the object of obtaining some relief or other outcome beneficial to himself. Among the forms of relief relevant to the law of tort are, first and foremost, *damages*. Damages are monetary compensation for a wrong, and are assessed, subject to certain rules, in such a way as to make up to the plaintiff for his loss. An award of money retains its character as damages even though a subjective element enters into the assessment. For example, in most personal injury cases there will be included in the plaintiff's damages an amount in respect of the pain and suffering endured and the future loss of bodily or mental faculty. From the purely pecuniary point of view this may mean that the plaintiff is better off than before the accident. But the compensatory principle remains intact because we treat money as the sole instrument for restoring the status quo.[12]

In one way the law of tort clearly aims at controlling conduct. Instead of claiming damages for a tort, or in addition to a claim for damages, the plaintiff may ask for an *injunction* – an order of the court directing the defendant not to do or continue the tortious[13] act. If the defendant subsequently disobeys such an order, he may be committed to prison. This may appear very like a criminal proceeding,

---

12 This and another more controversial example of the subjective element in damages – 'exemplary' damages – are considered in some detail in Chap 3, p 73, below.

13 This is the adjective derived from 'tort'. On the Continent, the name given to what we call tort is 'delict', with the adjective 'delictual' or 'delictal'; this adjective is sometimes used even in reference to the English law. The form 'delictal' is not given in the Oxford English Dictionary, but it is a pleasantly clean word which seems to have been invented by Salmond and was approved by Buckland and McNair, *Roman Law and Common Law* (1st edn) p 273. The editor of *Salmond on Jurisprudence* retains his author's invention, but the editor of *Salmond on Torts* goes back to the form 'delictual'.

but it is accounted civil because it follows civil procedure and is brought in the civil courts.

The injunction was the invention of the old Court of Chancery, whereas tort was distinctively a common law conception. Hence it is still the possibility of damages, rather than the possibility of an injunction, that characterises a wrong as a tort. If no action for damages can be brought for a wrong, the wrong is not a tort.[14]

Where chattels have been wrongfully kept from the plaintiff, he may claim a decree of *specific restitution*, which is another of the former equitable remedies that have now been made available in an ordinary action. Similarly, one who is dispossessed of land can recover it. But the wrongful detention of property is not only a ground for specific restitution but also a tort giving an action for damages. Here again it is the possibility of an action for damages that makes the detention of property a tort.

While on the subject of remedies, we may notice some legal proceedings of a public character that are not remedies in tort. One is *habeas corpus*, which is a proceeding whereby a man may recover his liberty. The wrongful deprivation of liberty is a tort, the tort of false imprisonment; but the writ of habeas corpus is not a remedy in tort, because it must be sought in a special proceeding which is not an action. Then there is the order of *mandamus*, which is very like an injunction except that the procedure for obtaining it is again a special one and it lies only for the failure to perform a *public* duty. Another remedy for breach of a public duty is a *relator action* for an injunction at the suit of the Attorney General. This is a civil action, injunctions being exclusively a civil remedy; but since no action for damages lies the breach of public duty that the Attorney General seeks to restrain is not

---

14 *Hulton v Hulton* [1917] 1 KB 813 at 820, 822–823, 824. However, if a wrong *is* a tort, an action for an injunction in respect of that wrong is an action in tort even though no damages are claimed.

a tort. A common use of relator actions is in respect of the crime of public nuisance (eg obstructing the highway or discharging oil into a navigable river). When an individual suffers particular damage as a result of a public nuisance, then he may bring an action in tort.[15] Sometimes a statute gives the Attorney General the power to sue for a *penalty* if the statute is infringed. Although the action for the penalty is civil in character, it is not an action for a tort, at any rate for some purposes,[16] because the penalty is not conceived, even in part, as a mode of compensating for the wrong. It is not, in other words, damages.

The distinction between actions in tort and public law remedies has become increasingly important.[17] The House of Lords has held that a person asserting a right to impugn and overturn the decision of a public authority must as a general rule use the special procedure of an application for judicial review,[18] unless his claim for damages is an ordinary action in negligence concerning his rights at common law, and does not raise any issue of public law.[19] For example, a person who wants to challenge the decision of a local authority to refuse to provide him and his family with accommodation as required by the Housing (Homeless Persons) Act 1977 is limited to the remedies provided by public law, although he is seeking damages for the

---

15 *A-G v PYA Quarries Ltd* [1957] 2 QB 169, [1957] 1 All ER 894. No private individual can sue in his own name solely to prevent a 'public' wrong from which he has suffered or will suffer no particular damage. He must have the consent of the Attorney General; the latter brings the action ex relatione the citizen (who has to pay the costs): *Gouriet v Union of Post Office Workers* [1978] AC 435, [1977] 3 All ER 70.

16 *A-G v Canter* [1939] 1 KB 318 at 326. Yet for some purposes the action was formerly regarded as being in tort: see Williams *Joint Torts and Contributory Negligence* § 2, n 1.

17 For a critique see Carol Harlow in (1980) 43 MLR 241; and *Compensation for Government Torts* (London, 1982). Cp. G. Samuel in (1983) 46 MLR 558.

18 *O'Reilly v Mackman* [1983] AC 237, [1982] 3 All ER 1124.

19 *Davy v Spelthorne BC* [1983] 3 All ER 278, [1983] 3 WLR 742.

authority's tortious breach of statutory duty.[20] On the other hand, a person alleging that he lost his chance to impugn a town and country planning enforcement notice and so suffered damage, as a result of the negligence of a local authority is entitled to proceed by way of an ordinary action for damages. This is because he does not seek to impugn or overturn the enforcement notice.[1] The public law remedies are less advantageous than an action in tort to the aggrieved citizen. First, there is a 'filter': leave of the court is required to proceed. Second, a three-month time limit applies (compared to six years for actions in tort, and three years in respect of personal injuries). Third, the citizen must have sufficient 'interest' to claim the remedies, and the granting of these is a matter for the court's discretion, unlike common law damages which may be claimed as of right. The full implications of this recent distinction between 'private' tort actions and 'public law' remedies are yet to be worked out; 'it is a consequence of the development that has taken place over the last 30 years of the procedures available for the control of administrative action,'[2] which procedures are distinct from an ordinary action for damages in tort.

EXTRA–JUDICIAL REMEDIES

It is not always necessary to go to court when a tort has been committed. Various forms of self-help are recognised by law. One class of these extra-judicial remedies is known as *abatement of nuisances*. The word 'abatement' comes from the law–French *abatre*, to beat down. For instance, if a person has

---

20 *Cocks v Thanet District Council* [1982] 3 All ER 1135, [1982] 3 WLR 1121.
1 *Davy v Spelthorne BC* [1983] 3 All ER at 283.
2 Per Lord Diplock in *O'Reilly v Mackman* [1983] AC 237 at 277; [1982] 3 All ER 1124 at 1128. See Chap 4, p 103, below, regarding the possible limits on the liability of public authorities in respect of the tort of negligence.

a right of way across land and finds a gate barring his path he can remove the obstruction. The expression is now applied to any termination of a nuisance by the act of the party aggrieved.

A number of rules govern the exercise of the remedy, in particular as to when notice of the intention to abate a nuisance must be given; but here we must be content with one example to indicate its limits. An occupier of land is entitled to lop off the branches of trees overhanging his land, without giving any notice, provided he does not go outside the boundaries of his land to do so. But he must not burn the wood or consume fruits that he finds on the branches he has cut off; that would be conversion. And he must act reasonably: if his neighbour pegs out washing and the wind occasionally blows the line so that the linen flaps over his garden he would not be entitled to take a pair of scissors to it. From one point of view abatement is a superior remedy to an action for damages because the nuisance may be abated although no actual damage has been suffered (as in the example of the overhanging branches).

Another form of self-help is *distress damage feasant*.[3] This is the right to take things that are wrongfully doing damage or (possibly) encumbering land and to retain them by way of security until compensation is paid. For example, the occupier of land is not obliged to return a cricket ball that has broken his window-pane, before being reimbursed for the damage.

There was a time when this remedy was an important form of protection against straying animals. In origin it was a mitigation of the right of executing summary vengeance upon an offending chattel. In the Dark Ages a man had the right to kill any animal that he found trespassing upon his land. There is clear evidence for that in the Anglo-Saxon laws, and in the form of local custom the practice survived

3 Pronounced 'feezant'.

into the Middle Ages. Thus it was the custom of Portsmouth that if one found a hog in the street one could smite off the snout. By the end of the Anglo-Saxon period the principle had developed that the landowner was no longer to destroy the animal but could keep it until the owner paid for the damage it had done. This common law right in respect of animals has now been abolished by statute.[4] In its place there is a new right to detain trespassing livestock.[5] The rules that have to be observed are somewhat complicated, and the harassed suburban householder whose garden is invaded by straying animals will find it simpler to drive them away.

Whilst on the subject of self-help mention must be made of the related, but distinct, right of 'private defence'. As a general principle it is legitimate to take reasonable steps to defend oneself, or anyone else, or property in one's possession, against direct physical damage that is not done in pursuance of a legal right. As an example of this principle, the owner or lawful occupier of premises may resist trespassers (with no more force than is reasonably necessary) until he is ejected. But once pushed out he cannot force his way back merely on the ground that he is the owner, unless he is a 'displaced residential occupier' who is allowed to use reasonable force.[6] One may keep a guard dog for protection against trespassers if the keeping of an animal for that purpose is not unreasonable.[7] A dog worrying or about to worry livestock may be shot; indeed, even the unfortunate

4 Animals Act 1971, s 7(1).
5 Ibid s 7(2). Since the definition of 'livestock' (s 11) does not include cats one cannot detain (let alone, drown) members of this wandering species.
6 Criminal Law Act 1977, s 6. Section 7 of the Act gives further protection of the criminal law to the displaced residential occupier. An occupier who has technically become a 'trespasser' upon expiry of his tenancy may not, however, be evicted without due process of law: Protection from Eviction Act 1977, as amended by Housing Act 1980, s 69(1).
7 Animals Act 1971, s 5(3)(b); but see the Guard Dogs Act 1975 which prohibits the use of guard dogs except on agricultural land and in private houses and gardens.

dog that *has been* worrying livestock, has not left the vicinity, and is not under anyone's control, may be killed if its owner cannot be found by any practicable means.[8]

The discussion so far supports the definition of a tort as a *civil* wrong giving rise to an *action for damages*. It is a civil, not a criminal, wrong; and the plaintiff may always, if he wishes, ask for the monetary compensation known as damages. He may, however, ask for some alternative remedy such as an injunction, a decree of specific restitution, or a simple declaration of his rights, or he may resort to some permitted extra-judicial remedy.[9] If we can say 'so far, so good', that is only, unfortunately, because we have been saving the real difficulties of definition till last.

TORT AND BREACH OF CONTRACT

The definition as it stands is too wide. A breach of contract, also, is a civil wrong giving rise to an action for damages. How can we distinguish it from a tort?

The easy answer is that a breach of contract is the breach of a promise to behave or not to behave in a certain way; in tort, there need not have been any promise. An assault, for example, is tortious although the defendant never promised not to assault the plaintiff.

However, this distinction is of diminished utility where the defendant has made a promise and yet is liable in tort. For a tortious wrong may be a breach of promise, and so not only a tort but a breach of contract. An example would be where a surgeon, employed privately, negligently leaves a swab inside the patient. The surgeon is liable in contract, for

---

8 Animals Act 1971, s 9(3). The deterrent effect of action after the event can arise only in the long term.

9 However, the discussion of extra-judicial remedies indicates that self-help may be permissible although no tort has been committed.

breach of his implied promise to use due care; but he is also liable in tort for negligence. Of course, the surgeon cannot be made to pay double damages in such a case; but the plaintiff can rest his claim either on the tort or on the breach of contract or on both.[10] In case of doubt, he would plead both causes of action, hoping to win on one or other of them. It used to be thought that this concurrent liability was restricted to those in certain common callings, such as innkeepers and carriers, who by the 'custom of the realm' owe duties to provide their services to the public. But it is now established that whenever someone, in the course of his trade or business, undertakes to perform a service for another person who relies on that undertaking, a duty of care may arise in both tort and contract.[11] Even a nonfeasance, an omission to act, can be actionable in tort and not merely in contract.[12]

It will be seen from the example of the surgeon just given that a man may be liable in tort when he has made a contract with the plaintiff, although, but for the contract, he would have had no opportunity to commit the wrong. True, the action in tort can here be distinguished from the action in contract by saying that in contract the plaintiff has to rely on the defendant's implied promise, whereas in tort the question of promise is immaterial. However, the proof of a

---

10 *Edwards v Mallan* [1908] 1 KB 1002 (dentist). In other words, the plaintiff may 'plead' both the tort and the breach of contract. If he sues in tort, he cannot afterwards sue in contract, since the judgment in the first action will make the matter res judicata. Nor would the plaintiff be allowed to pursue two distinct actions at the same time for substantially the same grievance. Either the two actions would be consolidated, or one would be stayed as being frivolous and vexatious.

11 *Midland Bank Trust Co Ltd v Hett, Stubbs and Kemp* [1979] Ch 384, [1978] 3 All ER 571 (solicitor); *Batty v Metropolitan Property Realisations Ltd* [1978] QB 554, [1978] 2 All ER 445 (builder); *Ross v Caunters* [1980] Ch 297, [1979] 3 All ER 580 (solicitor).

12 See, however, the cautionary notes by Jolowicz in [1979] CLJ 54 and Stanton in (1979) 42 MLR 207.

promise is sometimes an essential part of the plaintiff's cause of action even in tort (as with some claims founded on a gratuitous undertaking), and here the differentiation is more difficult.

For present purposes, the most important of the differences between contract and tort relates to the object of compensatory damages. The law of contract gives the plaintiff damages to compensate him for the disappointment of his expectations under the contract, while the law of tort does not generally do this. In tort, the plaintiff can usually recover compensation only for a deterioration of his existing position.[13] This is known as *restitutio in integrum*, or the indemnity measure of damages. For example, if A sells a painting to B for £10,000, fraudulently or negligently representing it as the work of a famous artist, whereas it is in fact an imitation worth only £100, and if B is suing for the tort of deceit or negligence, his damages (if he has paid the contract price) will be £9,900, the amount necessary to put him in the position he would have been in had he not bought it. He will not be compensated for loss of an expectation of profit. On the other hand, let us suppose that B can prove that A warranted, as a term of the contract, that the painting was genuine, and that B could have resold it on the open market for £15,000 had it been as warranted; then B's damages in contract will be £14,900, that is, the difference between what it would have been worth had the warranty been true and its present selling price.

A breach of contract may result not only in loss of bargain (the expectation interest) but also in actual pecuniary loss, for example, B's expenses in storing the painting. In that event, tort-type indemnity damages may be recovered in an action in contract.

This last example indicates that the law of tort does not

---

13 The idea of preventing wrongful disruption of the status quo also lies behind the other major remedy in tort, the injunction: see below, Chap 3, p 68.

enjoy a monopoly in protecting the status quo. This can sometimes be done by the law of contract, either in conjunction with the protection of an expectation interest or on its own.[14] For its part, the law of tort has recently been expanding to protect the expectation interest in certain circumstances. For example, in *Ross v Caunters*[15] a solicitor who had been instructed to draw up a will negligently failed to ensure that the will was properly witnessed. As a result the gift to a beneficiary was void. Had the mistake been discovered during the testator's lifetime, the testator (the solicitor's client) could have recovered damages (in contract or tort), although these would have been limited to the cost of making a new and valid will, or otherwise putting matters right. But it came to light only after his death. The court decided that the solicitor was liable in tort to the disappointed beneficiary for the loss of the expected gift.

Another important development in the same direction has been the recognition, by the House of Lords,[16] that a person who relies on the skill and judgment of a builder may recover damages from him for the cost of repairing any defect in the building due to the builder's negligence, even in the absence of a contractual relationship. These damages may include not only the cost of replacement but also the

---

14 For examples in the reports see the cases applying the rule in *Bain v Fothergill* (1874) LR 7 HL 158 (purchaser of land entitled only to recovery of deposit and expenses of investigating title where seller transfers late or fails to transfer due to defect in his title), and *Anglia Television Ltd v Reed* [1972] 1 QB 60, [1971] 3 All ER 690 (damages for pre-contract expenditure where loss of profits could not be ascertained); cp. *C and P Haulage v Middleton* [1983] 3 All ER 94. Arguably, such damages can be claimed even where the plaintiff has made a bad bargain: see the discussion by A. S. Burrows in (1983) 99 LQR 217 at 226–32.

15 [1980] Ch 297, [1979] 3 All ER 580.

16 *Junior Books Ltd v Veitchi Co Ltd* [1983] 1 AC 520, [1982] 3 All ER 201; cp. *Balsamo v Medici* (1983) Times, 31 October; see further below, Chap 4, p 107.

consequential economic losses, including the loss of profits while the repairs were being done.[17] By analogy this decision could be applied to protect the expectations of the consumer of shoddy goods against a negligent manufacturer with whom he has no contract.[18] Distinctions between the extent of damages available in contract and tort have also been whittled down, although not entirely removed, in recent years.[19]

Where does this leave the classification of tort and contract? The answer must be that the traditional models of contract, as a system protecting expectations, and tort, as a system protecting the status quo, are breaking down. We are in the process of a gradual, and not always clearly perceived, transition towards a general conception of obligations.[20] The notion that contract is mainly about what the parties *intend*, while tort is about what they *do* has come under

---

17 Some writers argue that this simply protects the status quo interest of the plaintiff because the property is worth less than he paid for it, or the expenditure is to prevent future harm: see Burrows, op cit at 227, n 27. This does not change the fact that the damages are essentially the same as would have been obtained for breach of contract in similar circumstances.

18 See Chap 4, below, p 109.

19 Eg damages for non-pecuniary losses, previously limited to tort, have been regarded as being 'within the contemplation of the parties' in actions in contract such as *Jarvis v Swan Tours Ltd* [1973] 1 QB 233, [1973] 1 All ER 71 (disappointed holidaymaker awarded damages for mental distress and inconvenience on account of a breach of contract to provide holiday); *Cox v Phillips Industries Ltd* [1976] 3 All ER 161, [1976] 1 WLR 638 (damages for depression, anxiety and illness for breach of contract of employment); and *Heywood v Wellers* [1976] QB 446, [1976] All ER 300 (damages for mental distress caused by solicitor's negligence). There are, however, still doubts whether the rules as to remoteness of damage are the same in contract and tort: *Koufos v Czarnikow* [1969] 1 AC 350, [1967] 3 All ER 686 and compare *H Parsons (Livestock) Ltd v Uttley Ingham & Co Ltd* [1978] QB 791, [1978] 1 All ER 525. Exemplary damages are not recoverable in contract (on tort, see below, Chap 3, p 73).

20 This includes restitution, on which see below, p 22.

increasing pressure.[1] One line of attack is that what is often taken as the enforcement of a promise is in reality the compensation for an injury sustained by the plaintiff because he relied on the defendant's promise. Similarly, acts of reasonable reliance will often create liability in tort. If a newspaper offers free financial advice to its readers and negligently gives bad advice which causes loss to a reader, whose question was published in the paper, the reader may claim damages. Seventy-five years ago the courts had to base this sort of decision on the finding of an artificial contract, namely the exchange of a promise to provide sound information for an (implied) consent to the publication of the question.[2] Twenty years ago, the House of Lords was able to lay down a general principle that for the purpose of the tort of negligence a duty of care arises from an express or implied undertaking by the defendant that he will exercise care in giving information or advice, and this undertaking need not be supported by consideration.[3] The principle of reliance is being developed into a general source of legal obligation, the will or intention of the parties being merely evidence of the undertaking and reliance.[4]

It may be objected that cases such as these involve a

1 The writings of Professor P. S. Atiyah have been in the forefront, in particular *The Rise and Fall of Freedom of Contract* (Oxford, 1979); see too (1978) 94 LQR 193, and *An Introduction to the Law of Contract* (3rd edn, Oxford, 1981) especially Chaps 1 and 2. An amusing American attack on the promise principle will be found in Grant Gilmore *The Death of Contract* (Columbus, Ohio, 1974); see too, Morton J. Horwitz *The Transformation of American Law 1780–1860* (Cambridge, Mass., 1981) Chap 6. Strong support for promise as the moral basis of contract law will be found in Charles Fried *Contract as Promise* (Cambridge, Mass., 1981), and for the protection of the expectation interest through traditional classifications by A. S. Burrows in (1983) 99 LQR 217. Cp. J. Holyoak in (1983) 99 LQR 591.

2 *De la Bere v Pearson Ltd* [1908] 1 KB 280.

3 *Hedley Byrne & Co Ltd v Heller & Partners Ltd* [1964] AC 465, [1963] 2 All ER 575 (Hepple and Matthews, pp 105, 517).

4 See Atiyah in (1978) 94 LQR at 207–9 on contract; and *Junior Books Ltd v Veitchi Co Ltd* (n 16, above) on reliance in tort.

voluntary assumption of responsibility, while the typical tort case involves a chance event between strangers, such as a road accident. But whatever may be the typical tort case, the fact is that in the nineteenth century the law of tort expanded to cover voluntary relationships, as in the actions by passengers against railway companies, by employees against employers, and by entrants of buildings against the occupiers. Moreover, it is just as artificial to say that the seller of goods submits to his legal obligations to the consumer as it would be to say that the driver of a vehicle submits to the law of the road.[5] If the driver of a bus negligently causes injuries to passengers and pedestrians, there is no valid reason for distinguishing between the classes of victim, when all have suffered harm as a result of their reliance on the driver using the vehicle with due care and attention.[6] Both the law of contract and the law of tort have been moving towards subjecting all obligations, whatever their precise origin, to standards of reasonableness and fairness; and this, no doubt, reflects the movement away from the laissez faire philosophy of the nineteenth century, with its emphasis on individual choice, towards the welfare philosophy of the twentieth century.

Despite these trends, for a number of practical purposes the distinction between contract and tort remains important. This is true in relation to the limitation of actions. There is a limitation period of six years for bringing an action in contract and tort,[7] and in the case of personal injuries this is limited to three years.[8] The time limit begins to run from the date on which the cause of action accrues, and in determining this date there is a crucial difference

---

5 See Atiyah *Introduction to the Law of Contract* at pp 17–25 on the restrictions on free choice in contracts.
6 An example suggested by Atiyah in (1978) 94 LQR at 221.
7 Limitation Act 1980, ss 2, 5. If the contract is under seal the period is 12 years: s 8(1).
8 Limitation Act 1980, s 11(1).

between contract and tort. Time generally runs from the moment of breach in the case of contract, but only from the time that the damage is suffered in tort. For example, if a building is negligently constructed so that cracks later appear in the walls, the cause of action for breach of contract accrues when the building was completed (which was the breach of the promise to build properly), while the cause of action for the tort of negligence arises only when the cracks occur (which is when the harm is suffered).[9] There are several other procedural differences between actions in tort and contract,[10] and some limitations on liability in tort that do not apply to contract.[11].

TORT AND EQUITABLE WRONGS

There is also a difficulty with equitable wrongs, such as the breach of trust. If a trustee commits a breach of trust, as by making off with the trust property, he can be made to pay compensation to the beneficiaries. This compensation is not technically called damages, but that is only a verbal point. In essence it is damages; yet the trustee is not regarded as committing a tort. The reason for distinguishing tort and breach of trust is the historical one relating to the distinction that existed before the Judicature Act 1873 between the courts of common law and the Court of Chancery: as said above, tort is primarily a common law matter. Neither

---

9 *Pirelli General Cable Works Ltd v Oscar Faber & Partners* [1983] 2 AC 1, [1983] 1 All ER 65.

10 For a summary of these see *Street on Torts* (7th edn, London, 1983) pp 442–3.

11 The Crown is answerable in tort only for a restricted class of 'servants' (Crown Proceedings Act 1947, s 2); a trade union is not liable for certain torts not authorised or endorsed by a responsible person within the union (Employment Act 1982, ss 15, 16, 17); the Post Office cannot be sued in tort in relation to the post (Post Office Act 1969, s 29(1)); and British Telecommunications have a similar immunity (British Telecommunications Act 1981, s 23(1)).

before the Judicature Act nor since have breaches of trust had applied to them the general rules of tort, and trusts are still, in the main, administered in a separate department of the High Court, the Chancery Division.

The difficulty of separating tort from equitable wrongs may be illustrated by reference to the legal protection of confidential information. The information may be literary ideas, the details of a person's private life, or trade secrets. The courts have laid down a broad equitable principle of good faith: 'he who has received information in confidence shall not take advantage of it'.[12] Equitable remedies are available for a breach of this principle: in particular an injunction to restrain a person from making use of confidences reposed on him. We shall see later[13] that wherever the Court of Chancery could have issued an injunction, the courts can now give damages in lieu of an injunction. Consequently, even on the definition of a tort as a wrong giving rise to an action for damages, an equitable wrong like a breach of confidence can be regarded as a tort, provided one is willing to cast aside the historical peculiarity of the remedy. There may, in addition, be a remedy in damages for breach of confidence where no equitable remedy would be granted. Let us say that the defendant did not derive a profit, and did not consciously make use of the information and so was in good faith; an injunction (or damages in lieu) would not be granted, and there would of course be no account of profits (another equitable remedy). In these circumstances, the innocent misappropriation of the information can be treated as akin to the misappropriation of tangible property and damages will be awarded and assessed on the analogy of the tort of conversion, that is, the value of the information taken. Once the damages are paid the

---

12 *Seager v Copydex Ltd* [1967] 2 All ER 415, [1967] 1 WLR 923, per Lord Denning MR at 417, 931.
13 See below, Chap 3, p 70.

information becomes the property of the defendant.[14] This example shows that insistence upon the difference between equity and law makes the definition of tort unnecessarily technical, and there is a convincing case for the view that at the present day the conception of a tort may well be extended to include some 'equitable torts'.[15] Breach of trust, however, must be excluded from the field of tort because it is a department of the law that has grown up separately with its own principles.

TORT AND RESTITUTION

The law of civil obligations is not confined to contract, tort and equitable wrongs. Another group of civil claims is founded on the conception of unjust enrichment. At the present day these claims are studied under the title of *restitution*, which includes the topic of quasi-contract. The root conception of quasi-contract is that the law gives the plaintiff a remedy on the basis of a fictitious promise by the defendant to pay him what is fair by way of restoration of the enrichment. (The advantage of the fiction of promise

14   *Seager v Copydex Ltd (No. 2)* [1969] 2 All ER 718, [1969] 1 WLR 809. P. M. North in (1972) 12 JSPTL 149 discusses the problems raised by this case. Gareth Jones, (1970) 86 LQR 463 at 475–477, criticises the decision on the ground that if liability is based on a duty to act in good faith (the equitable wrong), it is hard to see how a wholly innocent defendant can be in breach of that obligation. Against this, it can be argued that in the actual case the plaintiff recovered damages based on the same principles as those in conversion, although he was denied equitable remedies, because of a de facto fusion of law and equity. This is a development that helps the plaintiff who has suffered considerable loss by a breach of confidence although the defendant has not made a profit (and so cannot be made to account).

15   Another example is the developing concept of 'economic duress' ('coercion of the will which vitiates consent') which may be coterminous with tort, but need not be: *Universe Tankships Inc of Monrovia v International Transport Workers' Federation* [1983] 1 AC 366, [1982] 2 All ER 67. Enlightenment on this must be left to the books on restitution and labour law.

formerly was that it enabled the plaintiff to bring the same form of action, assumpsit, as if there had been an express contract.) For example, if P pays D money under a mistake of fact, there being in truth no money due, P can recover back the payment in quasi-contract. So also where money is paid on a consideration that subsequently fails. The defendant has not in fact contracted to repay the money, but the law treats him as if he has. All quasi-contractual claims are for money − never for a chattel − and the money claimed is usually a precise amount (a 'liquidated' sum).[16]

Apart from quasi-contract, there are other restitutionary claims founded upon the principle of unjust enrichment − for example, equitable relief from undue influence, and claims in equity analogous to quasi-contractual claims to recover money paid under mistake.[17]

The theoretical distinction between tort and quasi-contract is subtle − almost, one might say, metaphysical. The claim in quasi-contract is not founded upon a wrong, except indeed the wrong of keeping the plaintiff out of his money. A tort presupposes two distinct duties: a duty imposed on the defendant that an event shall or shall not happen, and, upon violation of that duty, a sanctioning duty on the defendant to pay damages for the wrong.[18] In quasi-contract, there is simply a duty to make monetary return in respect of an unjust enrichment; the enrichment need not have occurred by way of legal wrong, and the monetary return is not properly called damages. Hence in restitution there is only a single duty, namely to pay money.

---

16 Some claims in tort, also, are for a liquidated amount (eg a claim for the conversion (misappropriation) of £100), and some claims in quasi-contract are for unliquidated sums, ie are at large until fixed by the court (eg a claim against a person of unsound mind, who has no contractual capacity, for the reasonable price of necessaries supplied).

17 Goff and Jones *The Law of Restitution* (2nd edn, London, 1978) pp 3–5.

18 Although this is undoubtedly the theory of the law, we shall see (Chap 4) that strict and vicarious liability in tort do not fit well with it.

If this distinction is thought to be too mystical, a second point of difference is that in quasi-contract the emphasis is on the benefit unjustly received by the defendant, whereas in tort the emphasis is on the loss sustained by the plaintiff. Quasi-contract restores the benefit; tort remedies the loss. The fact that the two approaches may often yield the same monetary result does not affect the fact that they are different in principle. It is this difference that gives practical point to the possibility of 'waiving a tort' and suing in quasi-contract. A party who can prove that a tort has been committed may elect to sue in quasi-contract to recover the defendant's unjust benefit rather than sue in tort to recover damages.[19] For instance, if the tortfeasor has converted (ie misappropriated) a chattel and sold it for a sum in excess of its value at the date of the conversion, the plaintiff can waive the tort and claim the proceeds of the sale. There are several other procedural and substantial advantages of waiving a tort and proceeding in quasi-contract.[20]

CLAIMS FOR STATUTORY COMPENSATION

Somewhat analogous to quasi-contractual claims are *claims for compensation under statute*. An Act of Parliament may provide that the Government can requisition a chattel or expropriate land for public purposes – for example, for building a highway. Compensation is payable, and it may be provided that this shall be assessed by the ordinary courts or by some special tribunal. In the case of acquisition of land the compensation is assessable by a Lands Tribunal. An instance of compensation being assessed by the ordinary courts for an act done under statutory powers is the Manchester Ship Canal Act 1897, which provides that if a vessel is sunk in the

---

19 Goff and Jones op cit Chap 32.
20 Ibid pp 479–84; and see Burrows in (1983) 99 LQR at 236–9.

canal, the canal company may raise the vessel and recover the expenses from the owner in an action of debt in the ordinary courts.[1] This statute, notwithstanding that it gives an action in the High Court, does not fall within the common law conception of quasi-contract, since it does not depend upon an unjust enrichment obtained by the defendant; nor does it create a new tort. To sink a vessel in the canal, if without negligence, is not a tort, or a wrong to the canal company, but the canal company has a statutory right to recover its expenses. The expenses are an unliquidated sum until fixed by the court (for although the amount the company has spent may be known, there may be argument on whether the expenditure was reasonable or extravagant); but the expenses are not properly called 'damages', which is a word normally used to mean a sum of money payable as compensation for a wrong.[2]

The question may be asked whether the foregoing account of the differences between a claim in tort and a quasi-contractual or statutory money claim represents reality or whether it is merely a matter of legal language. Is there really any legal point in saying that an action for damages in tort presupposes a wrong by the defendant? Is not this 'wrong' a matter of morals, or even a mere matter of words, rather than an effective rule of law?

An illustration can be put that makes the distinction appear very thin. Suppose that the Government wants to acquire my motor car in time of emergency. It may do so in either of two ways. As one method, it may requisition the car under statutory powers, paying compensation assessed by a compensation tribunal. Alternatively, the Government may simply seize my car without bothering to act under any powers. In the latter case, the seizure will be a wrong and a tort, and I can sue the Crown for damages for the tort of

---

1 *The Stonedale (No. 1)* [1956] AC 1, [1955] 2 All ER 689.
2 See *Hall Bros SS Co Ltd v Young* [1939] 1 KB 748, [1939] 1 All ER 809.

conversion. When the Crown pays the damages under the judgment, the property in the car (ie ownership of the car) will pass to the Crown, because it is a rule that a satisfied judgment in conversion vests the property in the goods in the defendant. To put it simply, the position is that when the defendant pays the value of the goods under the judgment of the court, there is a sort of fictitious sale to him. Now the question may be asked whether there is any substantial difference between these two modes of procedure. The first mode, statutory expropriation, is supposed not to involve any legal wrong. The second is supposed to do so. Yet in both instances the Crown gets the car, and in both it has to pay compensation based on its value. So close is the similarity between the two cases that a famous American judge, Justice O. W. Holmes, was led to deny any real difference.[3]

It is now generally recognised that Holmes J was mistaken, and that several important differences exist. One example is the right of recaption of goods wrongfully taken. If the Crown takes my car unlawfully, I may seize it back if I am able. But if the Crown requisitions the car under statutory powers, the property in the car vests in the Crown and I may not legally use force to get it back. In the first case, there is a wrong which is remediable by self-help; in the second there is none. Another difference is that tort damages are assessed on the basis of restoring the status quo, while a claim for compensation in public law, particularly war damage, may be guided by the principle of sharing losses equitably among all those affected.[4]

---

3 (1897) 10 HLR 457.
4 See Carol Harlow *Compensation and Government Torts* (London, 1982) pp 102–15; and *Maharaj v A-G of Trinidad and Tobago (No 2)* [1979] AC 385, [1978] 2 All ER 670, where doubt was expressed whether a claim for compensation can ever include an exemplary or punitive award (for the position in tort see below, Chap 3, p 73).

SUMMARY OF THE DEFINITION OF TORT

The reader will now be waiting for a compendious definition of tort. It is not easy to give one. The most accurate definition, consistent with brevity, is to say that *a tort is a civil wrong recognised by the common law, or by statutory extension of the common law, or (possibly) in equity (but not being merely a breach of contract or breach of trust), the remedy for which is an action for damages.* But there is not much virtue in attempting to compress the scope of a department of law into a single sentence, particularly when the sentence is as clumsy as this.

THE AIMS OF THE LAW OF TORT

What has been said on the definition of a tort may become clearer if we look back at some of the distinctions drawn from a somewhat different angle, namely what the law of tort is trying to do. Speaking of legal proceedings generally, and not only of actions in tort, it may be said that they are generally brought for one or other of six purposes.[5]

1 *To give to the plaintiff what the defendant has promised him, or at least to give him damages for not getting what the defendant has promised.* As already said, it is usually the law of contract that protects the expectation interest of the plaintiff, ie his justifiable expectation that the promise will be performed; but we have seen that an action sounding in tort may sometimes protect an expectation interest – even that of a person other than the promisee.

5 The purposes of the law of tort in particular are examined in (1951) 4 CLP 137.

2   *To compensate for harm, or to prevent the continuance or repetition of harm.* This is the most important function of the law of tort, but it is also part of the function of the law of contract, and of other departments of the law as well (eg breach of trust). All these branches of law protect the plaintiff's 'reliance'[6] or 'status quo' interest,[7] aiming to put him in as good a position as he was before the wrong was committed.

3   *To restore to a person what another has unjustly obtained at his expense.* This department of the law has come to be known generically as restitution. Restitution may be effected through the operation of a number of legal rules. Where the thing obtained is money, the person deprived of it can generally obtain redress by means of an action in quasi-contract, which, as we have seen, is an action proceeding upon a fiction of promise by the defendant to repay the money unjustly obtained. But an action in contract proper may also be used to enforce restitution where there is a contractual relationship between the parties and the courts can imply a term that the defendant shall make restitution; or the law of constructive trusts may be used to achieve a similar result. Finally, the law of tort may be pressed into service. If the thing unjustly detained by the defendant from the plaintiff is not money but some chattel or land, no action in quasi-contract lies (because that action is limited to money), and the plaintiff must sue in tort for the wrongful detention of the chattel or land.[8] Thus it has to be said that one of the aims of the law of tort is the restoration of unjust enrichment, and to this extent tort belongs to the law of restitution.

6   This is the term coined by Fuller and Perdue in their classic article in (1936–37) 46 Yale LJ 52, 373.
7   This term is preferred by Burrows in (1983) 99 LQR at 219–20.
8   This will be an action for the tort of conversion in the case of goods and an action of ejectment in the case of land.

4 *To punish for wrongs and to deter from wrongdoing.* This is the historic function of the criminal law. Yet the law of tort also has it as one of its purposes – as is shown by the frequent remark that a new offence should not be created if the civil sanction is sufficient. The punitive element is particularly obvious when exemplary damages are given for a tort. But even ordinary damages can be regarded as having a two-fold aspect: although in theory they are compensation to the plaintiff for what he has undergone, in fact they are also a punishment to the defendant for what he has done.[9]

5 *To decide the rights of the parties.* There is one action, called the action for a declaration, that is specifically designed to declare the rights of the parties when nothing is in issue but the question of right. However, almost any action can incidentally have the effect of settling rights. An action for damages in contract determines contractual rights; and an action for damages in tort may determine all kinds of rights. For example, it may be used to establish the right of the plaintiff to land or to a chattel. The court, in awarding damages for wrongful detention of the land or chattel, necessarily declares that the plaintiff has some kind of title to it – even if only a possessory title.

6 *To decide or alter a person's status.* The most obvious examples of proceedings to alter status are divorce, where the court is asked to dissolve a marriage and restore the parties to the status of unmarried persons, and adoption, where the court is asked to transfer parental rights from the natural parents to the adopting parents. An action in tort never alters a person's status, but it may occasionally be used to declare it. Thus suppose that Mrs D writes that Mrs P is

---

9 But the aim of punishment is not explicit in the law, and consequently the measure of damages in tort is based on the loss to the plaintiff, not the gain to the defendant see below, Chap 3, p 74.

not married to Mr P. This is a libel upon Mrs P, and Mrs P can bring an action in tort, which will have as an incidental result a declaration by the court that Mrs P is properly married. This declaration may be much more important to Mrs P than the money damages she gets.

This brief review of legal proceedings shows that an action of tort may serve almost all the purposes for which people go to law. The great variety of functions performed by the law of tort gives this topic its great legal and social importance, but also adds in no small measure to its complexity. Of all the possible purposes of an action in tort, however, the most important is certainly that numbered 2. The compensatory purpose underlies the great majority of actions in tort, and it is this purpose, expressed in the action for damages, that, as has been seen, enters into the technical definition of a tort. Scots law emphasises its importance by giving this branch of the law the general name of 'reparation'.

In recent years there has been growing emphasis in legal writing[10] and in university courses on the compensatory aspect of the law of tort, particularly in regard to claims arising from personal injuries and death. Fact-based classifications of the law,[11] which break down conventional concepts like 'contract' and 'tort' into functional groupings that reflect the facts of social and economic life, have much to commend them, particularly when one wishes to study matters of policy and law reform. An intelligent approach must involve examining the social functions of the law of tort, and testing the legal rules critically in the light of those functions.

Before we can do this, however, we must step inside the door of the house of tort and meet some ghosts that haunt it.

---

10 See the list of Further Reading, below, p 221.
11 The phrase is suggested by J. A. Jolowicz in his paper under that title in *The Division and Classification of the Law* (ed. Jolowicz) (London, 1970) p 1.

2 The ghost story

Those who cannot remember the past are condemned to repeat it.
                                     Santayana *Reason and Common Sense*

This chapter is on the historical side, but its object is the practical one of explaining the classification of torts at the present day. The modern law of tort has been considerably influenced by the forms of action, that is to say the old categories of legal claim, which were governed by strict rules. These rules, and the forms of action themselves, were abolished in the nineteenth century, yet they have had an enduring effect upon the arrangement and also upon some of the details of the law. 'The forms of action,' said Maitland 'we have buried, but they still rule us from their graves.'[1] Their spectral existence can be perceived in three ways: in the chapter-headings of a modern book on tort; in the way a tort action is pleaded; and in rules as to the necessity for proof of damage. The first two matters will be considered immediately, the third in the next chapter.

OLD RULES AS TO THE FORMS OF ACTION

To begin with, we may remind ourselves of the importance of the writ in the middle ages. Bracton, writing during the reign of Henry III, stated the rule that no action could be brought in the king's courts of common law without the king's writ. The rule was not invariable in his time, but it

---

1 For a general account see Maitland *Forms of Action* (1936 edn) pp 1–11, 48–72; Sutton *Personal Actions* Chap 4.

became completely true afterwards. Even today, claims for any relief or remedy for a tort must ordinarily be begun by a writ, and the sovereign's association with the administration of justice is indicated by a replica of the Royal Arms at the top of the writ. But whereas nowadays there is only one type of writ whatever the cause of action, in former times there was a distinct writ to start each main type of claim, and these writs differed from each other on a number of points. In technical language, each writ was appropriate to a particular form of action. And each form of action was a separate pigeonhole having its own procedure and its own substantive law. The law applicable to the action of trespass was different from the law applicable to the action upon the case. The law applicable to the action upon the case differed in many ways from the law applicable to the action of detinue. And so on with all the other forms of action. If the plaintiff brought one when he ought to have brought another he lost the case, and it was not much comfort to him to know that after paying the costs of the unsuccessful proceeding he could begin all over again with the proper form of action.

THE ABOLITION OF THE FORMS OF ACTION

This disease of 'hardening of the categories' is one of the worst that can afflict a legal system, and strong measures were necessary for the cure. After a palliative in 1832, forms of action were theoretically abolished by the Common Law Procedure Act 1852, which was superseded by the more thorough-going provisions of the Judicature Act 1873 (which came into operation in 1875). Today the precise form in which an action is framed is not usually material; as Scrutton LJ observed, 'the courts find out the facts, and having done so, endeavour to give the right legal judgment on those facts.'[2] Or, as Diplock LJ said, 'a cause of action is simply a factual situation the existence of which entitles one

2 *Oakley v Lyster* [1931] 1 KB 148 at 151.

person to obtain a remedy against another person.'[3] The present-day writ is appropriate to any cause of action; and when the plaintiff draws up his statement of claim he is not expected to plead the law on which he relies, but need plead only the facts. It is true that the courts require the facts to be pleaded with sufficient particularity to enable the defendant to make his defence; and for this purpose, and to save the time of the court by particularising the issue, the plaintiff may be required to state his cause of action.[4] But if he states the claim wrongly, the court will generally try to help him over the difficulty either by giving leave to amend the pleading, or even (sometimes) by ignoring the mistake. Stable J said: 'The question is not now one of the appropriate forms in which to clothe the right, but whether or not the right exists, although the absence of any clothing that fits may be an indication of the non-existence of the right.'[5] In similar vein Lord Atkin, harking back to Maitland's epigram about the forms of action, said: 'When these ghosts of the past stand in the path of justice, clanking their

---

3 *Letang v Cooper* [1965[1 QB 232 at 242–3.

4 Lord Halsbury once said, in *The Calliope* [1891] AC 11 at 13: 'I cannot help thinking that this case affords a somewhat important illustration of the necessity of calling upon litigants to place in some written form of pleading the precise cause of action upon which they rely, for I think that the time during which your Lordships have been occupied and the time which has been occupied in the courts below has to a considerable extent been the result of an oscillation in the minds of the advisers of the plaintiff as to what was their cause of action.' Although a court that takes this attitude may penalise a plaintiff in costs for not obeying the rules of pleading, and this is a fact to be reckoned with by counsel, it may be doubted whether judges are really justified nowadays in frowning upon an 'oscillation in the minds of the advisers of the plaintiff'. Since the forms of action have been abolished, the advisers of the plaintiff are entitled to refrain from making up their minds as to the proper form of action, and to leave this question to the judges. There is certainly nothing improper in bringing an action based expressly upon two or more causes of action.

5 *Dies v British and International Mining and Finance Corpn Ltd* [1939] 1 KB 724 at 738; approved in *Rivoli Hats Ltd v Gooch* [1953] 2 All ER 823 at 825, [1953] 1 WLR 1190 at 1193.

medieval chains, the proper course for the judge is to pass through them undeterred.'[6]

In order to understand this better we must revert to certain matters of procedure. Today, as said before, there is only one form of writ to commence every action. The following is a specimen. (In the county court the forms and procedure are simpler.)

[Royal Arms]

In the High Court of Justice   1983 S No. 4567
Queen's Bench Division
[Group   ]
[District Registry]

BETWEEN   John Doe   PLAINTIFF
AND   Richard Roe   DEFENDANT

TO THE DEFENDANT Richard Roe
of 777 Fleet Street, in the City of London

THIS WRIT OF SUMMONS has been issued against you by the above-named Plaintiff in respect of the claim set out on the back.

Within [14 days] after the service of this Writ on you, counting the day of service, you must either satisfy the claim or return to the Court Office mentioned below the accompanying ACKNOWLEDGMENT OF SERVICE stating therein whether you intend to contest these proceedings.

If you fail to satisfy the claim or return the Acknowledgment within the time stated, or if you return the Acknowledgment without stating therein an intention to contest the proceedings, the Plaintiff may proceed with the action and judgment may be entered against you forthwith without further notice.

Issued from the Central Office [or   District Registry] of the High Court this   th day of December 1983.

Important

Directions for acknowledgment of service are given with the accompanying form.

6 *United Australia Ltd v Barclays Bank Ltd* [1941] AC 1 at 29. Lord Wright thought that this decision rendered the forms of action 'as dead as mutton'

On the back of the writ is an indorsement setting out the nature of the plaintiff's claim and the relief or remedy sought. This may be in general language, without much detail (formerly called a 'general indorsement'). For example:

The plaintiff's claim is for
(1) Damages for personal injuries, loss and expense caused by the negligent driving of the Defendant or his servants on the 21st day of August 1983 at Ludgate Circus in the City of London.
(2) Interest thereon pursuant to the Law Reform (Miscellaneous Provisions) Act 1934 and the Administration of Justice Act 1969.

To give the defendant more precise notice of what is alleged against him, and so enable him to prepare his defence, where the writ has been indorsed in this general way, the plaintiff must subsequently serve on the defendant a full statement of claim. Alternatively, the writ may be indorsed with a full statement of claim (formerly called a 'special indorsement'). The statement of claim is divided into numbered paragraphs setting out the facts on which the plaintiff relies, and the relief that he asks for, including particulars of special damage. The following is an example:

(1) On or about the 21st day of August 1983 the plaintiff travelled by omnibus from St. Paul's Cathedral to Ludgate Circus in the City of London.
(2) On arrival at Ludgate Circus, the plaintiff having waited for the said omnibus to stop at the recognised stopping place alighted from the said omnibus and proceeded to cross the road.
(3) While the plaintiff was crossing the road as aforesaid the defendant so negligently drove a motor car along the said road that he knocked down and injured the plaintiff. The plaintiff has thereby been put to loss and expense and has suffered damage.

(57 LQR 184). Lord Atkin's sentiment was approved by Lord Denning MR in *Letang v Cooper* [1965] 1 QB 232 at 239 ('the distinction between trespass and case is obsolete').

(A) Particulars of Negligence

The defendant was negligent in that he –
  (i) drove too fast;
 (ii) drove on the wrong side of the road;
(iii) failed to keep any proper look-out;
 (iv) failed to give any sufficient warning of his approach;
  (v) passed too close to a stationary vehicle, from which passengers were or might be alighting.[7]

(B) Particulars of Injury

The injuries suffered by the plaintiff were:
  (i) compound fracture of the lower third of the left tibia and fibula;
 (ii) concussion;
(iii) abrasions and lacerations of the thighs;
 (iv) shock.

Plaintiff was treated as a hospital in-patient for two weeks. Under general anaesthetic the fracture was manipulated and immobilised in a plaster. The plaster was removed at the end of three months, and the Plaintiff attended hospital as an out-patient for exercise to mobilise the knee and strengthen the leg. There is some stiffness in the ankle and the Plaintiff limps somewhat. There is still a 25% loss of normal movement and stiffness in the toes.

(C) Particulars of Special Damage

The plaintiff suffered the following special damage:
  (i) Loss of wages from 22.8.83 to 21.11.83 at £100
      per week   £1,200.00
 (ii) Home help's wages while Plaintiff was incapacitated,
      22.8.83 to 21.11.83 at £25.00 per week   £ 300.00
(iii) Damage to clothing   £   50.00
 (iv) Ambulance fee 21.8.83   £   2.00
  (v) Prescription charges and other medical fees etc.   £ 500.00
 (vi) Hospital treatment   £ 432.00

---

7 The first four of these particulars of negligence are common form in running-down cases. The last is added to meet the facts of the particular case.

And the plaintiff claims

(1) Damages
(2) Interest thereon pursuant to the Law Reform (Miscellaneous Provisions) Act 1934 and the Administration of Justice Act 1969.[8]

Now the point is that on this writ and statement of claim the court will give the plaintiff any relief to which he is entitled in law, and the plaintiff does not run the risk of being told that although he has a good claim he has chosen the wrong form of action to enforce it. Moreover a plaintiff is now allowed to join any number of claims in a single action, provided that they are not so diverse as to be embarrassing to the defendant. He may, for example, sue both in contract and in tort, or he may sue both in tort and in quasi-contract, electing at the last moment to take his judgment for the one or the other,[9] if the circumstances make such an election necessary. He cannot, of course, recover double damages by relying on two causes of action.

In view of this development, it is no longer strictly accurate to speak of an 'action *of* trespass' or an 'action *of* negligence'; strictly speaking it ought to be 'an action *for* trespass', 'an action *for* negligence'. In other words there is only one action for all cases, although the statement of claim in the action may allege liability in trespass or in negligence according to the old distinctions. Still, old language dies hard, and as a matter of convenience we continue to use the old terms – to speak of an action of trespass, of case, of conversion, even in connection with modern law. The student

---

8 This form is based upon those in Atkin's *Encyclopaedia of Court Forms in Civil Proceedings* (2nd edn, London, 1976) vol 29. The other practitioner's work of this character is Bullen and Leake *Precedents of Pleadings*. A set of pleadings in an industrial compensation claim will be found in Hepple and Matthews, Chap 1.

9 For tort and quasi-contract this was decided in *United Australia Ltd v Barclays Bank Ltd* [1941] AC 1.

must understand that these expressions refer to a generic action in which the statement of claim alleges trespass, negligence, and so on, or at any rate alleges facts from which some cause of action arises.[10]

THE INFLUENCE OF THE FORMS OF ACTION ON LEGAL CATEGORIES

One of the features of the American landscape is the Petrified Forest of Arizona, where the form and shape of ancient trees remain, whilst every particle of vegetable substance has disappeared, having been replaced by infiltrating minerals. In somewhat the same way, the vanished forms of action have left our legal thinking eternally moulded to their shape. Dead and gone, they are immortalised in our nomenclature. Lawyers are accustomed to fit facts into legal categories, and the old categories still control the meaning of legal terms. When we speak of a trespass, we mean a wrong that in former times would have been remedied by the writ of trespass. Similarly a nuisance is a wrong that would formerly have been remedied by the action upon the case for nuisance. The forms of action continue to rule us through the dictionary. The classic works on the law of tort – Pollock, Salmond, and Winfield – are strongly influenced in their arrangement by the old categories. In American legal writing and a few modern English works, however, an effort has been made to break away from the classification according to traditional torts, and to expound the law according to the plaintiff's interest that has been violated. There are the plaintiff's interests of personality – freedom from assault, false imprisonment, etc; his interests in family

---

10 The court may give judgment for the plaintiff on ground A, when this appears from the facts stated in the particulars, even though the particulars expressly mention ground B: *Drane v Evangelou* [1978] 2 All ER 437, [1978] 1 WLR 455.

relations; his proprietary interests; his interest in reputation, economic security, and so on. This classification by the interest affected has to be further divided according as the tort is intentional or merely negligent, for the principles applicable to these two varieties are by no means the same. It means that some of the traditional compartments have to be divided and rearranged: the tort of negligence, in particular, must be divided according to the interest invaded, while the tort of trespass must be divided not only according to the interest invaded but according to the type of fault. The advantage of this form of presentation is not only that it makes for the orderly arrangement of a textbook or – if we ever come to have one – a code. By directing attention to the interest of the plaintiff that it is socially desirable to protect, and to the degree of protection given it, one can better perceive the gaps and inconsistencies in the legal scheme.

THEIR SURVIVING IMPORTANCE IN PLEADING

Occasionally it may happen that the plaintiff pleads in his statement of claim that the defendant has committed a trespass, or a nuisance, or something of the sort, and the court may think that according to traditional language the wrong legal term has been used and that the defendant has in fact committed some other kind of wrong. This mistake on the part of the plaintiff will not usually matter, because the court will give him liberty to amend his pleading, or if specially indulgent may even overlook the malapropism without amendment and give judgment against the defendant for the tort that he is proved to have committed.

The plaintiff obtains no *procedural* advantage by pleading his cause of action under one legal category rather than another. For example, it will make no difference to the time-barrier should he plead his case as one of trespass rather than negligence. By statute, causes of action are generally barred by the lapse of six years.[11] Actions for damages for 'negligence, nuisance or breach of duty' in respect of personal injuries are barred after the shorter period of three years.[12] A plaintiff cannot avoid the shorter period in an action for damages for personal injuries by the expedient of labelling his claim as one for 'trespass to the person'. It was held in *Letang v Cooper*[13] that the words 'breach of duty' include all tortious breaches of duty including trespass to the person. This is so whether the injuries are unintentionally[14] or intentionally[15] inflicted. Under rules of court[16] it is even permissible, by amendment with leave of the court, to add a new cause of action after the limitation period has expired, provided that the writ was issued before the period expired and the new cause of action arises out of substantially the same facts as those on which the original cause of action was based.

Nevertheless, the levelling of procedural barriers has not robbed the forms of action of all their legal importance. To some extent it remains true to say that the ectoplasm of the forms of action still controls *substantive* rights. If the facts on which the plaintiff's claim is founded cannot be fitted into any of the old forms of action, one is on the way to saying that the plaintiff has no remedy. A defendant may set out to show that before 1875 the plaintiff could not have brought an action of trespass, an action upon the case, an action of detinue, and so on, in order to persuade the court that at the

---

11 Limitation Act 1980, ss 2, 5.
12 Limitation Act 1980, s 11(1).
13 [1965] 1 QB 232, [1964] 2 All ER 929. This was the main reason given by Danckwerts LJ and the alternative line of reasoning of Lord Denning MR and Diplock LJ.
14 Ibid.
15 *Long v Hepworth* [1968] 3 All ER 248, [1968] 1 WLR 1299 (Cooke J).
16 RSC Ord 20, r 5(5). This rule was revised in 1964 and now overcomes some of the former difficulties which stood in the way of such amendments.

present day the plaintiff has no action at all. Thus the search for an appropriate form of action under the old law is still, in some situations where the legal position is doubtful, part of the mental process of the competent lawyer.[17]

This point must not be pressed too far, because the law has been growing since 1875, just as it grew before that date, and it is therefore not a conclusive answer for the defendant to say that the claim would not have been recognised before the Judicature Act. Since the Judicature Act judges have been slowly emancipating themselves from the forms of action; they have begun to think in terms of broad rules of law which are not related to the old categories. An outstanding example is the case of *Wilkinson v Downton*,[18] decided by an eminent judge of the Victorian era, Wright J.

> Mr Downton, in joke, told Mrs Wilkinson that her husband had been 'smashed up' in an accident and had both his legs broken. The lady suffered a serious shock entailing weeks of suffering and incapacity. At the risk of seeming to have no sense of humour she sued Downton for damages. Wright J held that the action well lay.

There was no precedent for this decision before the Judicature Act. The plaintiff could not have brought an action for trespass, which lay only for the direct physical infliction of harm (or the threat of it). Here the plaintiff had been physically injured, but only as the result of her mental shock following upon the words spoken. She could not have sued for this mental suffering in deceit, because an action for deceit could be brought only where the defendant had made a fraudulent statement on which the plaintiff was intended to rely, and did rely to his detriment; here the plaintiff was

---

17 An example of a refusal by a modern court to extend the old forms of action – a refusal arising from some hostility to the type of claim – is *Best v Samuel Fox & Co Ltd* [1952] AC 716, [1952] 2 All ER 394.

18 [1897] 2 QB 57 (Hepple and Matthews, p 50); followed in *Janvier v Sweeney* [1919] 2 KB 316 (Hepple and Matthews, p 52).

not claiming in respect of damage resulting from any conduct on her part in reliance upon the truth of the statement. The damage resulted merely from her belief in its truth, and from the effect that that belief had upon her mind. Notwithstanding these difficulties, the judge felt able to assert the existence of a principle of law whereby the intentional infliction of bodily harm is a tort. He did not attempt to relate his decision to any of the ancient writs, as by saying that the concept of trespass to the person could be extended to a 'psychological assault'. Instead, he assumed the existence of a general principle of law according to which a person who intends without justification to cause fear or anxiety to another, in circumstances where grave effects are likely to follow, is responsible if such effects do follow. The judge's attitude can perhaps be expressed in Horatio's words: 'There needs no ghost, my lord, come from the grave to tell us this.' The decision is an outstanding example of the greater readiness of the courts at the present day to lay down general principles of liability instead of indulging in mere historical research.

THE ACTION OF TRESPASS

Enough has been said to show how the forms of action have moulded legal thought, and so, perhaps, to render more palatable the following very short exposition of the old law.

The modern law of tort springs from three actions: of trespass *vi et armis*, case and detinue. Detinue (wrongful detention of goods) was abolished by the Torts (Interference with Goods) Act 1977.[19] The action for conversion now lies in every case in which detinue would formerly have been

---

19 Section 2(1).

available. This can be left for specialised study elsewhere, but the first two actions are so important that they need some consideration.

The action of trespass *vi et armis* – otherwise called 'general trespass', 'common trespass', or 'trespass' simply – commenced early in the thirteenth century, under King John, as a combined civil and criminal proceeding. It operated not only to give the plaintiff damages but to punish the defendant by a fine payable to the Crown. Later these two aspects became separated, and we are concerned only with the civil one.

According to the mature theory of the law, trespass was the appropriate remedy for any act causing a direct and forcible injury – in other words for any direct invasion of a right by some physical interference.[20] To the layman, trespass means trespass to land, but the lawyer recognises in addition trespasses to the person and to chattels. If the trespass was to the person, the action used to be, and still is, called assault, battery, or false imprisonment, according to the circumstances. If the trespass was to goods, it was generally trespass *de bonis asportatis* – the wrong of carrying away chattels from the possession of another. (But it was equally a trespass to damage goods, even though they were not carried off.) If to land, it was trespass *quare clausum fregit* – the defendant was summoned to show wherefore he broke the plaintiff's close. The word 'close' bore a Pickwickian meaning, as is so often found with legal expressions: originally, no doubt, it signified land that was really enclosed by a fence, but very soon it became extended to all land – even an open heath. The word 'land' in law includes buildings, so any trespass in or damage to buildings was covered by the writ.

---

20 Blackstone *Commentaries* iii 123, 208. The earlier meaning was wider: see 73 LQR 65.

The allegation of force and arms (*vi et armis*) may at first have been an allegation of a real fact, but speedily became a legal fiction. Any physical interference came to be regarded as *vi et armis* in law, so that, for instance, spitting upon a man was as much an assault and battery as beating him with a bludgeon. Moreover, if a person were lawfully on land with the permission of the occupier, but then the permission were revoked, he would, under the doctrine of continuing trespass, become a trespasser from the moment when he wrongfully failed to leave.

The three limitations upon the notion of trespass were that there had to be an *act* by the defendant that amounted to a *direct* and *forcible* invasion of the plaintiff's rights. There had to be an act: there could be no liability in trespass for a mere omission. (The doctrine of continuing trespass was an exception to this.) The act had to be by the defendant: hence if the defendant were forcibly carried upon the plaintiff's land by third parties,[1] or by a runaway horse,[2] he was not liable in trespass. The requirement of some 'forcible' interference with the plaintiff's right meant that merely causing economic loss, as by deceit, was not a trespass. The concept of a 'direct' injury was a subtle one; perhaps the rule would better be expressed by saying that the injurious consequence had to be 'immediate' upon the act – not necessarily immediate in time, but immediate in causal sequence. If the injurious result followed only after a protracted chain of causation, it was said to be 'consequential' and trespass would not lie.[3]

---

1 *Smith v Stone* (1647) Sty 65, 82 ER 533 (Hepple and Matthews, p 382).
2 Cp. *Gibbons v Pepper* (1695) 1 Ld Raym 38, 91 ER 922.
3 Sometimes the courts showed benevolence to the action, as in the well-known squib case of *Scott v Shepherd* (1773) 2 Wm Bl 892, 96 ER 525 (Hepple and Matthews, p 40). Lord Ellenborough, some 40 years afterwards, remarked that it 'went to the limit of the law' (3 East 593).

THE ACTION UPON THE CASE

The origin of the action upon the case has long been wrapped in obscurity, but an impressive piece of historical detection by Professor Milsom[4] enables us to state the development with some confidence. Originally the word 'trespass' meant any wrong – a meaning that it still bears in the traditional English rendering of the Lord's Prayer. Most trespasses, or wrongs, were redressed in the local (county) courts, and the king's courts were reluctant to hear them unless a breach of the peace were involved or there were some other royal interest. Putting this in another way, Professor Milsom says that in the thirteenth and fourteenth centuries the *concept* of trespass was unlimited. For the royal courts, the only question was a jurisdictional one: 'Is this the kind of trespass that the court can or will handle?' It would handle an action of trespass alleging *vi et armis*, because this wrong was menacing to the national security; and it would also handle an action of trespass that did not allege a forcible wrong provided that a sufficient case could be made for the intervention of royal justice. For example, actions of trespass were heard in the king's courts for failing to repair river walls, the duty to repair these being regarded as of a public nature; and similarly actions were heard for interfering with the plaintiff's franchise of market, as by preventing people from coming to his market, or selling outside his market. In actions of this type, the writ would recite the special right of the plaintiff (his right to have the wall repaired, or his franchise of market) which the defendant had infringed. This peculiarity of the wording of the writ led to a distinction between 'common trespass' (*vi et armis*) and 'special trespass'. Common trespass was an action for a forcible wrong like

---

4 *Historical Foundations of the Common Law* (2nd edn, London, 1981) Chap 11; and his earlier articles in (1958) 74 LQR 195, 407, 561; (1965) 81 LQR 496; [1954] CLJ 105.

assault, battery or breaking a close. It followed a standard formula and did not allege any special right in the plaintiff. Special trespass was also an action of trespass, but it did not follow a standard formula to the same degree as the other kind: it had, to some extent, to be specially framed to meet the particular grievance of the plaintiff.

It is unnecessary to enter further into the many complexities of the development: suffice it to say that in later medieval theory the writs of special trespass came to be regarded as belonging to a distinct form of action, the action upon the special case. As the local courts decayed, the royal courts came to entertain a wider variety of actions upon the case.

It is the action upon the case (otherwise called trespass on the case, or 'case' simply) that has given us the major part of our modern law of tort, as well as the whole of our law of simple contract. If one wishes to know how much of the law of tort is owed to the action of case, one can find the answer by simple subtraction. Every single tort except those redressed by the actions of trespass (*vi et armis*) and (formerly) detinue is the product of case. Defamation, deceit, conversion, negligence, nuisance, probably *Rylands v Fletcher*, and malicious prosecution – all these sound in case, and a number of others besides.

One of the best examples of the boundary between trespass and case in the mature common law is to be obtained by comparing the torts of false imprisonment and malicious prosecution. In false imprisonment, the defendant has unlawfully locked the plaintiff up, or otherwise deprived him of liberty. This is a direct, physical interference which used to fall properly within the writ of trespass. In malicious prosecution, the defendant has maliciously and without reasonable cause instituted criminal proceedings against the plaintiff, and the charge has been dismissed. Here the plaintiff has an action, but it was formerly an action upon the case, not trespass. A person who has been maliciously prosecuted has very likely been deprived of his liberty, either while waiting for trial or at least during the trial; yet his complaint does not fall within the definition of trespass. This is said to be because the defendant has not directly interfered with the plaintiff; he has moved a judicial officer (a magistrate or judge) to act against the plaintiff; and the discretion of this officer, who cannot be regarded as a mere agent of the defendant, has been interposed between the defendant's conduct and the injurious result to the plaintiff.[5] Thus the injury is merely 'consequential'.

Although this distinction is generally treated as though it rested on a self-evident difference between judicial and ministerial functions, its true basis is public policy. If everyone charged with crime could, upon acquittal, turn round and sue the prosecutor for damages, the public purse would be much depleted and prosecutors would be inhibited. Careful restriction of the scope of the tort of malicious prosecution is therefore necessary in the interest of law enforcement. The courts enabled themselves to impose such restriction by requiring the action for malicious prosecution to be framed in case; the plaintiff was then required to allege and prove much more than that he had been wrongly imprisoned. He had to show that the prosecution was brought maliciously and without reasonable and probable cause and was determined in his favour. These rules are still the law.

This example may suggest the generalisation that a defendant who has caused an injury by operating upon a person's mind and thus indirectly enabling himself to bring about an injurious consequence is not a trespasser. However, this generalisation would not explain all the specific rules of law. For example, if D orders X (who may be a policeman) to arrest P unlawfully, and X does so, D is liable to P in

---

5 *Austin v Dowling* (1870) LR 5 CP 534 at 540 (Hepple and Matthews, p 599).

trespass for false imprisonment. Yet D has not lifted a finger to procure P's imprisonment; he has merely spoken words, and operated upon the mind of the policeman. His wrong is not regarded as an indirect one. Again, suppose that D orders P to remain where he is, impliedly threatening force if he does not, and P complies. This is, in law, a false imprisonment of P, and a trespass; yet the defendant has achieved his object purely by psychological means, and moreover psychological means directed to the plaintiff himself.

Another example of what is meant by an indirect wrong is the comparison of trespass and nuisance. The favourite illustration of the difference between these two torts in the old books was as follows. If I throw a log into the highway and it hits you, you can sue me in trespass (battery), but if it falls into the road and you trip over it at night, your action is case.[6] Nowadays it would be called an action of nuisance or negligence. It is an obstruction of the highway, not trespass to the person. Again, if I drive a golf ball on to your land that is trespass, and even if I put a mound of rubbish on the edge of my land so that it inevitably slides down on to yours, that is trespass.[7] But if I erect a house with a roof so shaped that it shoots rain water on to your land, that is only case (nuisance).

Artificial distinctions of this kind were bound to give rise to moot questions, but the practitioner's worries were greatly reduced when it was decided in a line of cases culminating in a clear rule in 1833 that the action upon the case for negligence overlapped traspass. Even if the plaintiff had a cause of action in trespass, because there was a direct and physical wrong, he was not confined to this action, but could bring an action of negligence whenever he was in a

---

6 Per Fortescue J in *Reynolds v Clarke* (1725) 1 Stra 634 at 636, 93 ER at 748.
7 *Gregory v Piper* (1829) 9 B & C 591, 109 ER 220. The question has arisen in modern times whether it is technically trespass or nuisance to discharge oil in the sea whereby it reaches the plaintiff's foreshore: see (1951) 17 MLR 580.

position to prove that the defendant had been negligent.[8] The law was thus summed up by the author of a well-known student's manual of the nineteenth century. The permission to sue in case, he observed, relieved the practitioner of the distracting difficulties that had formerly arisen.

> For wherever there is the least doubt, and the plaintiff cannot show that the act complained of was done wilfully and designedly, he will take the prudent course, and sue in Case – in which form of action he may recover as great an amount of damages, as in Trespass. It is chiefly cases of accidents occurring in driving carriages, and navigating ships, which give rise to these questions: and the results of the numerous decisions on the subject may be thus stated. First, if the injury be both wilful and immediate, Trespass is the only remedy.[9] Secondly, if immediate, yet not wilful, either Trespass or Case may be maintained. Thirdly, when the injury is not immediate, but only consequential, Case alone will lie. Fourthly, when the act arises from the negligence of the defendant's servants, Case is the only proper remedy.[10]

THE ELEMENT OF FAULT IN TRESPASS

The passage just quoted will serve as an introduction to the problem of fault in trespass. In the modern law a claim for damages in respect of an injury which has been intentionally caused may be framed in negligence since it is no defence to say that the act was intentional.

> For example, when a youth of 15 deliberately and without warning pushed a man into a swimming pool, so causing him serious injury,

---

8 *Williams v Holland* (1833) 10 Bing 112, 131 ER 848. M. J. Prichard in [1964] CLJ 234–53, provides a detailed and illuminating account of the development of this rule.
9 This is no longer true. See below.
10 Samuel Warren *Introduction to Law Studies* (2nd edn, 1845) p 494. The Common Law Procedure Act 1852 introduced a further improvement by allowing the joinder of causes of action.

the judge decided that the youth by his intentional act had exposed the man to the foreseeable risk of injury and so was liable in negligence.[11]

The allegation in the pleadings that the defendant acted intentionally may in essence also be an allegation of trespass to the person, but no legal advantage flows from this because, whether the claim be labelled negligence or trespass, the damages must be calculated in the same way.[12] The only situation in which it is convenient to rely upon an allegation that an intentional act constitutes a trespass is when the plaintiff cannot prove actual damage since, as we shall see in the next chapter, an action for trespass may be used to vindicate a right without the necessity of proving damage. Where the act is only negligent there is no legal consequence whether the claim is called negligence or trespass,[13] because the plaintiff must, in any event, prove actual damage.

There is another possibility to be considered: may a trespass be committed without either intention or negligence? Can an inevitable accident amount to a trespass? Or, to frame the question in yet another form of words, is trespass a tort of strict liability?

This matter was long in dispute. If one goes back to the middle ages, one can certainly find instances where the issue of inevitable accident was introduced, if only as an appeal to the mercy of the jury.[14] In some later cases it was expressly

---

11 *Williams v Humphrey* (1975) Times, 12 February (Talbot J).

12 In *Letang v Cooper* [1965] 1 QB 232 at 239, Lord Denning MR suggests that 'if intentional, it is the tort of assault and battery. If negligent and causing damage, it is the tort of negligence.' This should not be taken to mean that, at the present day, an intentional tort cannot be pleaded as negligence: cp. Diplock LJ at 244 (Hepple and Matthews, p 35).

13 See especially Diplock LJ in *Letang v Cooper* [1965] 1 QB 232 at 244. The distinction between trespass to the person and negligence was drawn by Nield J in *Gorely v Codd* [1967] 1 WLR 19 at 25, but had no effect upon the outcome of the case.

14 See Milsom in (1958) 74 LQR 214, 582–3; and for a special plea see YB (1470) T 10 E4, Selden Society (47) 113.

recognised that the defendant could plead inevitable accident.[15] But they were not regarded as settling the law, and were notably opposed in a number of dicta in *Rylands v Fletcher*.[16] This was an important case in which the judges veered towards a philosophy of strict liability. Lord Cranworth said in the House of Lords:

> In considering whether a defendant is liable to a plaintiff for damage which the plaintiff may have sustained, the question in general is not whether the defendant has acted with due care and caution, but whether his acts have occasioned the damage. And the doctrine is founded on good sense. For when one person, in managing his own affairs, causes, however innocently, damage to another, it is obviously only just that he should be the party to suffer. He is bound *sic uti suo ut non laedat alienum*.[17]

This was not an action of trespass, but it was assumed in the judgments that trespass was a tort of strict (or, as it was then termed, absolute) liability. The court had been pressed with certain cases where accidents had happened on the highway, and where the plaintiff had taken it upon himself to prove negligence. These cases were dealt with by Blackburn J, delivering the judgment of the Exchequer Chamber before the case reached the House of Lords, by asserting that traffic accidents were an exception from strict liability.

> Traffic on the highways, whether by land or sea, cannot be conducted without exposing those whose persons or property are near it to some inevitable risk; and that being so, those who go on the highway, or have their property adjacent to it, may well be held to do so subject to their taking upon themselves the risk of injury from that inevitable

---

15 Eg *Weaver v Ward* (1616) Hob 134, 80 ER 284; *Dickenson v Watson* (1682) T Jo 205, 84 ER 1218. Cp. Holdsworth viii 455–6.
16 (1868) LR 3 HL 330.
17 Ibid at 341.

danger. . . . In neither case, therefore, can they recover without proof of want of care or skill occasioning the accident.[18]

This doctrine was expressed as one of assumption of risk, ie fictitious consent, a mode of statement that would now be regarded as objectionable. Moreover, there was no sufficient reason for Blackburn J's assumption that trespass was a tort of strict liability, and so there was no reason for him to invent an exception from that assumed liability.

Fortunately, when the matter arose for express decision, the doctrine of strict liability was rejected, and the tort of trespass was placed securely upon the basis of fault. This was in the case of *Stanley v Powell*.[19]

> The member of a shooting party fired at a pheasant, but the shot glanced off an oak tree and injured the plaintiff who was employed to carry cartridges. The jury found that the defendant was not negligent in firing the gun, and Denman J accordingly entered judgment for the defendant. He was not liable since he had not been at fault.[20]

Although this case fell for decision after the abolition of the forms of action, the plaintiff's claim would in the old days have been for trespass to the person, and the law relating to that form of action was regarded as being still important for determining the rights of the parties. The decision settled

---

18 LR 1 Exch at 286–7. The same judge repeated the principle (as Lord Blackburn) in somewhat different words in *River Wear Comrs v Adamson* (1877) 2 App Cas 743 at 767, as did Bramwell B in *Holmes v Mather* (1875) 10 LR Exch 261.

19 [1891] 1 QB 86. The classic discussion of the history of the matter was by Pollock *Torts* (15th edn) 101 ff. His editor, Mr Landon, stood in vigorous but solitary opposition to *Stanley v Powell*: see his Excursus B at p 128.

20 It is sometimes supposed that a defendant in trespass who contends that he was not negligent must show that he took not merely ordinary care but the greatest care: *The Schwan* [1892] P 419 at 429. It is now safe to say that this is a mistake: see *Fowler v Lanning* [1959] 1 QB 426 at 433; and cp. LR 10 Ex D at 268–9.

the law relating to trespass to the person, but it still remained an open and undecided question whether trespass to land or to goods might not be a tort of strict liability. However, with the decision in *Stanley v Powell* as it was, the answer to this further question could hardly have been in doubt. On no acceptable scale of values could the protection of property be put higher than the protection of life and limb. If, for example, Powell's ricochetting bullet had hit a sheep instead of hitting Stanley, it can hardly be imagined that Denman J would have awarded damages to the owner of the sheep, for it is written: 'How much is a man better than a sheep?' But we do not now need to rely on this *argumentum a fortiori*, because the point is covered by authority. It was held by the Court of Appeal in *National Coal Board v J E Evans & Co (Cardiff) Ltd*[1] that not only was *Stanley v Powell* rightly decided, but the principle of the case applied to trespass to property.

THE BURDEN OF PROOF

The decision in *Stanley v Powell* left open one important question, that of burden of proof. In an action for trespass is it for the plaintiff to prove fault, or for the defendant to

---

1 [1951] 2 KB 861, [1951] 2 All ER 310. American courts have taken the opposite view. Although the outcome of *National Coal Board v J E Evans & Co (Cardiff) Ltd* is satisfactory, the judgments are defective. In the first place, they fail to notice that the action was brought in respect of conduct of a servant of the defendants; such an action could not have sounded in trespass under the old law because trespass could not be used to enforce vicarious liability where there was no personal act by the defendant (153 LT 78). The discussion of the law of trespass was therefore unnecessary to the decision. Secondly, Cohen LJ held that a trespasser on land who could not succeed in negligence against the occupier was equally unprotected against a third party, but this opinion is contrary to authority.

disprove it? This point was settled for English law by Diplock J (as he then was) in *Fowler v Lanning*.[2]

> The writ claimed damages for trespass to the person, alleging that the defendant 'shot the plaintiff' and that by reason thereof the plaintiff had sustained personal injuries and suffered loss and damage. Diplock J held that this allegation disclosed no cause of action since it neither alleged fault nor gave particulars of negligence.

The rule that emerges is that in an action for damages for personal injuries, and presumably for property damage, the onus of proving fault lies on the plaintiff. This had been the rule since 1875 in highway cases, and Diplock J could find neither reason nor authority why a different rule should be observed in other cases. 'It is indeed,' he said 'but an illustration of the rule that he who affirms must prove which lies at the root of our law of evidence.'[3]

This decision is a welcome step in the direction of burying the forms of action.[4] The fact that the debate has survived the reforming movement of the nineteenth century is a striking illustration of the preoccupation of English law with remedies rather than with a framework of positive legal concepts. The English lawyer tends not to ask questions such as 'Is the underlying theory of the law one of Fault or is it one of Risk?' (as his Continental counterparts might do), but instead he asks 'In what circumstances can my client obtain damages on grounds of trespass or case?' If we are to

---

2 [1959] 1 QB 426, [1959] 1 All ER 290 (Hepple and Matthews, p 30).
3 At 439.
4 The puzzling feature of Diplock J's judgment, however, is to know what particulars of negligence he expected the plaintiff to give. The allegation 'the defendant shot the plaintiff' would seem to satisfy the requirements of the doctrine res ipsa loquitur (see p 115, below) as clearly as any allegation could; this being so it seems pedantic to require the plaintiff to set out particulars of negligence: [1959] CLJ 33. Ironically, at the ultimate trial of the action the plaintiff failed because he was unable to prove whose shot had caused the injury: (1959) Times, 21, 22 May; Dworkin in (1959) 22 MLR 535.

understand the raison d'être of the law of tort, we must examine in some detail the social functions the legal categories serve. The next chapter will discuss the concept of damage and the ways in which harm is redressed, and Chap 4 will explain the wide and expansible theory of fault upon which the modern law rests.[5]

---

5 The view expressed by one of the present authors in (1939) 7 CLJ 111 that the present heads of tortious liability and of non-liability are not fixed and immutable, and that the novelty of a case is not conclusive in favour of one party or the other, is thought to be now so widely accepted that the arguments will not be repeated here.

3 Damage

I cannot make you what amends I would,
Therefore accept such kindness as I can.

King Richard the Third IV iv

DAMAGE AND INJURY

'Damage' is a generic term meaning any injury or loss, physical or economic (financial). Physical damage to the person is called specifically 'injury' (but this term is sometimes used also in a wide sense, as synonymous with damage in general). An example of physical damage to property is the loss of a ship; of general economic loss, the making of an investment in a company which turns out to be insolvent.

The word 'injury' occasionally retains also its original meaning of *injuria* or legal wrong. Injuria is the infringement of a right, something contrary to jus. The phrase *damnum sine injuria* (loss without legal wrong) is an expression of sympathy for a plaintiff who has suffered loss without being able to show the commission of a tort. There are, in fact, various ways in which a person may suffer damage without having any cause of action. The standard example is 'fair trade competition', which may result in a trader's ruin and yet not be a tort to him.

A converse phrase sometimes met with is *injuria sine damno* (legal wrong without actual loss). This is used in connection with some torts that are actionable without proof of damage, or, in legal language, actionable per se (on their own account, merely on proof of the breach of duty). The primary principle is that a plaintiff in tort must prove damage, because the object of the law is to prevent and redress harm, and if there has been no harm there is no complaint. But in some torts the plaintiff is given 'nominal damages' in recognition of the fact that his legal rights have been invaded, though he has not suffered in the least.

NOMINAL DAMAGES AND THE FORMS OF ACTION

This distinction between torts that require proof of damage and others that are actionable per se connects up with the old forms of action. Trespass was actionable per se, and so, even at the present day, a person can sue for an invasion of his rights falling within the old writ of trespass without proving damage. If I walk over your field, even in winter when the ground is hard, you can put me in the county court, and no amount of apology, beating a hasty retreat, or even offer of pecuniary satisfaction, can save me from it.[1] In English law, said Pratt CJ, 'every invasion of private property, be it ever so minute, is a trespass. No man can set his foot upon my ground without my licence, but he is liable to an action, though the damage be nothing'.[2] This rule is to be explained partly by the fact that a continuing trespass, if not stopped, would eventually ripen into an easement by lapse of time. Also, the right of property in land is thought to carry what may be called a right of privacy on that land: the presence of the trespasser may be an unwelcome interference, even though he does no damage. Yet another justification for the rules is that the action in tort is used to try questions of title and obtain declarations of right. The award of nominal

---

1 The common belief that an offer of amends bars an action of trespass is contradicted by a case of 1681; see Williams *Liability for Animals* 196. It was, however, a defence to the old action of cattle-trespass: ibid.
2 *Entick v Carrington* (1765) 19 State Tr at 1066.

damages amounts to a declaration of the plaintiff's right; and, since the sum awarded, though small, is not usually utterly derisory,[3] it is also some kind of warning to the defendant and to others not to trespass in future. In modern times the courts have developed the 'action for a declaration' which achieves the same purpose by way of an explicit declaration of rights, without the award of damages.

Not only trespass to property but trespass to the person (assault, battery, false imprisonment) is actionable per se. My right to be free from personal molestation would be of small avail if people could lay offensive hands on me with impunity, whenever I could not prove actual damage. However, it seems that there is now an important limitation on the rule; in cases of *unintentional* trespass to the person there must be proof of actual damage.[4] Thus a librarian at closing time may lock the library forgetting that a reader is still inside; if he returns almost at once and releases the reader, so that no harm is done, it seems that the reader would not have an action for false imprisonment.[5] If appreciable harm were done he would have an action for negligence.

Sometimes the conduct of the plaintiff may have been so open to censure that the jury may give him only a derisory figure, say a halfpenny.[6] This is known as *contemptuous* damages which are in effect nominal damages awarded for the infringement of a right. Contemptuous damages are not generally met with outside libel,[7] and they are there used to

---

3 A shilling was sometimes given when money had another value. It is now generally a few pounds.

4 *Letang v Cooper* [1965] 1 QB 232 at 245, per Diplock LJ.

5 Although this point has not been directly tested since *Letang v Cooper*, it is the rule adopted by the American *Restatement of Torts* 2d, comment *h* on s 35(2).

6 'The smallest coin in the realm' — formerly a farthing, as in *Newstead v London Express Newspaper* [1940] 1 KB 377, [1939] 4 All ER 319 (Hepple and Matthews, p 563).

7 But for an instance in assault see *Read v Coker* (1853) 13 CB 850, 138 ER 1437.

express the fact that although the plaintiff has technically been libelled, the plaintiff has such a bad character that the libel was very nearly justified. It is always in the discretion of the judge whether to order that either party shall pay the other's costs, and where the plaintiff has only gained the pyrrhic victory of contemptuous damages the judge will be very likely to exercise his discretion to refuse to make an order for costs in the plaintiff's favour, even though the plaintiff has technically won.[8]

In trespass to the person and to goods, the maxim *de minimis non curat lex* (the law takes no notice of trifles) is allowed some play. An ordinary social contact, such as lightly tapping a man on the shoulder to attract his attention,[9] is not a trespass to the person, though 'the least touching of another in anger is a battery' (Holt CJ).[10] Similar contact with another's chattel is also innocent, for example, pushing a parked car in order to reduce the obstruction it causes; it has even held that striking another man's horse that is standing outside your door in order to get it away is not actionable in the absence of actual damage.[11] No precise reasons were given for the decision, but it might well be rested on 'social contact', or necessity, or the

---

8 An example is *Dering v Uris* [1964] 2 QB 669, [1964] 2 All ER 660n (Hepple and Matthews, p 591) which ruined the successful plaintiff who was ordered to pay the defendant's costs, but since he was unable to contribute materially to these costs amounting to about £20,000 the defendants had to bear them. The exercise of the judicial discretion depends not on the precise figure awarded but on all the circumstances. A plaintiff may be refused costs if he brings a vexatious action on a 'trifling' ground – 'an action in which the damages given would be, I will not say the contumelious farthing, but possibly a shilling' – per Bramwell LJ, *Dicks v Brooks* (1880) 15 ChD 22 at 40–41.

9 This is doubtless the law. *Coward v Baddeley* (1859) 4 H & N 478, 157 ER 927 is frequently cited upon it, but that case only decides the point for criminal law, and expressly leaves the tort rule open.

10 *Cole v Turner* (1705) 6 Mod Rep 149, 87 ER 907 (Hepple and Matthews, p 42).

11 *Slater v Swann* (1730) 2 Stra 872, 93 ER 906.

abatement of nuisance. If the striking were so violent that damage were caused to the horse, this would go beyond the exemption and the striker would be liable for trespass to goods.

We now come to the action upon the case. The original principle was that this required proof of damage,[12] which rule still holds in a number of applications – in actions of negligence, of malicious prosecution, of deceit, of inducement of breach of contract, and of conspiracy. Here damage is, in legal parlance, the gist of the action. This is not to say that the plaintiff has to particularise his damage down to the last detail; it is enough that he shows a reasonable probability that damage has occurred.

A number of exceptions have been developed to the proposition that the action upon the case requires proof of damage. The most important relate to property rights. Many actions in respect of wrongful interferences with property are brought in order to vindicate the plaintiff's title to the property, and, accordingly, an action for violation of property rights may be brought without proof of actual damage, even though the particular action used to be an action of case.[13] This is true of conversion[14] and even of nuisance.[15] The judgment for nominal damages, which the plaintiff gets in the absence of proof of actual loss, is in the nature of a declaration of the plaintiff's title, or of the fact that his right has been infringed. For much the same reason, nominal damages may be given, without proof of actual damage, for a breach of contract.

---

12 Old authorities are: Brooke's *Abridgement, Action sur le case* 68 (but cp. ibid 86, 89); *Williams v Morland* (1824) 2 B & C 910 at 916, 107 ER 620 at 622.
13 The rule goes back to 1618: *Hunt v Dowman* (1618) Cro Jac 478, 79 ER 407.
14 *Williams v Peel River Land and Mineral Co Ltd* (1886) 55 LT 689.
15 *Nicholls v Ely Beet Sugar Factory Ltd* [1936] Ch 343 (held that a person who has rights of fishing in a stream may sue for interference with his rights by the discharge of refuse into the stream, without proof of actual damage). Cp. *Price v Hilditch* [1930] 1 Ch 500 at 509.

The tort of defamation is in a special position. Defamation is of two kinds, libel and slander. Roughly speaking, libel is written defamation while slander is spoken defamation. Damages may be given for libel, and some types of slander, without proof of loss, and these damages may be not merely nominal but substantial, by way of punishment to the defendant and comfort to the plaintiff. 'The jingling of the guinea helps the hurt that honour feels.' The justification here, as in the case of the substantial damages that may be given for assault, is that if the law did not provide an effective remedy for affronts the victim might be tempted to take private revenge; besides, there is always a distinct possibility that a libel does cause damage, even though of an intangible kind.

On the whole these distinctions are fairly intelligible. But some confusion has been caused by the judgment of Holt CJ in *Ashby v White*,[16] which is well known to students of constitutional history.

> The facts were that the plaintiff, whose vote at an election was improperly rejected, sued the returning officer for damages for refusing his vote. The plaintiff had, in a sense, suffered no damage, because the candidate for whom he would have voted was elected. In the Court of Queen's Bench, Holt CJ alone was for allowing the action, and his dissenting judgment was upheld in the House of Lords, so that it has become the effective judgment in the case.

Celebrated as this judgment is, it rests upon a double error. Holt based himself in part on the proposition that the plaintiff had a right to vote, and that the returning officer by refusing the vote violated that right, and so committed a breach of duty to the plaintiff. This is a fallacy of a rather elementary kind. The word 'right' is frequently used in a wide sense to mean any legal interest; it encompasses *rights in the narrow sense* (correlative to duties), *liberties* and *powers*.

---

16 (1703) 2 Ld Raym 938, 92 ER 126.

Liberties and powers, though rights in the wide sense, are not rights in the sense that they have duties correlative to them. My right of free speech, or freedom of speech, is not correlative to a duty on your part *that I shall speak freely*. True, you are under a duty not to gag me, because that would be in law a battery, and I have a right not to be battered. But in arguing from a right in the strict sense to its correlative duty one must keep to the same form of words; so the right of freedom of speech is not correlative to a duty not to gag. Freedom of speech is a liberty. To say that people have a right of free speech merely means that they commit no crime or other legal wrong, generally, when they ventilate their opinions. Hence a right in the sense of a liberty to do something is a *no-duty not to do that thing*.[17] Similarly, my so-called right to make a will is a *power* to affect legal relationships by making a will; when I die my will will confer rights on various people. Nobody is under a duty that I shall make a will, so it is not a right in the strict sense. The same analysis holds for the right to vote. It is a power, when exercised in common with a sufficient number of like-minded people, to elect a member of Parliament, who will thereby obtain a particular legal status. We say, for example, that a person under age has no right to vote, meaning that he does not possess the franchise. If a minor votes at an election, his vote is invalid and, on proof of the facts, is struck out. On the other hand, if an adult validly votes at an election his vote is legally counted for the candidate in question, and may help to elect him. It does not follow from his possession of the franchise that the voter has, at the same time, a private right against the returning officer to have his vote accepted.

It is true that the returning officer is under a public duty to accept the vote. But when a public officer refuses to perform his public duty the usual rule is that no private action for

17 See Williams (1956) 56 Col L Rev 1129, reprinted in *Essays in Legal Philosophy* (ed. Summers) (Oxford, 1968) 121.

damages lies[18]; the person must seek his remedy in a writ of mandamus against the officer to compel him to perform his duty, or else in a criminal prosecution for breach of duty. Consequently, the existence of the public duty is not in itself a ground for inferring the private right of action. This is looking at the matter through modern spectacles. Holt regarded the right to vote as 'a matter of property', and this is perhaps understandable when the right to vote was possessed only by certain privileged people, often as incident to the ownership of a particular piece of land, in which case the right to vote added to the value of the land. It was natural for a judge to suppose that a property interest had to be supported by imposing suitable duties on other people to give effect to it. However, to assert that the right to vote was 'a matter of property' begged the question, because if the right to vote belonged to public law it was not a matter of private property.

With the advent of universal suffrage the decision in *Ashby v White* came to look anomalous, and it has been reversed by statute, so that no damages can at the present day be sought against a returning officer who refuses a vote. The voter still has the 'right to vote' in the sense of a power in public law. But he no longer has a private right to have his vote accepted. Instead, the franchise is protected through the criminal law, the returning officer being made subject to a penalty if he unlawfully refuses a vote.[19]

The distinction between a wide intangible 'right' and a 'right' in the strict legal sense, correlative to a duty, was relied upon by Sir Robert Megarry V-C as a reason for

---

18 The tort of misfeasance in a public office has generally been limited to cases of ill-will or an intention to injure (as by the corrupt returning officer in *Ashby v White*) or, in some Commonwealth jurisdictions, cases where the officer knows that he does not possess the power which he is purporting to exercise: see Jeremy McBride in [1979] CLJ 323, and see, *Dunlop v Woolahra Municipal Council* [1982] AC 158, [1981] 1 All ER 1202.
19 Representation of the People Act 1983, ss 63, 64.

refusing to recognise a tort of invasion of privacy by unauthorised telephone tapping.[20] In the absence of a trespass to his property, there could not be said to be a violation of a legal right. Nowadays judges less bold than Holt CJ will not step in to create new 'rights' where Parliament has feared to tread.[1]

A second fallacy in Holt's judgment was that because the plaintiff's right had been violated he necessarily had an action, even without proof of actual damage. 'Every injury,' he said, 'imports a damage, though it does not cost the party one farthing.' That may be technically true, but it again begs the question; in many cases there is no injuria in the legal sense, no legal wrong, unless there is damage; damage is a constituent element of the injuria. That is so in negligence and in the other instances given above of torts that are actionable only on proof of damage. Take the action of negligence, for example: there is no completed tort of negligence until the occurrence of damage, and for this reason the Limitation Act does not begin to run against the plaintiff until he suffers damage; until then, there is no cause of action, and no injuria. It was, therefore, no solution of the problem in *Ashby v White* to announce that every injuria was actionable. A better argument in support of Holt's conclusion would be that the refusal of a vote is damage to the voter, or at any rate is so closely akin to damage that it ought to be treated as such. Or it could be said that an omission by a public officer to perform his duty ought to be actionable per se, in order that aggrieved members of the public may be able to establish in the courts what the officer's duty is. Arguments of this kind, based upon the public policy of the case, may be acceptable where pseudo-logic is not.

20 *Malone v Metropolitan Police Comr* [1979] Ch 344, [1979] 2 All ER 620; and see the Report of the Committee on Privacy, Cmnd. 5012 (1972).
1 Carol Harlow *Compensation and Government Torts* (London, 1983) pp 43–4.

Holt CJ's judgment was relied upon in different circumstances by Birkett J in *Constantine v Imperial Hotels Ltd.*[2]

Constantine, the West Indian cricketer, was refused admission to the Imperial Hotel, London, on the score of his colour, though he was accommodated instead in the Bedford Hotel, another hotel in the same ownership. The law is that an innkeeper (which in modern language means a hotel-keeper) must admit any traveller who presents himself in reasonable condition, if there is room for him at the inn; and for breach of this duty the traveller may bring an action, which was formerly an action on the case. It was argued in *Constantine* that although the defendants had committed a breach of their duty, no action lay in the absence of proof of damage, and here the plaintiff had suffered no damage, because he had been accommodated elsewhere. The judge ruled against this contention, following Holt CJ's dictum in *Ashby v White* as though it afforded an automatic answer. The law provided a remedy for the violation of the plaintiff's right, and injury imported damage; QED.

In the particular circumstances of the case the conclusion was satisfactory, because it enabled the court to give Constantine five guineas nominal damages and the costs of the action, and to pronounce against a colour bar in hotels.[3] At the same time, the reasoning upon which the conclusion was founded begged the question as much as did Holt's in *Ashby v White*. It would be far better to treat the question frankly as one of policy, and to consider whether the particular kind of tort is one for which the court ought to be able to award nominal damages. If every technical violation of duty were allowed to found an action for nominal damages the result might be a great proliferation of actions which might be little more than blackmailing in character. It is also to be observed that in *Constantine*'s case there was damage, because the plaintiff was put to the inconvenience of going to another hotel, besides being subjected to

2 [1944] KB 693, [1944] 2 All ER 171.
3 In a case of this kind today, the victim could, in addition to any claim at common law, make use of the machinery of the Race Relations Act 1976.

annoyance. Damages for inconvenience are not always allowed in law, but there are some causes of action for which it is reasonable that they should be.[4] The judge pointed out that no special damage was alleged or claimed by the plaintiff, and he seems to have equated special damage with actual damage. This is a confusion. 'Special damage' is merely a technical pleader's term, and is a narrower conception than that of actual damage. Special damage means damage that must be specially claimed in the statement of claim if recompense is to be given for it, as opposed to general damage which need not be specially pleaded. In an action against an innkeeper for refusing admittance, the fact that the plaintiff was not allowed to enter the hotel is general damage, and accordingly there is no need to put a figure upon the plaintiff's inconvenience in the statement of claim as special damage.[5] An illustration of special damage properly so called would be a doctor's bill incurred as a result of catching cold when the plaintiff was refused admission to the hotel. It is true that Constantine did not suffer damage in this sense, but he did suffer the general damage of being kept out of the hotel; and this general damage remained measurable even though the defendants mitigated it by providing other accommodation. General damage can be actual damage just as much as special damage is. Thus the facts of the case did not necessitate a decision that the tort was actionable per se.

GENERAL AND SPECIAL DAMAGE

The confusion we have just noticed about the phrase 'special damage' illustrates the undesirability of using

4 See below, note 5.
5 Damages for inconvenience, disappointment and distress can be recovered even in contract which shows that this is regarded in law as actual damage: see above, Chap 1, p 17, n 19. In tort, damages for inconvenience are most commonly found in the torts of deceit, false imprisonment and nuisance.

technical expressions in double meanings. The unfortunate, though common, use of 'special damage' to mean actual damage should be avoided. The term 'actual damage' (or just 'damage') should be used where that is meant.

In the pleader's sense special damage means all damage upon which a sufficiently precise figure can be placed to make it reasonable to expect the plaintiff to give notice of the amount he claims. Pain and suffering are not special damage, because their translation into money terms is arbitrary, but if the plaintiff had his clothes ruined in the accident, and incurred hospital expenses, and loss of wages, the value of the clothes and other monetary loss up to the date of the trial would be special damage upon which he would have to put a figure. It will be remembered that special damage under these heads was mentioned in the illustrative statement of claim given in the previous chapter.

General damage,[6] on the other hand, is damage not accurately quantifiable in money terms, for which damages can be awarded even in the absence of any specific monetary claim in the plaintiff's statement of claim. All that the plaintiff has to do is to claim 'damages' at large and then the court will make some rough assessment. For example, if the plaintiff has been knocked down by the defendant's car and suffered pain and physical injuries, the court may award him such damages for these matters as it thinks right, and no precise figure need be claimed on the pleadings. In

---

6 It is often said that general damage is damage that the law will presume to have followed from the tort, but one may take leave to say that this is incorrect. For example, pain and suffering and physical injury are general damage, but they are not presumed to have followed from the tort; on the contrary, particulars of physical injury (without a translation into money terms) must be furnished by the plaintiff as part of his pleadings, and evidence must be given of it at the trial. To obtain substantial damages the plaintiff must always give evidence of the circumstances and consequences of the tort; there is no presumption to aid him. The only damage presumed to follow from the tort is that represented by an award of nominal damages.

discussions about the substantive law, little use need be made of this distinction between 'special' and 'general' damage.

INJUNCTIONS

Damages alone are often an inadequate remedy for the protection of a legal right, because they enable the wrongdoer to buy out his victim at a price fixed by the court. The view of the Court of Chancery was that the effective enforcement of the law often needed an order of the court commanding the defendant to comply with his legal duties, as by pulling down a house built in infringement of ancient lights, or ceasing to publish a libel. Such orders, called injunctions, may be granted in contract as well as in tort. The injunction may be *interlocutory*, issued provisionally until the trial of the action (in cases of urgency this may be done ex parte, ie in the absence of the respondent), the object being to keep matters *in statu quo* pending the trial of the action. Or it may be *perpetual*, issued on the merits, after the case has been decided in the plaintiff's favour. It may be *prohibitory*, telling the defendant not to do something, or it may be *mandatory*, telling the defendant to do something.[7]

The injunction was, as just said, a weapon fashioned by the Court of Chancery, but since the Judicature Act 1873 it may be had in the Queen's Bench Division and Family Division as well as the Chancery Division.[8] A plaintiff in any of these Divisions may, if he chooses, ask for both damages and an injunction at the same time, or he may ask for one of these remedies alone. The courts have always held that the

7 The principles upon which such an injunction may be granted were restated by Lord Upjohn in *Redland Bricks Ltd v Morris* [1970] AC 652 at 665, 666.
8 An application for an interlocutory injunction in the Chancery Division is made in open court; an application in the QBD is made to a judge in chambers. A leading work, Snell *Principles of Equity* (28th edn) p 646, accordingly advises those who desire privacy to issue the writ in the QBD.

remedy of injunction is discretionary, but that need cause little alarm to prospective plaintiffs, because the discretion is exercised upon fairly settled principles.

It is customary to say that an injunction will never be granted where damages would be an adequate remedy; but this is not very helpful, because the question is when the judges regard damages as adequate. At the present day injunctions are issued with such regularity that it is probably truer to put the proposition the other way round, and to assert that whenever an injunction can stop a tortious course of conduct it will be granted, except where the defendant acted in good faith and where the tort is trivial, or the plaintiff has acquiesced in the defendant's conduct, or in the rare cases where nothing but money is involved.[10]

Normally the injunction relates to an injury already committed, forbidding its continuance or repetition. But it may also be sought to prevent an injury not yet committed, if the plaintiff reasonably fears that one is about to be committed (quia timet[11]). For instance, suppose that your neighbour has started to build a house that, if completed according to plan, will cause an actionable obstruction of your ancient lights. The court has power to grant an injunction by way of prevention. But the plaintiff must generally show that this fear of harm amounts to a very strong probability – some courts even say a moral certainty – and moreover that the harm when it occurs will be virtually irreparable. The comparative rarity of this type of relief was indicated by Lord Dunedin when he said: 'No one can obtain a quia timet order by merely saying "Timeo" '.[12]

---

10 It used to be said that equity protected only rights of property, but 'property' was given a wide interpretation, and exceptions were also developed, as in libel. It seems that at the present day there is no restriction as a matter of law to proprietary rights. See 34 HLR 407; but cp. 8 Can B Rev 386.
11 'Because he fears.'
12 *A-G for Dominion of Canada v Ritchie Contracting and Supply Co Ltd* [1919] AC 999 at 1005.

Although, before the Judicature Act, damages were the primary common law remedy and injunction the primary equitable remedy for a tort, an Act of 1858, Lord Cairns's Act, had broken in upon the monopoly of the courts of common law by conferring upon the Chancery power to award damages as an alternative to an injunction. It had to be shown that the Court of Chancery had jurisdiction to issue an injunction, and, if it had, then it could award damages instead. At first sight that Act has nothing to do with us, for it was repealed in 1883; and everyone knows that a repealed statute ceases to be law. Nevertheless the House of Lords held, in 1924[13] that Lord Cairns's Act has had an enduring effect, for this reason: when the Act was repealed in 1883, by a Statute Law Revision Act (one of the scavenger statutes that clean up obsolete law from time to time), it was provided that the repeal was not to affect any jurisdiction conferred by the Act repealed. This meant that the High Court still had any jurisdiction possessed by the Court of Chancery under Lord Cairns's Act.

Now, as to wrongs actually committed, obviously there is no need to disinter Lord Cairns's Act. For the High Court can award damages in virtue of its common law jurisdiction, and it can grant an injunction in virtue of its equitable jurisdiction; in neither case is the Act needed.[14] But as to threatened wrongs, the case is different. For the House of Lords held, in the case just referred to, that Lord Cairns's Act gave to the Court of Chancery the fresh and unique power – for the common law courts had it not – of awarding damages for a threatened wrong, in lieu of a quia timet injunction. This power of the Court of Chancery, though never discovered by that court, was latent in the

---

13 *Leeds Industrial Co-op Society Ltd v Slack* [1924] AC 851. See Jolowicz in [1975] CLJ 224.
14 Note that both damages and injunction can be awarded. Thus damages can be given in respect of the past wrong, and an injunction to prevent the wrong being continued.

logic of the law, and notwithstanding the upheaval of the Judicature Act it was still retained by the High Court. So it was held that where the defendant proposed to build so as slightly to obstruct the plaintiff's ancient lights, and the plaintiff asked the court for an injunction, the court had a discretion to refuse him that and to give him instead damages by way of buying him out.

The decision to award damages in lieu of an injunction on the facts of the particular case has been criticised, as giving wrongdoers a means of expropriating their victims without the authority of Parliament. Lord Sumner, who delivered a strong dissenting speech, thought that the principle meant that the court could allow 'the big man, with his big building and his enhanced rateable value, and his improvement of the neighbourhood, to have his way, and solace the little man for his darkened and stuffy little house by giving him a cheque that he does not ask for'. 'What will be my remedy,' asked one writer, 'if persons use my ground as a convenient short cut to the railway station? Are they to be entitled to purchase a right of way to suit their own convenience, and to nullify my right to privacy?'[15] The courts have taken these misgivings to heart in subsequent cases. Where there is a continuing nuisance, for example, the court will rarely exercise its discretion in favour of granting damages in lieu of an injunction. So where a plaintiff built a house on land adjoining the premises of a motor boat racing club and the club subsequently increased its activities so as to hold large and noisy meetings at weekends, the Court of Appeal granted an injunction restricting the activities and declined to award damages in lieu of the injunction.[16]

Injunctions are regularly claimed in cases of nuisance. The

15 (1925) 41 LQR 4.
16 *Kennaway v Thompson* [1981] 1 QB 88, [1980] 3 All ER 329; cp. *Miller v Jackson* [1977] QB 966, [1977] 3 All ER 338 (action to restrain the nuisance of cricket balls landing in the garden of neighbours of an old-established cricket club; injunction refused and damages not awarded).

traditional attitude is that this is a discretionary remedy, and that the court may take various factors into account, such as whether damages would be an adequate remedy, the conduct of the two parties, and the hardship to the plaintiff of refusing the injunction or to the defendant of granting it. In later years, however, judicial policy has become more favourable to the remedy, and it has been laid down that if the plaintiff proves that his proprietary rights are being wrongfully interfered with by the defendant, who proposes to continue his wrong, the plaintiff is prima facie entitled to an injunction.[17] But he will be refused this remedy if he has unduly delayed in bringing proceedings (laches), or acquiesced in the invasion of his rights.

Another field in which injunctions are frequently more important than an award of damages is in the regulation of economic competition, particularly labour disputes.[18] Here the main objective of the plaintiff in issuing a writ is to obtain interlocutory relief to stop a boycott or industrial action which is damaging his business. In order to do this he may allege the commission of any of a large number of torts (for example inducement of breach of contract, interference with contracts, intimidation and conspiracy). So long as he can show that there is a serious issue to be tried the court will determine where the 'balance of convenience' lies. This nearly always favours the plaintiff whose tangible business interests are being threatened rather than the defendants (say, union officials calling a strike) whose industrial objectives are intangible. Once the interlocutory injunction

17 Per Evershed MR in *Pride of Derby and Derbyshire Angling Association Ltd v British Celanese Ltd* [1953] Ch 149, [1953] 1 All ER 179. For the older authorities see Pearce and Meston *Nuisances* 342 ff.

18 Felix Frankfurter and Nathan Greene called this *The Labour Injunction* in their classic work of that name (Harvard, 1930). Their critique was directly responsible for the Norris LaGuardia Act of 1932 which banned the use of the injunction in labour disputes in the USA. For an account of the problem in Britain, see P. Davies and M. Freedland *Labour Law: Text and Materials* (London, 1979) Chap 8, part 3; and S. Evans in (1983) 12 ILJ 129.

is granted the plaintiff usually has little interest in bringing the matter to trial and so the substantive issue – whether the torts were in fact committed – is never decided.[19] The view that this is unfair to those engaged in 'trade disputes' (the technical name given in Great Britain to most management–labour disputes) has resulted in certain statutory immunities for those acting 'in contemplation or furtherance' of such disputes,[20] and some restrictions on the grant of labour injunctions.[1]

AIMS OF DAMAGES: THE AWARD OF EXEMPLARY DAMAGES

The action for nominal damages – in order to determine rights – and the injunction – to secure observance of certain standards of conduct – emphasise the fact, if emphasis still be

---

19 An example is *J T Stratford & Son Ltd v Lindley* [1965] AC 269, [1964] 3 All ER 102, where the House of Lords, overruling the Court of Appeal, restored the judge's order for an interlocutory injunction against union officials in 1964. The order stood for nearly five years. The union officials then took out a summons to dismiss the action for want of prosecution. The Court of Appeal, [1969] 3 All ER 1122, upholding the decision of Chapman J, (1969) Times, 22 May, gave leave for the action to be discontinued and ordered each side to pay its own costs. So the officials (no doubt backed by their union) were left with a considerable financial burden although the substantive issues were never tried.

20 Trade Union and Labour Relations Act 1974, s 13, as modified by the Employment Act 1980, s 17, and the Employment Act 1982, ss 15–19.

1 Trade Union and Labour Relations Act 1974, s 17(1), which requires reasonable steps to be taken to give notice of the application and an opportunity to be heard to a party who acted in contemplation or furtherance of a trade dispute. Section 17(2) requires the court to have regard to the likelihood of the defendant establishing the 'trade dispute' defence, but despite this the courts have insisted on retaining their residual discretion to grant injunctions where this factor is outweighed by the 'disastrous' consequences of the industrial action to the employer or the public: *NWL Ltd v Woods* [1979] 3 All ER 614, [1979] 1 WLR 1294; *Express Newspapers Ltd v McShane* [1980] AC 672, [1980] 1 All ER 65; *Duport Steels Ltd v Sirs* [1980] 1 All ER 529, [1980] 1 WLR 142; and see generally, Christine Gray in [1981] CLJ 307.

needed, that compensation is not the only aim of the law of tort. But when we come to examine actions for substantial (as opposed to nominal) damages it is generally assumed that the object is, in words used by Lord Blackburn a century ago, to assess 'that sum of money which will put the party who has been injured, or who has suffered, in the same position as he would have been if he had not sustained the wrong for which he is now getting compensation or reparation.'[2]

A prominent exception to this principle is the award of exemplary (or punitive or vindictive) damages (the first epithet being generally preferred), which go beyond what is necessary to 'compensate' the plaintiff.[3] Such an award is apparently[4] limited to the torts of defamation, trespass to the person (assault, battery and false imprisonment) and trespass to or conversion of property. They are not appropriate in the ordinary road- or work-accident case in which the allegation is negligence or breach of statutory duty. The House of Lords has decided that even within these limits an award of exemplary damages can be made only in the following cases:[5] (a) where there has been 'oppressive, arbitrary or unconstitutional action by servants of the government'; (b) where 'it is necessary to teach a wrongdoer that tort does not

---

2 *Livingstone v Rawyards Coal Co* (1880) 5 App Cas 25 at 39. Where the tort has prevented the plaintiff from proving the amount of his loss, the court may make a presumption in his favour. In *Armory v Delamirie* (1721) 1 Str 505, 93 ER 664, the defendant by detaining a jewel and failing to produce it in court prevented the plaintiff from proving its value; damages for the detention were assessed on the basis that the jewel was of the finest water.
3 For a penetrating study see Clarence Morris in (1931) 44 Harv LR 1173.
4 According to dicta of Lord Hailsham of St. Marylebone LC and Lord Diplock in *Cassell & Co Ltd v Broome* [1972] AC 1027 at 1068, 1120.
5 Per Lord Devlin in *Rookes v Barnard* [1964] AC 1129 at 1226, approved by the House of Lords in *Cassell & Co Ltd v Broome* [1972] AC 1027, [1972] 1 All ER 801. Other common law jurisidictions have not imposed the restrictions.

pay'; and (c) where statute expressly authorises such an award.[6]

The first of these categories is an important historical legacy of the eighteenth-century cases in which awards of exemplary damages were used by the courts to defend civil liberties against high-handed governmental action. Such an award is sometimes made against a police officer who has grossly exceeded his powers, and may in fact be paid by the police authority; so the jury are enabled to express strong and effective disapproval of the conduct of the police.[7] The second category covers, in particular, cases where 'the defendant's conduct has been calculated by him to make a profit for himself which may well exceed the compensation payable to the plaintiff'. It also covers cases where the defendant acted to obtain property that he was unable to buy.[8] In assessing exemplary damages the means of the defendant may be taken into account so as to avoid crippling him financially.

The restrictions imposed by these rules can be partly evaded by distinguishing exemplary damages from a compensatory award in which the conduct of the defendant is said to *aggravate* the damages. Aggravated damages, in theory at least, are supposed to soothe the injured feelings of a plaintiff who has been distressed by the malice with which a wrongful act has been done, or the insolence or arrogance with which it is accompanied. The name 'aggravated

---

6 There appears to be only one statute clearly in this category, the Reserve and Auxiliary Forces (Protection of Civil Interests) Act 1951, s 13(2), which authorises exemplary damages in an action for conversion falling within the statute.

7 In *Huckle v Money* (1763) 2 Wils 205, 95 ER 768, £300 was awarded to plaintiff who was falsely imprisoned for six hours on suspicion of printing the *North Briton*, though 'treated very civilly with beef steaks and beer'. In *Reynolds v Police Comr* (1982) Times, 21 May where the plaintiff was unlawfully detained by the police for one day, the jury were upheld in awarding him £12,000 damages!

8 *Drane v Evangelou* [1978] 2 All ER 437, [1978] 1 WLR 455.

damages' is strange, for it implies damages aggravated beyond the amount required for compensation, which is just what they are not supposed to be. Allowing aggravated damages to be awarded as compensation for injured feelings, without the restrictions imposed upon awards of exemplary damages, involves a departure from the restraints traditionally imposed upon damages in many tort actions. It means, for example, that damages for injured feelings may now be awarded in actions for breach of contract and deceit.[9] Such damages are regarded as compensatory, and their award is not governed by any rule other than that they must bear a reasonable relation to the distress caused by the tort.[10] The court should first consider what sum is justified by way of compensation (which sum may be aggravated by the manner in which the defendant has behaved to the plaintiff); if the court thinks that this sum is insufficient to punish the defendant for his outrageous conduct, to mark their disapproval of such conduct and to deter him from repeating it, the court may proceed to add a further sum by way of exemplary damages if the case falls within the classes stated by the House of Lords. Even exemplary damages can be reduced on appeal if they are thought to be unjustly high;[11]

9 *Archer v Brown* (1983) Times, 2 November.

10 An action for aggravated damages survives the death of either party, but exemplary damages cannot be claimed after such death: Law Reform (Miscellaneous Provisions) Act 1934, s 1(2)(a).

11 In *Cassell & Co Ltd v Broome* [1972] AC 1027, [1972] 1 All ER 801 there was only a slender majority (4–3) for upholding – as a verdict that could have been reached by 12 reasonable jurors – an award of £25,000 exemplary damages in addition to £15,000 compensatory damages, in respect of a libel which had been deliberately published despite a clear warning that it was defamatory. In *Drane v Evangelou* [1978] 2 All ER 437, [1978] 1 WLR 455, where a tenant was forcibly evicted, an award of £1,000 was upheld as 'exemplary' damages for trespass; but Lawton and Goff LJJ agreed that this could also be justified as 'aggravated' damages. Goff LJ pointed out that the award need not specifically distinguish between aggravated and exemplary damages. Cp. *Devonshire v Jenkins* [1978] CA Transcript 283, 129 NLJ lxviii. Exemplary, but not aggravated, damages must be specifically claimed in the Statement of Claim in the High Court.

and the court should take account of any punishment that has been imposed by a criminal court. A moment's consideration will show that even when an action in tort results in an award of compensatory damages, it is too simple to say that the object of the law is to provide compensation for injury or loss.

Take the torts of causing personal injury. Since, as a general rule, English law requires proof of fault before damages may be awarded for such injuries, there cannot be said to be a comprehensive compensatory principle that one who has caused injury to another must always make good the damage. The law generally regards compensation as the expression of a moral principle: one who has by his fault caused damage to another ought as a matter of justice to make compensation.[12] The important practical effect of this principle of ethical compensation is that not all those who are injured are entitled to tort damages. Estimates made by the Pearson Commission indicate that only 6.5% of all personal injuries attract tort compensation.[13] The Commission's research found that of those who thought their injury had been caused by something another person had done or failed to do, some two-thirds took no steps towards making a claim in tort. Of these about a fifth either did not know that they could claim or were ignorant as to how to do so. Others felt that they would be unable to prove fault or that they would be in an unequal bargaining position or that it would be too costly.[14] Only 1% of tort claims reach the courts, the remainder being settled or withdrawn.[15] The uncertainties, costs and, above all, the delays involved in pursuing a case to court may lead a plaintiff who has suffered

12 The social purpose behind the fault principle is examined in the next chapter.
13 Pearson Report, vol 1, para 78 and Table 5. Road accident victims are more likely to recover compensation than those injured at work or elsewhere. See further Chap 4, below, p 137.
14 Pearson Report, vol 2, Chap 18.
15 Pearson Report, vol 1, para 79.

relatively serious injuries to accept a settlement for considerably less than the amount of damage inflicted upon him, especially if he is not backed by an insurance company or trade union. On the other hand, in the case of minor injuries, where only small sums are involved, relatively high amounts of compensation may be paid by the defendant's insurers because the claim is regarded as something of a nuisance and not worth the cost of litigation.[16] The result of the settlement process is that many seriously injured people are under-compensated, while some of those with minor injuries may be over-compensated.[17]

COMPENSATION FOR PERSONAL INJURY

A general question in the law of tort is how far damages, when they are intended to be restitutionary and not merely exemplary, are appropriate for inflictions that are not measurable in money terms. In fact the courts often award such damages. In relation to defamation, for example, an arbitrary line is drawn. Actions for slander (chiefly oral defamation) require proof of what is regarded as actual loss. The affront and distress caused by the attack upon the plaintiff's character is not regarded as such loss. Action for libel (chiefly written defamation), on the other hand, can found general damages for loss of reputation. In libel the 'compensatory' purpose of damages is said 'to operate in two

---

16 Jenny Phillips and Keith Hawkins in (1976) 39 MLR 497, explain the economic factors which affect this settlement process; see too, P. M. Danzon and L. A. Lilliard in (1983) 12 J Leg Stud 345.

17 The Pearson Commission survey of insurance claims disposed of in November 1973 revealed that the median amount of settlements was just over £200, and only 1% exceeded £5,000, although these accounted for 23% of the total amount paid out (vol 2, para 522). The median amount awarded by courts in England and Wales (1974) was £1,810. In recent years there has been a trend towards much higher awards by the courts and this has probably been reflected in the level of settlements.

ways – as a vindication of the plaintiff to the public and as consolation to him for the wrong done'.[18]

The somewhat haphazard operation of the law of tort has already been mentioned. Even those who manage to prove fault may be under- or over-compensated. This is owing in part to the common law method of making once-for-all lump sum awards. In the case of a living plaintiff this includes not only those pecuniary losses, such as lost earnings, that have been incurred up to the time of trial (the special damage)[19] but also an estimate of future pecuniary losses, in particular lost future income,[20] and an amount in respect of non-pecuniary losses (pain and suffering and loss of amenities).[1] For small claims this non-pecuniary loss is the predominant element.[2]

The attempt to compensate for future losses involves a likelihood of mistaken forecasts. These result in part from the uncertainties of medical prognosis. Assume that the medical evidence shows that there is a 10% probability that the accident victim will go blind at some future date as a result of the tort. The judge in awarding a lump sum as compensation will make an assessment on the basis of the losses the plaintiff will suffer if he goes blind and then discount this by 90%. If the plaintiff does go blind he will have been under-compensated; if he does not he will have been over-compensated. The difficulties can sometimes be lessened by postponing the date of the trial on the issue of the quantum of damages, but delays of this kind may increase the plaintiff's anxieties and financial difficulties.

18 Per Windeyer J in *Uren v John Fairfax & Sons (Pty) Ltd* (1966) 117 CLR 118 at 150; approved by Lord Hailsham in *Cassell & Co v Broome* [1972] AC 1027 at 1071.

19 Above, p 66.

20 Nearly 20% of all tort compensation is for future pecuniary loss, and 45% of all payments over £25,000 were under this head in 1973: Pearson Report, vol 1, paras 259, 553.

1 See below, p 83 for the meaning of these terms.

2 Pearson Report, vol 2, paras 519–21 and Tables 107 and 108.

Until recently, the general rule was that once the lump sum had been assessed the amount could not be redetermined even if it was later found to be woefully inadequate or grossly excessive. The Administration of Justice Act 1982[3] goes some way towards meeting the problem by authorising rules of court that will enable the court to award *provisional* damages in cases where there is a chance that at some time in the future the injured person will, as a result of the tortious act or omission, develop some serious disease or suffer some serious deterioration in his physical or mental condition. In these cases, damages will be awarded in two stages: first, damages assessed on the assumption that the development or deterioration will not occur, and then further damages at a later date if this does occur.

Apart from medical contingencies, many other uncertainties may affect the estimate of future loss of earnings. The traditional method is to compare the aggrieved person's expected income after the accident with the income he might have enjoyed had it not been for the tort. An estimate of net annual loss (called the multiplicand) has to take account, inter alia, of the likely duration of the incapacity, the chances of promotion or increases in earnings and, against this, the chances of loss of earnings and unemployment, as well as the advantages of receiving a capital sum that can be invested in interest-bearing securities. The award is worked out on the basis that the income and part of the capital will be spent each year so that the capital will be exhausted at the age until which the loss is assessed. In practice this means that the number of years' loss (the multiplier) rarely exceeds 16.

It might be thought that the courts would turn to experts for assistance. Actuaries use statistical techniques to work out expectancies and to discount capital sums so as to reflect

---

3 Section 6, inserting Supreme Court Act 1981, s 32A. At the time of writing the rules have not been made.

contingencies; but the courts are strangely reluctant to admit their evidence.[4]

The obvious solution would be to institute a system of periodical payments, adjusted according to the plaintiff's changing circumstances. Although this system is widely established in Europe,[5] in British social security legislation,[6] and in no-fault insurance schemes in the United States,[7] and was recommended by a majority of the Pearson Commission in respect of future pecuniary loss caused by death or serious personal injury,[8] it has not yet been accepted in Britain. The system does not appeal to private insurers, mainly because of the problem of estimating their contingent liabilities. It has been argued that periodical payments discourage the rehabilitation[9] of accident victims by tying payment to continued disability; but various devices have been used in other countries to overcome this objection: in particular the possibility of commuting periodical payments into a lump sum where this would help the victim's rehabilitation, and a rule limiting the periodical payments to a figure between 80 and 90% of lost earning capacity in order to provide an incentive for the victim to return to work.

A system of periodical payments would have the additional advantage that it would be capable of revision in the light of current inflation. At present the lump sum award generally takes no account of future inflation, partly because of the difficulty of forecasting.[10] The result is likely to be

---

4 *Mitchell v Mulholland (No 2)* [1972] 1 QB 65, [1971] 2 All ER 1205.
5 See J. G. Fleming in (1969) 19 Univ Tor LJ 295; Pearson Report, vol 1, paras 215–18.
6 Below, Chap 6.
7 Below, Chap 7.
8 Pearson Report, vol 1, para 573; for the very unconvincing reasons of the minority, see para 628.
9 Eg by a minority of the Pearson Commission, vol 1, para 620.
10 *Cookson v Knowles* [1979] AC 556, [1978] 2 All ER 604; *Lim Poh Choo v Camden and Islington Area Health Authority* [1980] AC 174, [1979] 2 All ER 910. In exceptional cases where the assumed annuity is large enough to attract tax at a high rate the multiplier may be increased or some other allowance made for inflation.

that in times of rapid inflation apparently large sums soon become inadequate. The victim may have to apply to the social security system for assistance,[11] so throwing responsibility on to taxpayers.

Difficult questions arise in deciding what the principle of ethical compensation requires. Suppose that the victim's life expectancy is reduced by the tort. Should he be awarded damages for loss of earnings during the years he will not live? An affirmative answer was given by the House of Lords, it being held that these damages should cover the whole period of the plaintiff's pre-accident life expectancy, with a deduction for living expenses that he would have incurred during the lost years.[12] The reason given was consistent with the principle of ethical compensation, namely that 'good health and sound earning' are an asset of present value for the loss of which compensation can be assessed, regardless of the particular 'needs' of the victim. This, however, was merely the formal reason, the real reason being the common sense one that the damages for the lost years were likely to improve the position of the victim's dependants, who were likely to inherit at least part of them.

The question whether to base damages on ethical compensation or on provision for the victim's need raises a sharper issue in cases where the victim's spouse or parent renders gratuitous services in order to help him cope with his disablement. The 'needs' or welfare approach would allow recovery of damages by the victim only if he could prove actual financial loss. The notion of ethical compensation, on the other hand, allows the court to place an objective 'value' on the services rendered, leaving it to the moral responsibility of the victim to recompense those who help him from

---

11 This was the conclusion of the Woodhouse–Meares Report in Australia (1974) paras 145–150.

12 *Pickett v British Rail Engineering Ltd* [1980] AC 136, [1979] 1 All ER 774. The decision accorded with the unimplemented recommendations of the Law Commission (No 56 para 87) and the Pearson Commission (vol 1, para 335).

motives of love or family bond. After much debate, the Court of Appeal adopted the latter approach.[13] For similar reasons, a plaintiff may recover damages for the loss of capacity to render gratuitous services to others; so an injured housewife is compensated for being deprived of her capacity to look after her family regardless of the fact that other members of the family may have absorbed her tasks.[14]

A further illustration of the extended interpretation of ethical compensation arises from the argument that it should not be cheaper to kill than to maim, and, further, that it should not be cheaper to injure a person so severely that he is incapable of obtaining any enjoyment from a sum awarded to him as compensation than to injure him less severely. These considerations are advanced to justify a rule that damages for 'loss of amenity' may be awarded although the victim has died or is unconscious or, although conscious, is totally insensible to his loss because of severe brain damage.[15] Were it otherwise the damages payable by the tortfeasor who inflicts moderate injuries would be greater than those due from one who kills or causes 'living death'. The theoretical argument in favour of the award of damages for loss of amenity is that life is regarded worth living quite apart from any happiness it may bring. Loss of amenity

13 *Donnelly v Joyce* [1974] QB 454, [1973] 3 All ER 475; *Cunningham v Harrison* [1973] QB 942, [1973] 3 All ER 463. Cp. the approach of the social security system to care allowances, below, Chap 6, p 184.

14 *Daly v General Steam Navigation Co Ltd* [1980] 3 All ER 696, [1981] 1 WLR 120.

15 *H West & Son Ltd v Shephard* [1964] AC 326, [1963] 2 All ER 625 (41-year-old housewife with serious brain damage helpless and unconscious – £17,500 for loss of amenity); this followed *Wise v Kaye* [1962] 2 QB 638, [1962] 1 All ER 257 (CA by majority awarded £15,000 to 20-year-old woman with no knowledge of her condition). In mid-1983 the level of awards under this head had reached £70,000 in the case of injuries of maximum severity: (1983) 7 CL 111. The Law Commission (No 56, paras 31–6) proposed no change in the rule, but the Pearson Commission (vol 1, paras 393–8) recommended that damages for loss of amenity should no longer be recoverable for permanent unconsciousness.

includes any loss or impairment of function and worsening of the plaintiff's health, apart from pain and suffering. Individual circumstances may be relevant: a plaintiff who loses a leg may be expected to be awarded more if he is a football player than if he follows a sedentary occupation. The judges have tended to favour a tariff, albeit an unwritten and rough and ready one, in respect of this kind of loss. Judges and those engaged in settling claims can obtain a fairly accurate guide as to the amount that a particular disablement is 'worth' by consulting the standard practitioners' works. This tariff approach to the loss of amenity is fairly recent. Before the 1950s the judges usually included an unspecified amount in respect of disablement under the general heading of 'pain and suffering'. Today loss of amenity is regarded as having an independent existence within the category of general damages. From a strictly compensatory point of view it can be argued that no one can really form an idea of what the plaintiff has lost, whether it be described in objective terms or in terms of what the injured person knows and feels about his deprivation.[16] Yet large awards continue to be made in cases of permanent unconsciousness for loss of amenity.

It is traditionally said that damages for personal injuries do not include any compensation for wounded feelings or mere mental suffering. But the exceptions to this rule are so important that it would seem nearer the truth to say that mental suffering will be compensated for provided there is clear evidence that it was reasonably prolonged. Psychiatry tells us that mental distress can give rise to disorder just as real as physical illness. The House of Lords has recently removed cases of 'recognisable psychiatric illness', excluding

---

16 Damages for loss of amenity are very similar to the former damages for loss of expectation of life. Although claims under the latter head were abolished by the Administration of Justice Act 1982, s 1(1)(a), this factor can still be taken into account in assessing damages for pain and suffering in so far as the victim is aware that his life has been shortened: s 1(1)(b).

transitory distress, from any special categorisation in the law of negligence,[17] and Parliament has acknowledged the feelings of mourners by a new head of damages for bereavement.[18] Awards for 'pain and suffering' stand on a special footing. The court will take into account the pain caused by the injury and subsequent treatment and the suffering caused by awareness of physical disability, shortened expectation of life, and the embarrassment or humiliation of disfigurement and so on. Judges and claims negotiators can find guidance in the books about appropriate awards. There is a strong attachment to such awards in England. One reason may be that they supplement what might otherwise be rather inadequate lump sums for pecuniary loss. But they also give solace to the victim, and in a system based on the fault principle they have a basis in the principle of ethical compensation. The main objection that has been raised against awards for pain and suffering is that they tend to over-compensate the victim – particularly in the less serious cases, where insurance companies are forced into inflated settlements because of the 'nuisance' value of the claim.[19] In a no-fault system the reasons for non-pecuniary damages are less compelling than in a fault system, and the need to effect administrative savings may lead either to the elimination of pain and suffering awards, as in the British social security system (which does however provide disablement benefits for non-economic loss),[20] or to a statutory limit on the amount that can be awarded.[1]

17 *McLoughlin v O'Brian* [1983] 1 AC 410, [1982] 2 All ER 298, discussed below, Chap 4, p 105.
18 Administration of Justice Act 1982, inserting a new s 1A in the Fatal Accidents Act 1976: see below, p 87.
19 See above, p 78, and O'Connell and Simon *Payment for Pain and Suffering – Who Wants What When and Why?* (Champaign-Urbana, Ill, 1972).
20 Below, Chap 6, p 182.
1 As in no-fault schemes, below Chap 7, p 194.

THE EFFECT OF DEATH ON CLAIMS IN TORT

If a person who is tortiously injured recovers damages and then dies, the damages will pass, like the rest of his property, under his will or on his intestacy. If his life was shortened by the injury he may have recovered damages for loss of earnings in the lost years; and since most people leave the bulk of their property within their own immediate family, the result is likely to be that the victim's dependants will benefit by the damages. But there is no inevitability about this; if the victim has bequeathed the residue of his estate to charity, it may be the charity that gets the damages for the lost years, for the victim's pain and suffering, and so on.

Suppose that the victim is killed instantaneously, or otherwise dies before bringing his action. In that case the general rule is that his personal representatives (executors or administrators) can bring the action as though the victim were still alive, and the damages will swell his estate.[2] There are certain exceptions; in particular, the claim for damages for lost years does not survive.[3]

This arrangement still leaves it possible that the victim's dependants are left unprovided for owing to circumstances over which they have no control. To remedy this, the Fatal Accidents Act 1976 (continuing earlier legislation) creates an exception to the general principle that one person cannot sue in respect of a tort to another, by providing that the dependants of a person who dies as a result of a tort can sue

---

2 Law Reform (Miscellaneous Provisions) Act 1934. The damages are, in general, calculated in the same way as if the victim was still alive for the period between when he suffered the injury and his death. Where the death was instantaneous, the only claim under the 1934 Act will be for funeral expenses.

3 Administration of Justice Act 1982, s 4(2), trenchantly criticised by Peter Cane and Donald Harris in (1983) 46 MLR 478 as a 'lesson in how not to reform the law'.

for the loss of support.[4] The lump sum recoverable under this Act is assessed on a different basis from that on which the deceased could have recovered. First there is a claim for damages for bereavement, currently fixed at £3,500, which may be brought only by the husband or wife of the deceased or by the parents of an unmarried minor (ie under 18).[5] Second, a far wider class of dependants may recover damages in respect of the loss of 'prospective pecuniary advantage' from the life of the deceased. The plaintiff has to establish a reasonable probability of a direct financial contribution by the deceased had he lived. This means that the parents of a young child are unlikely to recover damages for loss of support even if they have invested a large amount in the child's education.[6]

It will be seen that the Fatal Accidents Act partially recognises the function of the law of tort in providing security against loss, and extends protection beyond the

4 The 1976 Act, substantially amended by the Administration of Justice Act 1982, is the modern version of the Fatal Accidents Act 1846, promoted by Lord Campbell, against the fierce opposition of the railway companies who feared a flood of claims by the dependants of victims of their activities. Although later Acts have broadened the categories of dependants who may sue, not all of those who are factually dependent upon another have a cause of action (eg a couple who have not been living together as husband and wife for the minimum period of two years: s 2(3)(b) of the 1976 Act, as amended by the 1982 Act).

5 If he was illegitimate, only the mother can claim. This head of damages, which has for long existed in Scotland in respect of 'loss of society', was introduced by the Administration of Justice Act 1982, inserting a new s 1A in the Fatal Accidents Act 1976; it follows recommendations of the Law Commission and a majority of the Pearson Commission: vol 1, para 424.

6 Whatever the dependants received by way of inheritance used to be set-off against their damages under the Fatal Accidents Act, but this rule has now been abolished by the Administration of Justice Act 1982. Special provision is made for funeral expenses, which may be claimed by a dependant under the Fatal Accidents Act 1976, s 3(5), as amended, except that if the personal representatives incurred them the claim is brought under the 1934 Act, s 1(2)(c). In either event the claim is for something more than 'compensation', because the only 'loss' is that the date of the funeral has been brought forward.

person immediately injured. Nevertheless, like the rest of the law of tort, it provides a measure of security only to those who can establish that what is regarded as a wrong has been committed. We must now consider the fault basis of liability.

Damage: Any injury or loss, physical or economic. Varieties of damage:

(A1) Pecuniary: loss of existing assets and of future advantages, profits and earnings.

(A2) Non-pecuniary: loss of assets that have no pecuniary equivalent, such as loss of amenity.

(B1) General damage, which need not be specifically claimed.

(B2) Special damage, upon which a precise figure can be put, and which must be claimed in the statement of claim.

Damages: A sum of money awarded by a judge or jury. Varieties of damages:

(i) Contemptuous – where the judge or jury disapproves of the plaintiff's conduct; sometimes treated as a variety of (ii) below.

(ii) Nominal – where the tort is actionable per se and the action is merely to establish the right.

(iii) Substantial – the amount whereby the plaintiff is worse off by reason of the defendant's wrong, as nearly as money can represent it.

(iv) Aggravated – an amount to compensate the injured feelings of the plaintiff where the defendant has acted with insolence, arrogance or malice. Not always easy to distinguish from (v) below.

(v) Exemplary, or punitive or vindictive – a tort 'fine'

which goes beyond what is necessary to compensate the plaintiff.

Lump sum awards: The lost net average annual income (multiplicand) × the number of years during which the loss will continue (the multiplier). The multiplicand includes an allowance for future prospects. The multiplier is scaled down for future contingencies and for the advantage of receiving an immediate capital sum (usually between 8 and 16, but shorter the closer the victim is to retirement).

Component items of claims for personal injuries:
   (a) Pain and suffering before judgment.
   (b) Pain and suffering that plaintiff will probably suffer in the future, either permanent or temporary.
   (c) Disability and loss of amenity before judgment.
   (d) Disability and loss of amenity that plaintiff will probably suffer in the future, either permanent or temporary.
   (e) Loss of earnings before judgment.
   (f) Loss of earnings, either partial or total expected in the future, either permanent or temporary.
   (g) Loss of earning capacity (eg handicaps if plaintiff seeks future employment).
   (h) Expenses before judgment (medical, value of services rendered by others, etc).
   (i) Expenses expected in future, either permanent or temporary.

Component items of claim under Fatal Accidents Act
   (a) Bereavement of spouse/parent (£3,500).
   (b) Loss of dependency.

4 Fault

Condemn the fault and not the actor of it?

Measure for Measure II ii

Why is it thought necessary to insist upon compensation being made for torts? If one goes back to the beginning, the reason can be found in the desire to prevent civil strife. A wrong meant retaliation by the injured person and his family, so the law intervened to require the offender to buy off the victim's wrath.

In time a more sophisticated reason came to be accepted. It was thought to be just that a wrongdoer should compensate his victim, and should be compelled to do so by the law, irrespective of the question whether the victim would otherwise exact vengeance. This assumed principle of justice, that a wrong requires compensation, is still a powerful motive behind the law of tort and, as has been seen, explains some of its principal features. The law of tort does not provide compensation for those who suffer from a natural misfortune where no human being is responsible, such as falling ill, nor does it generally provide compensation for those who are injured by their fellow-creatures by pure accident. The law of tort generally operates only in the case of harm caused by fault, which means wrongful intention or negligence: because, according to the traditional view, it is only in this case that justice requires reparation to be made. Persons who wish to be legally protected against other harms must cover themselves by private insurance, or else must rely on social security benefits. Before considering this justification of the fault principle we must first analyse the forms of fault.

THE FORMS OF FAULT: INTENTION, RECKLESSNESS AND INADVERTENT NEGLIGENCE

Legal fault is of three kinds: wrongful intention, recklessness, and inadvertent negligence.

Intention (otherwise called wilfulness) is the state of mind of willing the act (or being aware of the omission), knowing the circumstances and desiring the consequences. As regards the first element, to speak of willing an act is perhaps pleonastic, because every act is necessarily willed if it is to be an act at all. This can be shown by considering a bodily movement that is not willed. If some third party jerks my arm, the movement of my arm would not be said to be an act on my part, because it is not the exercise of my volition.

There may, of course, be an unintended consequence of a (voluntary) act. When a motorist presses the accelerator, the movement of his foot is an act, and it is an intentional in the sense of voluntary act. Moreover, the increased speed of the car is an intended result of the act. Nevertheless, if, owing to the speed of the car, a pedestrian were killed, it would be grievously misleading to say that the killing was the result of the motorist's intentional act. The term 'intentional' would be understood in such a context to imply desire of the consequence of the act, namely the killing of the pedestrian, and with this implication the statement would become false. It is desirable, therefore, to speak of intended *consequences*, when that is meant, rather than of intentional *acts*.

The term 'intention' is further extended to cases where the consequence, though not itself desired, is foreseen as the *certain* accompaniment of what is desired.[1] Summing this up,

---

[1] This point has more importance in the criminal than in the civil law: see Williams *Textbook of Criminal Law* (2nd edn, London, 1983) § 3.5.

a consequence is said to be intended when it is either (a) desired or (b) foreseen as the certain consequence of the actor's conduct. If it is neither desired nor foreseen as certain, but is nevertheless foreseen as possible, and if the actor is not justified in running such a risk, the conduct is said to be *reckless* as to the consequence. It is also possible to speak of recklessness as to circumstances, as when a deceitful statement is made, not caring whether it is true or false. In the law of tort, recklessness is nearly always classed with intention, either being sufficient to establish liability.

Some torts can be committed only intentionally or recklessly. Examples are deceit, malicious prosecution, and inducing a breach of contract. Most torts, however, can be committed not only intentionally or recklessly but even by mere *inadvertent negligence*. Inadvertent negligence is where the actor[2] does not realise the possibility of causing harm (or of the existence of a circumstance) but where he ought to have realised it. It is distinguished from recklessness, otherwise called advertent negligence, where the actor does realise the possibility. The common example of inadvertent negligence is in the running-down case. A careless motorist does not foresee the possibility of causing injury, other than the usual possibility which is inherent in lawful driving, but in fact his driving is such that it causes an increased and unreasonable risk to others. From an objective point of view, therefore, his conduct is stigmatised as negligent. Difficulty is caused in this conceptual scheme by a decision of the House of Lords[3] in a criminal case extending recklessness to cover circumstances where a person creates a risk without thinking. Previously this had been regarded as an instance of negligence not recklessness. The new rule is of very questionable policy, and the question of applying it to tort cases has not yet arisen.

2   The word 'actor' is intended to include one who in breach of duty omits to act.
3   *Metropolitan Police Comr v Caldwell* [1982] AC 341, [1981] 1 All ER 961.

In ordinary speech, any damage occurring without intention is frequently termed an 'accident'. Lawyers sometimes speak of an *'inevitable accident'*, the adjective 'inevitable' signifying that the accident was not caused by negligence. It means an accident not avoidable by taking reasonable precautions. The expression 'inevitable accident' is a relative one, because the same damage may be an inevitable accident for one person but not for another. If damage is physically caused by A and B together, and A is negligent but B is not, this is an inevitable accident for B but not for A. Hence the full definition of an inevitable accident is that it is damage brought about without the fault of the defendant or of a person for whom he is responsible in law.

The reader should notice how the definitions of fault, strict liability and inevitable accident are interrelated. Strict (sometimes called absolute) liability means liability without the necessity for showing fault, that is, liability where fault is not a relevant issue, whether or not it in fact exists. Inevitable accident means damage caused without fault, for which, therefore, there is no liability unless the case is one of strict liability. Certain defences are generally allowed, such as the plaintiff's contributory negligence; so that the liability is not really absolute in the sense of being unqualified, and it is for this reason that the phrase 'strict liability' is preferred. Examples of torts of strict liability are the conversion (wrongful misappropriation) of chattels, the keeping of dangerous animals, and liability for escape of dangerous things from land (the rule in *Rylands v Fletcher*, which will be considered later.)[4]

---

4 Below, p 128. The expression 'strict liability' was first proposed by Winfield in substitution for 'absolute liability' which was then current ((1926) 42 LQR 37). Although the expression has been adopted by some judges, they do not always use it in the precise meaning proposed by its inventor. For instance, so good a judge as Scott LJ said (in *Haseldine v Daw & Son* [1941] 2 KB 343 at 355) that 'so-called "strict liability" similar to the responsibility

The foregoing definitions may be summarised for convenience.

Fault: intention or negligence.

Intention: awareness of circumstances and desire of consequence or foresight that the consequence is certain to follow from the actor's conduct.

Negligence: causing unintended damage that the defendant ought to have avoided. Varieties of negligence:

(i) Advertent negligence, or recklessness, where the consequence was foreseen as possible but not desired (or where a circumstance was realised to be possible).

(ii) Inadvertent negligence (commonly called 'negligence' simply), where the consequence was neither desired nor foreseen, but should have been foreseen and avoided (or where the possibility of the circumstance should have been realised). Two sub-types must now be distinguished.

(a) Where the actor negligently comes to the conclusion that there was no risk.

(b) Where the actor negligently failed to consider the question of risk. This is now regarded, at least sometimes, as not merely negligence but as equivalent to recklessness under (i) above; but the law is highly unsatisfactory.

---

of an insurer' applies to dangerous things and under *Rylands v Fletcher*; but on turning over the page one finds that he does not mean this at all, for there he speaks merely of a 'duty of care which is higher than usual because of the obvious danger of the situation'. Legally, there is a sharp difference between a strict or absolute liability which is irrespective of fault, and a duty of care which, though perhaps high, is still not broken if there is no fault at all. As regards the instances given by the Lord Justice, he was correct in describing *Rylands v Fletcher* as creating a strict duty and wrong in saying that it created a mere duty of care; he was correct in saying that there was a high duty of care for dangerous things and wrong in saying that the liability was strict.

NEGLIGENCE AS AN INDEPENDENT TORT

Negligence is both a way of committing various torts and a tort on its own. To give an example of the first type, a libellous statement may be made negligently, and from this point of view negligence is merely a way of committing the tort of libel (though it is only in certain circumstances that a plaintiff suing for libel has to prove negligence). On the other hand, negligence is a tort on its own, because it is capable of giving a remedy in circumstances falling outside the other nominate torts.

It might be natural to suppose that the action upon the case for negligence is a comparatively modern development, linked perhaps to the invention of dangerous machinery, but this would be to over-simplify matters. The action for negligence, as applied to damage to the person and property, is old. There is an instance in 1676, where the action was held to lie when the defendant negligently sent his servant to break in some unruly horses in Lincoln's Inn Fields, among a large concourse of His Majesty's lieges, whereby the plaintiff was kicked.[5] Other instances are found centuries before that, as in the well-known Humber ferryman case of 1348, where a ferryman was held liable for overloading his boat, so that the plaintiff's horse was tipped into the water and drowned. In time the action came to be extended from positive acts of negligence to negligent omissions, and from physical damage to general financial loss.

This generalisation of the action of negligence does not mean that all carelessness causing damage is actionable. In order to succeed in the tort of negligence, the plaintiff must establish the following.

(1) The situation must be one in which the law attaches legal liability to carelessness. This is called the 'duty of care' or the 'notional duty'.

5 *Mitchil v Alestree* (1676) 1 Vent 295, 86 ER 190.

(2) There must have been a breach of that duty, that is the defendant's conduct must have fallen short of the standard of care required of a reasonable person in the circumstances. This is referred to as the 'negligence' or 'carelessness' issue.

(3) There must have been a reasonably close connection between the defendant's conduct and the resulting damage suffered by the plaintiff. The popular legal test is to regard as relevant only a cause 'but for which the damage would not have happened', and, having determined this in a broad commonsense way, to ask whether it was reasonably forseeable that the defendant's conduct would cause damage to the plaintiff. The kind of damage must, broadly speaking, have been within the risk created by the plaintiff. This is usually referred to as the question of 'remoteness of damage'.

The defendant may escape liability if the plaintiff voluntarily assumed the risk (*volenti non fit injuria*), or the plaintiff's damages may be reduced if he contributed to them by his own fault.

THE DUTY OF CARE

Some writers argue against the utility of the first of these requirements, that of a duty of care, but we shall try to show that in some form or other it is a necessary notion. Foreign lawyers, indeed, frequently assert that in their systems there is a general theory of liability, and that they do not have a restrictive concept of duty of care. It may safely be said that this claim is unfounded. They may not use the expression 'duty of care', but they will use some expression having the same meaning, such as 'the plaintiff's interest is not protected'.

The restriction upon liability imposed by the requirement of a duty of care applies particularly to omissions. There is no general duty to succour one's neighbour, to play the Good Samaritan. It would be impracticable for the law to be made coextensive with the moral duty of kindness and charity, though a legal duty to help others can arise out of specific situations.

Before the case of *Donoghue v Stevenson* in 1932,[6] the requirement of a duty of care exercised a severely restraining effect even in respect of positive acts of negligence. Many rules limited the type of relationship that gave rise to a duty of care, the kind of person who could claim the benefit of the duty, and the kind of damage for which he could recover. The courts followed precedent, occasionally extending the remedy slightly but expressing apprehension lest they be too venturesome.

Donoghue v Stevenson marked a turning point, more significant perhaps in retrospect than it seemed at the time. All that it actually decided was that the purchaser of a bottle of ginger beer who was (it was assumed[7]) injured by drinking the contents, which had been fouled by a snail in the bottle, could recover damages for negligence from the manufacturer who had bottled the drink. In itself this only went one step further than the previous authorities. The importance of the decision was its insistence upon the expansible nature of the action of negligence. Lord Macmillan said:

> The grounds of action may be as various and manifold as human errancy; and the conception of legal responsibility may develop in adaptation to altering social conditions and standards. The categories of negligence are never closed.[8]

---

6 [1932] AC 562 (Hepple and Matthews, p 64). The full title is *M'Alister (or Donoghue) v Stevenson*; for this idiosyncracy of Scots cases see Williams *Learning the Law* (11th edn, London, 1982) p 19.

7 The case was decided on the pleadings, and since it was later settled, it never was determined whether there was a snail in the ginger beer: see (1955) 71 LQR 472.

8 [1932] AC at 619. Conceivably, Lord Macmillan may here have been speaking as a Scots judge. But much the same remark was made by Evershed MR in *Denny v Supplies and Transport Co Ltd* [1950] 2 KB 374 at 379–80.

But the more celebrated statement of the new principle was that of Lord Atkin in the same case. He began by stating, and approving, the traditional principle.

> Acts or omissions which any moral code would censure cannot in a practical world be treated so as to give a right to every person injured by them to demand relief. In this way rules of law arise which limit the range of complainants and the extent of their remedy.

He followed this with a generalisation.

> The rule that you are to love your neighbour becomes in law: You must not injure your neighbour, and the lawyer's question: Who is my neighbour? receives a restricted reply. You must take reasonable care to avoid acts and omissions which you can reasonably foresee would be likely to injure your neighbour. Who then, in law, is my neighbour? The answer seems to be persons who are so closely and directly affected by my act that I ought reasonably to have them in contemplation as being so affected when I am directing my mind to the acts or omissions which are called in question.[9]

This much-quoted and very influential passage is in some respects strange. Lord Atkin calls his answer 'a restricted reply', but a moment's consideration will show that it is far from being restricted. The question 'Who is my neighbour?' was, of course, asked of Jesus (Luke X, verse 30), and the answer given was the parable of the Good Samaritan. Now it is quite clear that the law would not attach liability to the priest and the Levite who passed by on the other side, even though they might be literally 'careless' of the welfare of the man who fell among thieves. They were not under a duty of care to take positive action for his benefit. Yet they fell within Lord Atkin's generalisation. They were morally guilty, as Lord Diplock has pointed out, of 'an omission which was likely to have as its reasonable and probable

9 [1932] AC at 580.

consequence damage to the health of the victim of the thieves, but for which the priest and the Levite would have incurred no civil liability in English law.'[10] The logical objection to Lord Atkin's 'neighbour' dictum is that it makes the test of the existence of a duty of care the same as the test of breach of that duty, so that if accepted it would in effect abolish the need for a duty. The duty of care is broken if the defendant does not behave like a reasonable man; but the 'neighbour' dictum says that he is always under a duty to behave like a reasonable man, which if accepted means that the duty concept ceases to control the scope of liability for carelessness. In fact it has not been accepted to this extent. Rules relating to duty still exist as limiting factors upon the notion of negligence.

For example, the courts have denied that there is a duty on a landowner to prevent the subsidence of his neighbour's adjoining premises as a result of his careless abstraction of underground water flowing in undefined channels.[11] If a burglar, while making his getaway in a stolen car, drives dangerously and so injures another participant in the crime, the court will express its moral disapproval of his activities by denying a duty of care.[12] A judge owes not duty of care to the litigants before him, 'otherwise no man but a beggar or a fool would be a judge.'[13] Advocates cannot be sued by their clients in respect of alleged negligence in the conduct of a trial or in work intimately connected with the litigation, for

---

10 *Home Office v Dorset Yacht Co Ltd* [1970] AC 1004 at 1060. For the reasons of policy behind the legal rule see Atiyah *Accidents, Compensation and the Law* (3rd edn, London, 1980) pp 95–112, and Millner *Negligence in Modern Law* (London, 1967) pp 30–5.

11 *Langbrook Properties Ltd v Surrey CC* [1969] 3 All ER 1424, [1970] 1 WLR 161.

12 *Ashton v Turner* [1981] QB 137, [1980] 3 All ER 870. The policy is sometimes expressed in the Latin maxim *Ex turpi causa non oritur actio*.

13 Stair *Institutions* Bk 4, tit 1, s 5, quoted by Lord Fraser in *Arenson v Casson Beckman Rutley & Co* [1977] AC 405 at 440; and see *Sirros v Moore* [1975] QB 118, [1974] 3 All ER 776.

a number of policy reasons related to the administration of justice.[14]

The arguments advanced to support these rules are open to debate, and the rules are now very much the exception. *Donoghue v Stevenson* wrought a change of attitude. When judges wish to cut away from restrictions imposed by the precedents, they can happily quote the 'neighbour' dictum to justify (or appear to justify) the imposition of liability upon the careless defendant. Nevertheless, the process of expansion has been cautious, at least until recently. In 1963, when the House of Lords wished to remove the restrictions on liability for careless statements causing economic loss, they were unwilling to apply Lord Atkin's dictum literally. It was said that negligent words were different from negligent acts,[15] that acts causing physical harm were distinct from words causing economic loss,[16] and that to apply the 'neighbour' principle 'would be a misuse of a general conception and it is not the way in which the English law develops'.[17] Instead the Law Lords strove to delimit the boundaries of the new duty of care not to cause loss by negligent statements, saying that there had to be some 'special relationship' between the parties to give rise to this duty. Although they did not speak with one voice when describing the 'special relationships' which could found liability, the common factor in their speeches was *reliance*. In subsequent cases in England[18] the principle has been taken to

14 *Rondel v Worsley* [1969] 1 AC 191, [1967] 3 All ER 993; *Saif Ali v Sydney Mitchell & Co* [1980] AC 198, [1978] 3 All ER 1033.

15 *Hedley Byrne & Co Ltd v Heller & Partners Ltd* [1964] AC 465, [1963] 2 All ER 575, per Lord Reid at 482, 580 (Hepple and Matthews, pp 105, 517).

16 Ibid, per Lord Pearce at 534, 615.

17 Ibid, per Lord Devlin at 524, 607.

18 A majority of the Privy Council (in an appeal from the High Court of Australia) took a narrower view in *Mutual Life and Citizens' Assurance Co Ltd v Evatt* [1971] AC 793, [1971] 1 All ER 150; but it was the minority opinion of Lords Reid and Morris in that case that has been adopted in England: *Esso Petroleum Co Ltd v Mardon* [1975] QB 819, [1975] 1 All ER 203.

be that when a person in the course of his trade or business knows that his skill and judgment are being relied upon and gives advice or information without qualification or warning he places himself under a duty to take such care as is reasonable in all the circumstances. What remained uncertain, after this development, was whether it represented an exception to a general principle that a duty of care could arise only to avoid physical harm to another, or provided a basis for expanding the duty of care to situations of pure economic loss.[19] This is a problem to which we shall return after considering the law-making function of the judges.

PRINCIPLE AND POLICY

In the 1970s, the judges – led by Lords Reid[20] and Denning[1] – came to recognise more clearly than before that the question whether a duty should be imposed by the courts is one of public policy, and that changing notions of policy can justify changes in the scope of the duty. A major breakthrough occurred in *Anns v Merton London Borough Council*,[2] when Lord Wilberforce articulated a two-stage approach:

[T]he position has now been reached that in order to establish that a duty of care arises in a particular situation, it is not necessary to bring the facts of that situation within those of previous situations in which a duty of care has been held to exist. Rather the question has to be approached in two stages. First one has to ask whether, as between the alleged wrongdoer and the person who has suffered damage, there is a

19 For an explanation of these terms, see below.
20 *Home Office v Dorset Yacht Co Ltd* [1970] AC 1004 at 1027, [1970] 2 All ER 294 at 297.
1 Eg in *Spartan Steel and Alloys Ltd v Martin & Co (Contractors) Ltd* [1973] QB 27, [1972] 3 All ER 557; *Dutton v Bognor Regis UDC* [1972] 1 QB 373, [1972] 1 All ER 462.
2 [1978] AC 728 at 751–2, [1977] 2 All ER 492 at 498.

sufficient relationship of proximity or neighbourhood such that, in the reasonable contemplation of the former, carelessness on his part may be likely to cause damage to the latter, in which case a prima facie duty of care arises. Secondly, if the first question is answered affirmatively, it is necessary to consider whether there are any considerations which ought to negative, or to reduce or limit, the scope of the duty or the class of person to whom it is owed or the damages to which a breach of it may give rise.

The requirement of 'a sufficient relationship of proximity or neighbourhood' is too vague to operate as a restriction upon the rule, though it may be used by the courts in particular types of case to deny a duty. In ordinary cases the test is simply the reasonable contemplation of the defendant. It is the same test as that applied when deciding whether the defendant was negligent in fact. So the new rule seems to be that anyone who is negligent in fact can be found to be in breach of duty, unless there are considerations of policy the other way. The significance of the new formulation was that it changed the 'neighbour' principle from being an argument to support new areas of liability, if there were policy considerations in favour of doing so, into a principle that would apply unless there was a policy justification for excluding it. The onus of argument shifted, with 'policy' operating only as a long-stop where the logical application of the factual test of reasonable forseeability would lead to obviously undesirable social or financial consequences.[3]

The new approach makes it dubious whether some of the older precedents restricting the duty of care will survive, such as the decision that an employer is under no duty to take reasonable care of an employee's clothes when he is required to change them at work,[4] or that a university is under no

---

3 See Neil MacCormick *Legal Reasoning and Legal Theory* (Oxford, 1978), especially pp 159, 263.
4 *Edwards v West Herts Group Hospital Management Committee* [1957] 1 All ER 541, [1957] 1 WLR 415; *Deyong v Shenburn* [1946] KB 227, [1946] 1 All ER 226.

duty of care to candidates in examinations.[5] If the new approach still does not make the priest and the Levite liable for failing to alleviate the distress of the victim of an attack, this will hardly be because there is no sufficient relationship of proximity or neighbourhood (neighbourhood in the purely physical meaning of the term certainly exists). It will be because the courts are chary of commencing to impose a general duty of benevolence, even in comparatively simple and clear cases like that in the parable. It would be strange if liability for what might be very large damages were theoretically imposed on every one of perhaps hundreds of people who passed by with averted gaze. It is true that if these people were all regarded as tortfeasors, they would be concurrent tortfeasors with rights of contribution between each other if the victim exacted all his damages from one of them; but the probability is that he would be unable to ascertain their identities. If legal liability is to be created in such circumstances, it should be imposed by statute as a matter of criminal, not civil, law.

Another area where the courts will still be hesitant to recognise an extensive duty of care is where the harm arises from the exercise of statutory powers. In the *Anns* case (above):

> The plaintiff purchased dwellings in Wimbledon which turned out to have defective foundations. He sued the builder, who put up no defence. He also sued the local authority for negligence in allowing the building to proceed even though the foundations had not been taken to a sufficient depth as required by regulations made by the council under the Public Health Act 1936.

The House of Lords decided that there was a prima facie duty of care because it was within the reasonable contemplation of the council that failure to comply with the

5 *Thorne v University of London* [1966] 2 QB 237, [1966] 2 All ER 338.

regulations might give rise to a defect causing damage to the safety and health of owners and occupiers. But the House of Lords also considered the possible policy limitation on this duty. This was that 'the local authority is a public body, discharging functions under statute: its powers and duties are definable in terms of public not private law'.[6] The prerequisite of liability would be for the plaintiff to show that the council had acted ultra vires, that the action taken was not within the limits of a discretion bona fide exercised, before he could begin to rely on a common law duty of care. In order to determine this difficult question, the House of Lords divided discretionary power into an area of policy or planning and an operational area. It would be a policy decision for the council to decide on the scale of resources it was willing to allocate to its public health functions, but once it had decided on the degree of inspection there could be liability in negligence for the 'operational' failure of the inspector to carry out a reasonable inspection. On the facts of the case the council were held liable for negligence at this operational level. On the other hand, where a local authority lacked the resources to grit all roads in icy weather and took the policy decision to grit only major roads, they were not liable to a person who slipped and was injured on a minor footpath.[7] Behind this restriction of liability for negligence lies the policy of public law: compensation to individuals is not regarded as the proper remedy for harm resulting from the policy decisions of public authorities.

For some time there was hesitation in applying the neighbour principle to impose liability for recognisable psychiatric illness (quaintly called 'nervous shock' by lawyers, to distinguish it from mere mental suffering for which damages are not recoverable unless accompanied by physical harm). Two different principles were propounded.

6 [1978] AC at 754A.
7 *Haydon v Kent CC* [1978] QB 343, [1978] 2 All ER 97.

According to the 'impact theory' shock is only an extension of physical injury, and before he can recover for shock-induced psychiatric illness the plaintiff must show that he was within the area of reasonably forseeable injury by impact. According to the 'shock theory' nervous shock is a distinct kind of damage and the only test is that of reasonable forseeability of the plaintiff being injured by nervous shock as a result of the defendant's negligence.[8] Most English, Commonwealth and American cases have tended to support the 'shock theory', and in *McLoughlin v O'Brian*[9] the House of Lords unanimously and resoundingly adopted that theory as the basic principle.

> The plaintiff's husband and three of her children were injured in a collision due to the admitted negligence of the first defendant, the driver of a lorry, employed by the second defendant. At the time the plaintiff was at her home about two miles away. Two hours later the accident was reported to her and she was taken to the hospital, where she was told that her youngest daughter was dead and she saw the other injured members of her family in extremely distressing circumstances. The plaintiff (it was assumed) subsequently suffered from severe shock, depression, and a change of personality.

The Court of Appeal held that although the shock to the plaintiff was reasonably foreseeable, considerations of public policy led to the rejection of her claim, the defendant's duty being limited to those on or near the highway at the time of the accident. The House of Lords agreed that the shock was reasonably foreseeable but disagreed with the Court of Appeal's view that policy considerations negatived the prima facie duty of care owed to the plaintiff. In particular the argument that this would open the floodgates of

8 See *Bourhill v Young* [1943] AC 92, [1942] 2 All ER 396. The 'impact theory' was generally supported by the speeches of Lords Thankerton, Russell and Macmillan in this case, the 'shock theory' by the speeches of Lords Wright and Porter.

9 [1983] 1 AC 410, [1982] 2 All ER 298.

litigation was emphatically rejected. Accordingly the plaintiff was entitled to damages.

However, the speeches of the Law Lords showed
remarkable differences of opinion about the role of policy in
limiting the reasonable foresight test in relation to nervous
shock. Lord Scarman, while apparently conceding that
'policy considerations will have to be weighed' when
formulating principles,[10] denied that policy could justify a
judicial decision where to draw the line. His reason was, in
effect, that the forensic process is not suited to deciding upon
desirable goals or the means of achieving them. To draw a
hard-and-fast line between 'principle' and 'policy' within
the context of the present fault-based tort system is artificial
and unconvincing. To state a 'principle' of liability to all
reasonably foreseeable 'neighbours' is to enunciate a presup-
posed policy goal for the shifting of losses; to state a policy
that losses should be shifted in this way is to lay down a
principle. Policy and principle are inextricably linked. Lord
Scarman's rejection of the 'policy' limitation puts a strain on
the neighbour principle that it is incapable of bearing. One
can sympathise with Lord Edmund-Davies' emphatic
rejection of Lord Scarman's statement as 'running counter to
well-established and wholly acceptable law'.[11] In Lord
Wilberforce's words in this case: 'foreseeability does not of
itself, and automatically, lead to a duty of care.'[12]

The most important result of the decision in *McLoughlin v
O'Brian* has been to remove nervous shock from any special
categorisation in the law of negligence. If the issue is

---

10 [1982] 2 All ER 298 at 310–11. Lord Bridge, whose speech Lord Scarman
said 'cannot be improved or strengthened' (at 310), similarly thought there
were no policy limitations (at 320), while Lord Russell, who 'would not
shrink from regarding in an appropriate case policy as something which may
feature in an judicial decision' (at 310), could find no policy arguments for
limiting liability for nervous shock.

11 [1982] 2 All ER 298 at 308–9, citing a number of examples.

12 Ibid at 303.

approached from the standpoint of reasonable foresight, then factors of space, time and the relationship of the plaintiff to the victim as well as the nature of the victim's injuries are all relevant, and this is left to the 'good sense' of the judge 'enlightened by progressive awareness of mental illness'.[13] This may still exclude the ordinary bystander at an accident, because he or she is assumed to be reasonably strong-nerved and able to withstand the horrors of daily life, but the judges should now be willing to admit intimate relationships other than parent and child or husband and wife and there are no hard and fast lines between those who suffer shock in the immediate period after the accident and those who learn of the tragedy only some time later. Distance of time and space may, however, make it difficult to prove as a fact that the psychiatric illness was shock-induced.[14]

Finally, in relation to the scope of the duty of care, we may return to the problem of economic loss. If a person buys a product which causes him injury when he uses it because of a defect in the product (like the snail in the ginger-beer bottle) we call this physical harm; and it was with this situation that *Donoghue v Stevenson* was concerned. On the other hand, if a buyer simply has the defective product repaired, or if he suffers a loss of profit because the defect prevents him from using it in his business, this is described as an economic or financial loss. The distinction is not sharp, because economic loss can follow from physical harm. Where the loss is purely economic and arises in the course of a commercial transaction, the duty of care in tort usually plays a supplementary role to duties in contract; but, as we have

---

13 Per Lord Bridge at 320.
14 See generally, Harvey Teff in (1983) 99 LQR 100, who suggests that from a medical viewpoint 'the crucial determinant of whether the plaintiff is so affected as to suffer from a "recognised psychiatric illness" is almost invariably the nature of his relationship with the victim' (at 104).

seen,[15] the distinctions between contract and tort are beginning to wear thin in situations where one person suffers harm as a result of placing reliance on the words or conduct of another. Here a major, but still problematical, development took place in *Junior Books Ltd v Veitchi Co Ltd*.[16] A majority of the House of Lords extended the duty of care beyond the recognised situations of a duty to prevent harm being done by faulty work, to a duty to avoid such faults being present in the work itself. The result was that a building sub-contractor who did the work badly was made liable in tort for economic losses (including loss of profits) to the owner of the building who had to move out of the defective building while repairs were undertaken. There was no contract between the sub-contractor and the owner, but the situation was clearly very close to a contractual one.[17] One could also regard all the economic losses as being consequential upon the defects in the building and in that extended sense it was physical harm. However, the majority of the House looked upon it as a case in which there was no physical harm. Nor, they held, was the loss incurred in preventing or mitigating damages to the health or safety of any person or damage to any other property of the owner; and they rejected any difference in principle between economic loss caused by physical loss and 'pure' economic loss. This conclusion – 'the next logical step forward in the development of this branch of the law'[18] – was reached by applying the two-stage approach set out by Lord Wilberforce in *Anns* (above). There was a prima facie *Donoghue v*

15 See above, Chap 1, p 16.
16 [1983] 1 AC 520, [1982] 3 All ER 201. Like *Donoghue v Stevenson* this was an appeal from the Scottish courts; but the relevant principles of English and Scots law are the same.
17 The reports are silent as to why the pursuers had not taken the obvious course of alleging a collateral contract with the defenders, who were nominated sub-contractors.
18 [1982] 3 All ER 201 at 214, per Lord Roskill.

Stevenson duty because of the admitted 'proximity' of the parties (the owner of the building and sub-contractors nominated by the owner's own architects). The 'floodgates' argument and other policy objections to liability were then rejected.

One of the controversial issues arising from this decision is the *degree* of proximity required. The principle of reliance, which formed the basis of liability in the cases on negligent statements (above) has some importance on this. Lord Roskill said that the concept of proximity 'must always involve, at least in most cases, some degree of reliance'.[19] The imprecise nature of the notion of reliance is shown by the highly questionable view of Lords Fraser and Roskill that an ordinary consumer of products would be denied recovery on the ground that he had relied upon the retailer from whom he purchased the product rather than the manufacturer. Most purchasers of well-known branded articles these days rely upon the reputation of the article and its maker rather than upon the supplier. Even if the opinion of the two Lords is accepted, it may be supposed that if the manufacturer described the product as being of a particular quality, say Grade I, and the consumer relied upon this when purchasing from the retailer, he would be able to recover damages from the manufacturer for the diminished value.

The *Junior Books* case leaves it unresolved how cases in which there is no element of reliance fit into the picture. No reference was made to cases, such as *Ross v Caunters*,[20] where,

---

19 Ibid, at 214; see too Lord Fraser at 204; and (1983) 46 MLR at 216–17. This approach may be compared with that of the High Court of Australia in *Caltex Oil (Australia) Pty Ltd v Dredge Willemstad* (1976) 136 CLR 529, especially the test suggested by Gibbs and Mason JJ that the defendant must know that a particular person, not merely as a member of an unascertained class, would be likely to suffer economic loss in consequence of his negligence.

20 [1980] Ch 297, [1979] 3 All ER 580 (Hepple and Matthews, p 535). See above, Chap 1, p 16 and *Ministry of Housing and Local Government v Sharp* [1970] 2 QB 233, [1970] 1 All ER 1009 (Hepple and Matthews, p 533).

it will be remembered, an intended beneficiary was allowed to recover damages in tort for loss of a prospective gain against solicitors who had been negligent in the preparation of a will for their client (the testator). Lord Roskill required reliance 'at least in most cases', but if reliance is not required in *all* cases, what is the test of proximity where it is not? The authorities give no answer.

A particular form of the problem arises where property is negligently damaged but the action is brought not by the owner of the property but by someone who merely has some contractual or other relation with the owner. This is sometimes called the 'relational interest'. Take as an example the case of *Spartan Steel and Alloys Ltd v Martin & Co (Contractors) Ltd.*[1]

> Contractors digging up a road negligently damaged an electricity cable under the road, so interrupting the electricity supply to the plaintiff's nearby factory for $14\frac{1}{2}$ hours. The power failure led to a diminution in value of metal then in their arc furnace, causing them a loss of profit. In addition, they were prevented from putting 4 more melts through the furnace during the power failure and lost profit of £1,767.

The Court of Appeal agreed that the plaintiffs were entitled to damages in respect of the metal in the furnace at the time of the power failure, since this was damage to property suffered as a result of the defendants' negligence; but a majority held that the plaintiffs could not recover damages for the loss of profits on the undamaged melts which had not been put into the furnace. The question before the court was said to be 'at bottom . . . a question of policy'; and a variety of reasons were put forward for the distinction that was drawn – in particular the possibility of 'business interruption' insurance,[2] self-reliance by businessmen in respect of

1　[1973] QB 27, [1972] 3 All ER 557 (Hepple and Matthews, p 106); see too, *SCM (UK) Ltd v Whittall & Son Ltd* [1971] 1 QB 337, [1970] 3 All ER 245.
2　See Hepple and Matthews, p 705 for a specimen.

this kind of hazard, and the dangers of false claims and of opening the floodgates of litigation.

Despite the doubts which have been expressed about the correctness of this decision,[3] it seems sensible to distinguish cases where a person suffers economic loss as a result of reliance upon another's undertaking from cases in which the loss results from some dependency upon a third person. For example the loss of a breadwinner is treated differently from losses resulting from personal injuries.[4] So too, commercial dependency (such as the loss of electricity supply due to a power failure, for whatever reason) could be regarded as a risk of capital against which the businessman can insure and so protect himself.[5] However, this economic consideration conflicts with the strong moral view of judges that a person who suffers loss as a result of another's fault is entitled to damages.

NEGLIGENCE AS A CONFLICT OF VALUES

Every negligence issue involves a conflict of values. This is not generally obvious, because the scales are usually weighted heavily on one of the two sides. No one would doubt that a motorist must keep a proper look-out when driving, and is liable in negligence for injury caused through

---

3 [1982] 3 All ER 201 at 214, per Lord Roskill. *Street on Torts* (7th edn) pp 101–2, contends that Edmund Davies LJ's dissenting judgment would now be preferred, but is more doubtful about cases such as *Weller & Co v Foot and Mouth Disease Research Institute* [1966] 1 QB 569, [1965] 3 All ER 560 (cattle infected with virus which defendant negligently allowed to escape; auctioneer who could no longer hold auction sales denied a remedy).
4 See above, Chap 3, p 86.
5 The judgment of Lloyd J in *Schiffahrt und Kohlen GmbH v Chelsea Maritime Ltd, The Irene's Success* [1982] QB 481, [1982] 1 All ER 218 at 222, supports the distinction suggested in the text; the economic rationale is, however, a matter of controversy: compare W. Bishop (1982) 2 Oxf J Leg Stud 1 with M. Rizzo (1982) 11 J Leg Stud 281.

failing to do so. There can be no question that the pedestrian's interest in personal safety is superior to the driver's interest in saving energy by driving without paying attention to the road. But the conflict of values and the conflict of interests appears more clearly when we consider the factor of speed. Practically all road accidents could be prevented if vehicles went slowly enough; but this does not mean that keeping up a fair speed is necessarily negligence. We are prepared, as a society, to face the statistical certainty of some accidents in return for a fair measure of speed, and a line is drawn between this reasonable speed and the excessive speed that constitutes negligence.

In some cases it requires almost a judgment of Solomon to decide between the competing interests of the parties. Suppose that the defendant's airfield is situated near the plaintiff's silver fox farm; and the noise of the machines taking off and landing so disturbs the plaintiff's vixen that they refuse to mate. In such circumstances one or other of the parties must give up his business. One cannot solve the problem by asking whether the occupier of the airfield has behaved like a reasonable person, because this question must attend upon the other question: is he entitled to carry on his business at the expense of the plaintiff, the occupier of the fox farm? The answer to this question must be given as a matter of law, not as a deduction from the conduct of the reasonable person. The problem in this particular case is generally regarded as pertaining to the law of nuisance, but the principles of decision are the same whether it be regarded as a case of nuisance or of negligence. These principles are two in number. First, special sensitivity on the part of the plaintiff is not protected. Hence, if the keeping of silver foxes is regarded as an unusually delicate operation the plaintiff will have no remedy. But, secondly, if the plaintiff's activity is regarded as normal or usual, the defendant will be expected to prevent the escape from his premises, in unreasonable quantity, of any noxious 'thing', including noise. The consequence of this would be that the occupier of the airfield, if he could not reduce his volume of noise, would have either to obtain statutory authority or to close down.[6] It will be seen from this that the problem is resolved at common law not by weighing the relative public importance of a silver fox farm and an airfield, nor even by asking who came there first; but solely by fastening on the features of special sensitivity and 'escape'.[7] (Statute has added the overriding rule that no action lies in nuisance or negligence where the flight of an aircraft is at a reasonable height.)[8]

Where there is no noxious escape passing from the defendant's land to the plaintiff's land, this type of solution is not available. Suppose that there are two neighbouring farmers. One keeps bees. The other grows onions for seed; and to do this he has to allow his onions to flower. His neighbour's bees visit the onion flowers, and as a result the honey is completely spoilt. Has the bee-keeper any remedy to prevent the onion-grower from allowing his onions to go to flower? However the case is decided, one or other party must give up his business. The two are incompatible. Each is conducting his business in good faith, and in the absence of some rule of law it cannot be said that one is acting more unreasonably than the other. One must be sacrificed, and somehow a decision must be made between them. If the case arose the court would undoubtedly take its stand upon the technical point that there has been no noxious escape from the onion-grower's land, except, indeed, such escape as is assisted by the plaintiff's own bees. The case falls outside the accepted principles of liability, so the bee-keeper must put up with his loss.

---

6 Unless the court in effect allowed the defendant to buy the plaintiff out by awarding damages in lieu of a quia timet injunction (above, Chap 3, p 69).
7 This problem was dealt with in the Canadian case of *Nova Mink Ltd v Trans-Canada Airlines* [1951] 2 DLR 241, 26 MPR 389 (NSSC).
8 Civil Aviation Act 1982, s 76.

THE STANDARD OF THE REASONABLE PERSON

Assuming that the law recognises a duty of care in the circumstances, what standard of conduct is required to comply with it?

The word 'carelessness' is sometimes used (as it was in the above discussion) to connote conduct that becomes negligence when it is a breach of the duty of care. Although convenient, the word is misleading to the uninitiated because it wrongly suggests the idea of one who does not care. In truth the 'careless' man of the law may care very much about the consequences of his conduct. He may do his best not to cause injury, and yet be accounted careless and negligent when he does so. It is a defect in the expression 'careless' that it thus carries a connotation of moral blame which may be lacking in the actual case. The standard of care expected of the actor is that of the 'reasonable man' – meaning the reasonable person; this is an objective standard 'independent of the idiosyncracies of the particular person whose conduct is in question'.[9] The learner-driver is expected to observe the same standard of care as the skilled, experienced and careful driver, although his very inexperience makes it impossible for him to do so;[10] the home handyman must keep to the same standard as a reasonably competent tradesman doing the work in question;[11] and persons of unsound mind are responsible to the same extent as if they were sane.[12]

These examples reinforce the point that liability for negligence is not synonymous with moral blameworthiness. On the one hand, some of those who are at fault escape liability because of the absence of a legal duty; on the other

---

9 Per Lord MacMillan in *Glasgow Corpn v Muir* [1943] AC 448 at 457.
10 *Nettleship v Weston* [1971] 2 QB 691, [1971] 3 All ER 581 (Hepple and Matthews, p 148).
11 *Wells v Cooper* [1958] 2 QB 265, [1958] 2 All ER 527.
12 This point is, however, not free from doubt: below p 141.

hand, the morally innocent may be condemned to pay enormous sums by way of damages. This is because the standard of care of the 'reasonable man' is today applied indiscriminately to a wide range of human errors – such as momentary lack of attention or an unfortunate reaction to danger. It has been estimated that the average motorist commits one error every two miles he drives,[13] if one of these errors results in damage to another's person or property the motorist is legally negligent. A split-second's thoughtlessness may result in civil liability in both traffic and industrial accidents. Here the theory that liability is based upon fault bears little resemblance to reality.

The trend towards something that might almost be called 'strict' liability within the concept of negligence is pronounced when the facts are such that the court is willing to infer negligence from the mere happening of an event which causes damage. The classic example is the case in which a barrel fell on the plaintiff's head while he was walking down the street and it was shown that the barrel fell from the window of a warehouse in the defendant's occupation.[14] It was justly said: *res ipsa loquitur* – the thing speaks for itself. Used in this way the Latin tag is no more than a neat description of the argument that the defendant is put to a reply. But in many cases of liability for defective products, and in road and industrial accidents, res ipsa loquitur has been transformed into a rule that in the absence of cogent proof of innocence by the defendant the court must find for the plaintiff.[15] This is still not the same as strict liability as such, because it is open to the defendant to show that he complied with the standard of care of the reasonable person; but in practice it goes a long way towards it.

---

13 L. Norman *Road Traffic Accidents* (World Health Organisation, 1962); Pearson Report, vol 2, paras 196–7, on the causes of road accidents. See generally, A. Tunc in (1975) 49 Tulane LR 279.

14 *Byrne v Boadle* (1863) 2 H & C 722, 159 ER 299.

15 See *Henderson v Henry E Jenkins & Sons* [1970] AC 282, [1969] 3 All ER 756.

NEGLIGENCE AND STRICT STATUTORY DUTIES

The increasing stringency of the standard of care in the tort of negligence has been accompanied by the judicial imposition of tortious liability arising out of safety legislation, mainly in the industrial field.[16] A few Acts of Parliament and regulations expressly provide that breach of a particular statutory duty is to give rise to civil liability. For example, oil-rig workers who are injured as a result of a breach of the Mineral Workings (Offshore Installations) Act, or regulations made thereunder, may bring civil proceedings in respect of that breach in addition to the claim based on negligence.[17] But most Acts of Parliament are silent on this point: they create criminal liability, the liability to pay a fine, without specifying whether civil liability is also intended. The Law Commission recommended in 1969 that there should be a general statute creating a presumption that a breach of a statutory duty is intended to be actionable at the suit of a person who suffers or apprehends damage, unless a contrary intention is expressly stated;[18] but the recommendation has not been implemented. This has not prevented the courts from sometimes finding that breach of statutory duty can be a basis for an action for damages. The courts justify their creation of this kind of tortious liability by reference to the presumed intention of Parliament. A survey of the cases, however, shows one very striking fact. When it concerns industrial welfare, penal legislation results in strict liability in tort. In other cases, with only a few exceptions, it is

---

16 Historically the action upon the statute was one of the oldest common law remedies. The action is now generally limited to industrial legislation.
17 Mineral Workings (Offshore Installations) Act 1971, s 11.
18 Law Com. No. 21, 1969 (Interpretation of Statutes). There has been limited implementation of this proposal by the Health and Safety at Work etc. Act 1974, ss 47(1) and 71(1), below, p 122.

ignored.[19] The attitude of the judges towards industrial legislation reflects the desire to afford greater protection to injured workers than the common law of negligence would allow.

The effect of this construction of industrial legislation is that although the legislation is penal in form, it is applied much more by the civil than by the criminal courts. Whereas, in the criminal courts, the employer need fear no more than a modest fine, in the civil courts he can be made liable in heavy damages; and although he will be insured against these damages his premium may well be affected by his success in keeping clear of liability.

The advantage to the injured worker in being able to base his claim on a clearly-defined statutory duty is that the statute crystallises or 'concretises' the negligence issue. The employer's common law duty is to take reasonable care for the safety of his workers. It may be difficult for the worker to prove that the employer unreasonably failed to foresee and prevent the damage. However, if the duty is clearly set out in the statute the worker simply has to prove a breach of the statute and that the breach caused him damage. For example, if a construction worker falls off a working platform he does not have to prove that it would have been reasonable for his employer to provide a guardrail at a certain height; he may simply rely on a breach of the Construction (Working Places) Regulations 1966, reg 28 of which provides that 'every side of a working platform or working place, being a side thereof from which a person is liable to fall . . . more than 6 ft. 6 in., shall be provided with a suitable guardrail or guardrails of adequate strength, to a height between 3 ft. and 3 ft. 9 in. above the platform or place', etc. This kind of statutory duty writes out in black and white a definite code

---

19 Among the few examples of non-industrial legislation giving rise to civil liability are the compulsory motor vehicle insurance provisions: below, Chap 5, p 157.

of 'reasonable' behaviour instead of leaving the employer's obligations to be deduced from the general standard of care at common law.[20] Failure to observe the statutory standard is sometimes referred to as 'statutory negligence'.

The main aim of the legislation just instanced is to make explicit the height of the guardrail required and the circumstances in which the rail is required, thus saving the plaintiff from having to argue about what is a reasonable height and what are the reasonable circumstances in which a rail should be provided. However, since the statute is construed as creating a strict duty it has incidentally another effect. Even if the employer does all that is reasonable to provide the regulation guardrail, he can be in breach of duty if for some reason not his fault the rail is not provided at the time in question.

The last point cannot be stated simply or with assurance, because the courts are apt to make up exceptions to strict liability on the spur of the moment. 'Act of stranger' is frequently held to be an excuse, but not the wrongful intervention of an employee.

The important aspect of these statutory duties is that it is no defence to the employer that it was not reasonably or economically practicable to comply with the regulation. For example, s 14(1) of the Factories Act 1961 requires 'every *dangerous* part of any machinery' to be securely fenced. A grindstone wheel moving at 1,450 revolutions per minute was held to be 'dangerous' although the evidence showed that it would be impossible to provide a guard that would make the machine usable.[1] It is hard to imagine that Parliament really intended when it passed the Factories Act

---

20 The classic example of such a 'code' is s 48 of the Mines and Quarries Act – see *Brown v National Coal Board* [1962] AC 574, [1962] 1 All ER 81. Even in a case like this, however, the plaintiff must plead the specific breach of statute on which he relies: *Morris v National Coal Board* [1963] 3 All ER 644, [1963] 1 WLR 1382.

1 *John Summers & Sons Ltd v Frost* [1955] AC 740, [1955] 1 All ER 870.

that so common a machine as a grindstone should become unlawful. Nevertheless, that was the effect of the legislation, because the courts refuse to qualify the legislative mandate by the proviso 'if it is reasonably practicable so to do'.

Cases of the type just instanced are applications of the 'literal rule' of statutory construction, under which the courts refuse to read words into a statute that are not there. However, the so-called rules of construction are not so much binding rules as judicial practices or attitudes, and some cases apply not the 'literal rule' but one or other of opposing rules known as the 'golden rule' and the 'mischief rule'. The 'golden rule' allows words to be read into a statute to prevent an absurdity, and the 'mischief rule' allows words to be read in to suppress the mischief against which the statute was aimed.[2] It depends upon the temperament of the particular judge and the extent to which the facts of the case make an appeal to the emotions whether words are read into a statute or not.

Some legislation is more tender to the employer. It obliges him only to make reasonable efforts to achieve the statutory standard. An example is s 29(1) of the Factories Act 1961 which requires the factory occupier to provide safe means of access to the workplace 'so far as reasonably practicable' (but s 28 of the same Act retains strict liability as regards things such as floors, stairs and ladders which must be of 'sound construction'). Another example is s 157 of the Mines and Quarries Act 1954 which provides a general defence, in respect of any breach of the Act, for the defendant to prove that 'it was impracticable to avoid or prevent the breach'. These words limit the statutory duty.[3]

---

2 Williams *Learning the Law* (11th edn) Chap 7.
3 The word 'impracticable' should be compared with 'not reasonably practicable' (the latter being the expression used in the Coal Mines Act 1911, s 102(8), which was replaced by the 1954 Act). The change in wording implies that questions of reasonableness, eg expense, are no longer relevant.

Even where the duty imposed by the legislation is strict, judges sometimes retreat from the consequences of this construction by severely limiting the scope of the duty. So, as Lord Hailsham observed, 'some of the protection to the workman which at first sight might be thought available turns out on closer scrutiny to be illusory.'[4] These words are amply justified by the curious and inconsistent decisions under s 14(1) of the Factories Act. For example, the danger against which fencing is required is held to be the danger that the worker's body will come into harmful contact with a moving part. It does not include the ejection of flying material from the machine even though this is part of the machine itself;[5] and the worker is not protected if what comes into contact with the dangerous part is a hand tool operated by the worker instead of his body or (possibly) his clothes.[6]

The legislation under which these actions are brought is primarily intended to create criminal liability. It is only by 'interpretation' that the courts conjure up civil liability on the same facts. Now it is supposed to be a principle of the criminal law that in case of ambiguity penal statutes are to be construed 'strictly', that is to say, narrowly, in favour of the defendant and against the prosecutor. The rule originated at a time when many crimes were punished with death and even lesser penal sentences were almost incredibly severe. Since the statute is basically penal, and therefore subject to 'strict' construction, it may appear logical to say that the same strict construction must apply to the statute in its civil application, since it would be strange if the duty created by the statute were interpreted differently in a civil action than it is in a criminal prosecution. This may perhaps explain some of the decisions attaching pedantic limitations to the

---

4 *Johnson v F E Callow (Engineers) Ltd* [1971] AC 335 at 342.
5 *Close v Steel Co of Wales Ltd* [1962] AC 367, [1961] 2 All ER 953.
6 *Sparrow v Fairey Aviation Co Ltd* [1964] AC 1019, [1962] 3 All ER 706.

scope of statutory duties. But in general the explanation has less force than might appear. Even the criminal courts have come to pay little attention to the principle of strict construction of penal statutes. They are much more likely to interpret the statute to repress the mischief against which it was aimed. Pradoxically, the rule of strict construction is now more often enunciated by the civil courts, in actions for breach of statutory duty, than by the criminal courts in other criminal cases. Even so, it is only exceptionally that the rule or strict construction has a visibly constricting effect. Cases in which statutes have been restrictively interpreted can be matched by others where they have been given an interpretation generous to the injured workman, and the latter approach is now dominant. For example, it has been held that an employee who is injured when going to a part of his employer's premises where he has no business to be (and hence is trespassing) may claim compensation for breach of the strict statutory duties under the Factories Act 1961[7] and Offices, Shops and Railway Premises Act 1963.[8] This is an illustration of the *literal* interpretation of a statute (refusing to read in an unexpressed exception) prevailing over the *strict* interpretation (resolving what might be thought to be an ambiguity in favour of the defendant).

Surveying the legal scene, an official Committee of Inquiry (under the Chairmanship of Lord Robens)[9] reported in 1972 that some of the judicial interpretations of the safety statutes in the context of civil litigation for compensation 'have appeared to conflict with the intentions of the authorities responsible for framing and enforcing the accident prevention provisions'. The same committee pointed out that statutory duties are haphazard: there are

---

7 *Uddin v Associated Portland Cement Manufacturers* [1965] 2 QB 582, [1965] 2 All ER 213.
8 *Westwood v Post Office* [1974] AC 1, [1973] 3 All ER 184.
9 Cmnd 5034, paras 130, 435 and App 7 (which gives examples).

nine main groups of statutes controlling different industrial activities and these are supported by over 500 subordinate statutory instruments. These contain a mass of 'ill-assorted and intricate detail'; they show neither internal logic nor consistency, and until recently were far from comprehensive. Some 5 million of the 23 million workers in Great Britain were not, before 1975, subject to any occupational health or safety legislation.

As a result of the recommendations of the Committee, the comprehensive Health and Safety at Work etc. Act 1974 (in force since 1975) has been enacted. This places great emphasis on non-statutory codes and standards in promoting accident prevention, partly in supplementation of, and partly in place of, statutory regulations. The existing legislation (such as the Factories Act and subordinate legislation) will gradually be replaced by this new system for accident prevention.

This has considerable implications for claims for damages by injured workers. Although the Act of 1974 provides a general presumption that breach of the new regulations will give rise to civil liability unless the particular regulation provides otherwise, it is by no means clear that the new duties will be strict, nor that they will be as specific as some of those in existing legislation. They may allow defences – such as 'reasonable practicability' – which will at the very least be first cousins of the standard of care expected of the reasonable man. Industrial legislation that was once seen as the thin edge of the wedge of strict duties in tort may be returning to its proper place as 'codified negligence'. But much will depend upon the way in which the new regulations are framed.[10]

---

10 The Pearson Commission, vol 1, paras 914–17, concluded that the action for breach of statutory duty 'goes far enough' in the direction of strict liability for work accidents, and placed its faith in future regulations which would differentiate between civil and criminal liability.

The picture that emerges is that the law of negligence slips easily into something barely distinguishable from strict liability. Although the line between the two is sharp by definition, in practice it depends upon the stringency with which the court interprets the standard of care, the use of devices such as res ipsa loquitur, the willingness to create torts out of statutory duties, and the exceptions that will be read into the statute. The tendency to turn liability for fault into strict liability results from the sympathy felt for the injured victim. Even judges may feel a sense of satisfaction when they can be charitable at the expense of an insurance company.

NEGLIGENCE AND NUISANCE

The difficulty of distinguishing sharply between fault and strict liability may be further illustrated from the tort of nuisance.

Nuisances are either private or public. Private nuisance has been defined as 'unlawful interference with a person's use or enjoyment of land or some right over or in connection with it.'[11] Most instances concern the escape of noxious substances (or vibrations or noises) to neighbouring land. Public nuisance (for example, obstruction of the highway) is not generally a tort, but, exceptionally, it is actionable in tort by a person who suffers particular damage – damage over and above that suffered by other members of the public. (An example would be where a person is not merely delayed by an unlawful obstruction of the highway but crashes into it and has to go to hospital.) Another public nuisance is that committed by a factory-owner whose chimney emits

---

11 Winfield and Jolowicz, p 355.

noxious fumes over a wide area; if it affected only a few neighbours it would be a private nuisance. Air pollution is now partly controlled (administratively and penally) by legislation, but we are considering the tort action.

It is often said that the tort of nuisance does not require proof of negligence, but that may well be a mistake of analysis. Why should we not say that people are under a duty of care not to be noisy and not to allow a noxious escape of such a nature that the plaintiff cannot reasonably be expected to tolerate it? If these propositions represent the law it follows that nuisance is a branch of the law of negligence. It merely adds to the list of duties of care.[12]

The hypothesis certainly fits a large number of cases. Lord Wright said:

> The liability for a nuisance is not, at least in modern law, a strict or absolute liability.[13]

12 It is no objection to this hypothesis that some nuisances are intentional. Even in an action of negligence, it would not be open to the defendant to defend himself by proving that the injury was intentional. It is not generally realised that there is, in fact, a tort of intention, of wider ambit than the tort of negligence; and there is no need to refer to this specifically when speaking of negligence.

It will be observed that in the above formulation the question of reasonableness can occur twice. First, the nuisance must be such as the plaintiff cannot reasonably be expected to tolerate; and secondly, the defendant must have failed to take reasonable steps to prevent it. This double question of reasonableness is found also in ordinary actions of negligence. Someone brushes against me and knocks off my vaccination scar; or my car is recellulosed with slight blemishes. In an action of negligence, I must show both that the damage is one that I cannot reasonably be expected to put up with, and that the defendant could reasonably have prevented it. The first question relates to the nature of the damage, the second to the conduct of the defendant.

13 *Sedleigh-Denfield v O'Callaghan* [1940] AC 880 at 904. A point emphasised somewhat obscurely, by Lord Reid in *The Wagon Mound (No 2)* [1967] 1 AC 617 at 639: 'Although negligence may not be necessary fault of some kind is almost always necessary and fault generally involves foreseeability.'

The case of *Bolton v Stone*[14] illustrates the basic similarity of the torts of nuisance and negligence.

A cricket club had played for about ninety years on their ground and no ball had ever struck anyone on the highways near the ground until the unfortunate Miss Stone was hit, while standing in the road outside her house, by a ball straight-driven by a batsman playing for a visiting team. It was a rare occurrence for a ball to go over the fence during a match. The House of Lords decided that since the chance of such an accident happening was small, no reasonable persons in the position of the cricket club's committee would have taken precautions – such as raising the height of the fence around the ground. The claim based on negligence failed, and it was conceded that the case could not succeed for nuisance since negligence had not been established.

It is true that the courts frequently distinguish in words between nuisance and negligence, but this distinction is generally made without explaining whether it is anything other than verbal. As Dean Cecil Wright pointed out,[15] an examination of the cases indicates that the distinction is 'rather barren from the standpoint of actual solution of legal problems'. He continued:

We are, of course, fully aware that English courts have, from time to time, stated that nuisance and negligence must be clearly differentiated. In most of the cases, however, we must admit to a lack of understanding as to why this is necessary or whether, indeed, the very judges who said it was necessary so to separate them, actually kept them apart in practice.

The confusion on this subject must be attributed in considerable measure to a dictum of Lindley LJ in *Rapier v*

---

14 [1951] AC 850, [1951] 1 All ER 1078 (Hepple and Matthews, p 139). Although a different result was arrived at on the facts of *Miller v Jackson* [1977] QB 966, [1977] 3 All ER 338, by a majority of the Court of Appeal, they too equated negligence and nuisance.
15 (1943) 21 Can BR 517–18.

London Tramways Co,[16] which has been judicially quoted on several occasions.

> At common law, if I am sued for a nuisance, and the nuisance is proved, it is no defence on my part to say, and to prove, that I have taken all reasonable care to prevent it.

The meaning of this sentence must be understood in its context. The action was for a nuisance by smell coming from the defendants' excessively large and crowded stables, and the defendants had certainly not taken all reasonable care to prevent it – as they could have done, in the last resort, by reducing the size of the stables. The point is that in an action of nuisance it is no defence to show that you cannot carry on your business economically without creating the nuisance; if such be the case, you must reduce or give up your business, or else obtain statutory authority for creating the nuisance. A defendant who deliberately carries on a business in a place where it creates a nuisance cannot be acquitted of negligence. As Lindley LJ put it, in the same case:

> If the defendants are right in saying that they cannot concentrate their stables to such an extent as is desirable without committing a nuisance to the neighbourhood, then they must not concentrate their operations to such an extent. It is a mere question of money; it is nothing but economics which requires them to crowd their horses together.

The distinction is between a continuing nuisance and a sudden unforeseeable event. A person who allows a continuing nuisance on his premises is liable if he knows

---

16 [1893] 2 Ch 588 at 599–600. Cp. per Lord Simonds in *Read v J Lyons & Co Ltd* [1947] AC 156 at 183: '[In] nuisance negligence is not a necessary ingredient in the case. For, if a man commits a legal nuisance, it is no answer to his injured neighbour that he took the utmost care not to commit it.' This statement Lord Simonds substantially repeated in [1950] AC at 374. Contrast the view of Lord Wright quoted above.

what is going on or could know it by taking reasonable steps. But if a factory by some extraordinary mischance blows up and adjoining property is injured, the law of nuisance does not make the factory-owner strictly liable. Blast is regarded as an 'escape' and so comes within the law of nuisance, but, all the same, nuisance is not actionable without negligence.

Here, then, the law of nuisance does not differ basically from that of negligence. Whether the tort is called nuisance or negligence, the question is whether the defendant has acted reasonably. This is not to deny that there are certain peculiarities of the tort of nuisance; in particular, some authorities make an occupier vicariously liable in nuisance for the negligence of his independent contractors. These details are left for treatment in detailed textbooks on the law of tort. At this point we simply ask the reader to note that both negligence and nuisance involve drawing a line between what is and what is not reasonable.[17]

HAZARDS AND STRICT LIABILITY

Strict liability originated long before modern industrial legislation. In the early middle ages, a man who slew by pure misadventure could be adjudged guilty of felony; his rescue from the hangman's noose depended on royal clemency. Such a man 'deserved but needed a pardon'. It would hardly be surprising if this draconic attitude infected the law of tort, and in fact remarks recur in the books to the effect that liability in trespass was at least very high. As we have seen,[18] there was from quite an early period a current of authority in favour of the opposite view, that the issue in trespass was one

17 For a different view, see R. A. Buckley *The Law of Nuisance* (London, 1981), p 3.
18 Chap 2, above, p 50.

of fault, but it was only in the second half of this century that proof of fault was established as an essential requirement.

In the nineteenth century, strict liability could be presented as resting on a broad social value-judgment, that one who undertook activity for his own advantage should bear the risk inseparable from it. It was this notion that underlay the decision in *Rylands v Fletcher*[19] which created a new form of liability for the escape of dangerous things from land.

> The facts were that the defendants, Rylands and a partner of his, owned a mill and wished to construct a reservoir in order to supply it with water. They employed a competent engineer to construct the reservoir, and during the construction the workmen came upon some disused pit shafts, filled up with soil, of the existence of which no one was previously aware. The contractor failed to cover these shafts adequately, and, when the reservoir came to be filled, the water percolated through the shafts and flooded the mines of a neighbour, Fletcher. Fletcher failed to prove negligence on the part of Rylands and his partner. Nevertheless, the Exchequer Chamber and the House of Lords held that the defendants were liable without proof of negligence.

The best-known judgment is that of Blackburn J in the Exchequer Chamber. He pointed out that there were two ways of holding the defendant liable: either to say that he was absolutely liable, without proof of fault, or that, although fault had to be proved, the defendant was liable for the negligence of his contractor. The court preferred the first rule. Blackburn J expressed it as follows:

> The person who for his own purposes brings on his lands and collects and keeps there anything likely to do mischief if its escapes, must keep it in at his peril, and, if he does not do so, is prima facie answerable for all the damage which is the natural consequence of its escape.

19 The judgment of Blackburn J in the Exchequer Chamber, sub nom, *Fletcher v Rylands* will be found in (1866) LR 1 Exch 265; on appeal to the House of Lords sub nom *Rylands v Fletcher* in (1868) LR 3 HL 330 (Hepple and Matthews, p 345).

The judge constructed his rule by generalising from a number of narrower ones. He found in the law, as he thought, three examples of absolute or strict liability: liability for the escape of cattle, redressed by an action of cattle-trespass or distress damage feasant;[20] the *scienter* action for damage caused by animals; and the action for nuisance. In each of these three situations he perceived an 'escape' of a dangerous thing for which the plaintiff could sue without proof of negligence; and he regarded them merely as illustrations of a wider principle.

The common law, though in theory traditional, still develops: sometimes in response to changing ideas and conditions, sometimes through misinformation and mis-understanding. The rule in *Rylands v Fletcher* is an example of the second type of development. We have already seen that the action for nuisance is not an instance of strict liability. Strict liability for cattle is an anomalous survival: anomalous because of the view now accepted that trespass is not a tort of strict liability.[1] (The tort of cattle-trespass has now been abolished, and replaced by a statutory form of liability for damage caused by straying livestock.)[2] Strict liability for the purpose of distress damage feasant was a necessary conse-quence of the nature of the remedy, for the person who distrains animals which are doing damage is in no position to discover whether the owner was at fault in allowing an escape. One cannot, therefore, argue from the extra-judicial remedy to the judicial one. (Distress damage feasant, too, has now been abolished and replaced by a statutory right to detain straying livestock.)[3]

As for the *scienter* action,[4] which was founded upon the

---

20 See chap 1, p 11, for the meaning of this.
1 Chap 2, above, p 50.
2 Animals Act 1971, ss 1(1)(c), 4, 11. Unlike cattle-trespass there is no liability for personal injuries or death under s 4.
3 Animals Act 1971, s 7.
4 The medieval Latin writ that was used to start the action opened with the allegation that the defendant *knowingly* kept a vicious animal – *scienter retinuit*.

actual or presumed knowledge of an animal's propensity to attack persons or property, this was in origin an action of negligence. To keep an animal knowing that it has a dangerous proclivity is a kind of negligence. If a dog is given to worrying sheep, its owner is expected to kill it – as a matter of social obligation and quite irrespective of law. This custom is still firmly maintained in sheep-rearing districts. In former times the dog was hanged,[5] now it is usually shot. The old view was that if the owner of a sheep-worrying dog did not destroy the dog upon notice of its propensities, his failure to do so was negligence. If the dog then repeated its exploit the owner was liable, not necessarily because he was negligent on the subsequent occasion, but because he had already been negligent in not hanging the dog.[6] However, the *scienter* action was turned into strict liability by somewhat dubious legal reasoning.[7] The judges came to deny that the keeping of dangerous animals was unlawful in the sense of negligent. Instead of saying that the defendant was liable for negligence, the mere keeping of a dangerous animal being negligent, it was said that the defendant was liable without proof of negligence,[8] the obligation being to keep the animal safe 'at his peril'. Although there might not seem to be much difference between the old and new orthodoxies, the new one proved to be extremely complicated and inflexible. The *scienter* action now has been abolished by statute and replaced by a simplified form of strict liability for dangerous animals.[9]

One ambiguity runs through Blackburn J's judgment. Perhaps all that he meant to say was that nuisance was a tort of strict liability and that the defendants were liable in

---

5   The practice is echoed in the phrase 'hangdog look', and the proverb 'Give a dog a bad name and hang him'.
6   For numerous authorities see Williams *Liability for Animals* p 328.
7   See Williams, op cit.
8   The transition is marked by *May v Burdett* (1846) 9 QB 101, 115 ER 1213.
9   Animals Act 1971, ss 1(1)(a) and 2.

nuisance; the references to liability for animals were brought in to show that strict liability was well established for other types of 'escape'. Difficulties stand in the way of this interpretation: Blackburn J did not specifically say that he was deciding the case on the law of nuisance, as opposed to his asserted general principle; and his general principle did not well express the whole law of nuisance. (A landowner who has something on his land that emits highly unpleasant smells, noises or vibrations can hardly be said to 'bring on his lands and collect and keep there anything likely to do mischief if it escapes,' but he falls within the law of nuisance.) The more obvious reading of the judgment, and certainly the one that was finally adopted by the courts, was that it enunciated a new generalised principle of tort liability. In practice, *Rylands v Fletcher* has been taken to create a new tort, standing alongside the older torts of nuisance, negligence, trespass and so on; and it has generated its own complex law.

Enough has been said to show that the rule in *Rylands v Fletcher*, whatever slender support it may have had when originally formulated, stands uneasily in the modern law. The old actions for cattle-trespass and *scienter*, together with distress damage feasant, have been replaced by modern statutory rules; and the action for nuisance seems now to be in general based on fault. Blackburn J regarded it as a principle of justice that a person who imperilled his neighbour should indemnify him; however, many defendants have slipped through one or more of the limitations (eg on the class of 'things' for which there is liability) or the defences (eg Act of God, act of stranger). And, despite some doubts, it now seems that the rule has no application in actions by a non-occupier of land for compensation for personal injury or death.[10] Of those plaintiffs who have

---

10 This was part of the ratio decidendi of Lord Macmillan in *Read v J Lyons & Co Ltd* [1947] AC 156 at 173.

succeeded on the basis of the celebrated decision nearly all could have succeeded in negligence. The truth is that after 1866 most situations like that in *Rylands v Fletcher* came to be covered by the law of negligence and vicarious liability.

VICARIOUS LIABILITY

The basic postulate of liability based on fault is contradicted by the doctrine of vicarious liability. For upwards of two centuries an employer has been 'vicariously' liable for the torts of his employee ('servant' in the old terminology) committed in the course of his employment. The phrase 'vicarious responsibility' was coined by Pollock in the late nineteenth century, but the rule itself had been part of the law since about the year 1700; and the word 'vicarious' had also been current in literature and theology to signify something done by the hand of another.[11] 'Vicarious' comes from the Latin *vice*, in the place of; but this derivation is legally misleading because the employer is not liable in the place of the employee. The employer is liable for the employee's tort, but the employee remains liable as well. The pair are joint tortfeasors: each is fully liable, though of course the plaintiff can only recover his damages once. He can sue one, and collect the whole from that one; or he can sue both together, and collect part from each, or the whole from one.

Strict liability is found only in a few torts, but vicarious liability applies to practically the whole range of the law of tort. Where the tort requires fault, the employer is vicariously liable for his employee's fault; here fault remains in issue in the case, though the relevant fault is that of the

---

11 'My sister having so much to do was going to church vicariously, that is to say, Joe and I were going': Dickens *Great Expectations* Chap 4.

employee, not of the employer. Where the tort is one of strict liability, fault is not usually in issue at all.[12]

Many reasons have been suggested for vicarious liability, but the principal one is undoubtedly the desire of the judges to give the victim an effective remedy when he is injured by a person who is likely to have small means. Anyone can see that the the possibility of having an insolvent defendant is a serious defect in the law of tort as a means of restoring the disequilibrium caused by wrongful acts. So the employer is made liable because his pocket is deeper than the employee's. Although this is one of the psychological reasons for vicarious liability, it is hardly a philosophical justification. For it has to be recognised that vicarious liability, while it provides the plaintiff with a solvent defendant, contradicts the general principle of the law of tort that recompense is made on account of the defendant's fault. The employer may be totally free from blame; yet he is made to pay.

The most plausible explanations may be grouped under three main heads.

(1) According to the notion of *justice*, it is only fair and right that the employer should compensate for his employee's torts because he gets the benefit of the service and should therefore shoulder the losses. This principle[13] is exemplified by the rule that the employer is not responsible if the employee was acting wholly for his own purposes (on a 'frolic of his own'). There are certain difficulties, however, because not everyone who obtains a benefit from another's work thereby becomes liable for loss occasioned in the course of it. For example, a passenger by train is not liable for the negligence of the driver.

12 It is necessary to say 'usually' because certain defences (eg act of a stranger) which are open to the defendant let in the issue of fault.
13 Expressed in the ancient maxim: *Qui sensit commodum debet sentire et onus* (he who has obtained an advantage ought to bear the disadvantage as well). See generally on the theory of justice as applied to vicarious liability, P. Cane in (1982) 2 Oxf J Leg Stud 30 at 34.

(2) According to the *deterrence* theory, an employer is very often in a position to change his system of work, or to change his staff, in such a way to minimise acts of negligence. Vicarious liability gives him an incentive to do so.[14] Again, the employees of an organisation, particularly those in responsible positions, generally have some feeling of loyalty towards it. When the organisation is made responsible for 'its' torts, even those who work in the organisation feel that the organisation has made a slip; and steps may be taken to avoid a recurrence. A business enterprise is geared to reduce costs and produce profits; and liability in tort is a cost to be avoided where possible. Thus vicarious liability can affect the conduct of those who are not directly affected in their own pockets. The explanation does not go the whole way, because it does not explain why there should be liability even though it is demonstrably impossible to prevent such an accident from occurring. In the ordinary case where a lorry driver is involved in a negligent accident, the lorry itself being well maintained and the lorry driver having been chosen with reasonable care, the employer (whether individual or corporation) remains liable even though from his point of view the accident was quite unavoidable.[15]

(3) At this point a new theory of liability in tort may be allowed to make an entry: the *theory of social insurance*. It is invoked to explain vicarious and also strict liability, the other two theories being inadequate. According to the social insurance theory, vicarious liability is an economical way of distributing risk among the members of society at large.

It may be asked what warrant the judges have for introducing a system of social insurance. The decision to

---

14 This theory has been used to justify the liability of a car owner who delegates the task of driving to another: *Morgans v Launchbury* [1973] AC 127, [1972] 2 All ER 606.

15 It is this that contradicts the theory enunciated by Denning LJ (as he then was) in *Cassidy v Ministry of Health* [1951] 2 KB 343, [1951] 1 All ER 574, that the liability is based on personal fault in failing to prevent the damage.

introduce it would seem to be a political rather than a judicial matter. Moreover, the argument that a loss incurred by a firm can readily be borne as a business expense comes oddly from judges who profess to uphold rights of property. For the same argument would justify the operation of any shoplifter, burglar or confidence trickster. Again, if the purpose of strict liability is to provide a system of social insurance, it is an extraordinarily inefficient way of doing so.

AN EVALUATION OF THE FAULT PRINCIPLE

Strict and vicarious liability, then, are difficult to reconcile with the notion of a tort as a *wrong* requiring compensation. Moreover, strict liability as it now exists in the law hardly accords with what would be designed by a wise legislator, assuming that strict liability is to be accepted at all.[16] In statutory torts it depends on certain rules of interpretation of statutes, which may having nothing to do with the social policy of the matter. Again, there is no obvious reason why a farmer should be strictly responsible for his straying livestock or escaping water, but not for his dangerous farm machinery. One of the remarkable failures of the common law was the decision that a breach of the statutory duties regarding the use of defective vehicles on the highway did not give rise to civil liability.[17] And English courts (unlike the American) have been unwilling to impose strict duties in tort on manufacturers of defective products. Even where strict liability does exist – as under *Rylands v Fletcher* – large breaches in the principle have been allowed because it seems

---

16 See below, Chap 7, p 201, for a review of some proposed new forms of strict liability.

17 *Phillips v Britannia Hygienic Laundry* [1923] 2 KB 832 (Hepple and Matthews, p 277). Similarly there was a failure to utilise *Rylands v Fletcher*: see J. R. Spencer in [1983] CLJ 65.

unjust to condemn the actor in damages where he is not to blame. Sooner or later, therefore, one is driven back to the fault principle as the foundation of liability in tort. It is this principle that must be justified if one is to make out a case for the survival of the law of tort in its present form.

The two reasons commonly advanced have already been rehearsed in dealing with vicarious liability. The first is the principle of justice that one who has been damaged by the fault of another ought to be compensated by that other.[18] The second is that the award of compensation tends to deter people from committing such acts in future. There is little doubt that both these theories have been taken at different times as underlying the law, but the first is historically the older while the second has slowly increased in favour as apparently the more 'scientific' explanation.

The principle of justice comes as a ready explanation, particularly when applied to 'the other fellow'. 'He ought to have been more careful.' 'He should have kept a sharper lookout.' Commonsense morality suggests that a man who has been negligent ought to pay compensation to those whom he injures. Someone must bear the loss, and we think it better that this loss should rest on the person at fault than on the innocent person on whom it happens to fall. Like every other ethical proposition, this is an intuition which cannot ultimately be proved or disproved, but can only be held or rejected. However, it may be atrributed not to an eternal principle of justice but to a psychological reaction of a distinctly human kind. A person who has been wronged feels resentment, and society sympathetically identifies itself with the victim. The resentment of the victim and of society can be appeased by punishment (the criminal sanction) or

18 The Pearson Commission, vol 1, para 262 regarded this as 'elementary justice.' This looks at justice from the point of view of the victim and so may be called a principle of 'ethical compensation'. The other variant of justice, from the offender's viewpoint, is 'ethical retribution': see (1951) 4 CLP at 140 ff.

satisfied by reparation (the civil sanction). According to the classical philosophy of the criminal law, the harm inflicted on the victim is balanced by a punitive harm inflicted on the offender. According to the philosophy of the civil law, the harm inflicted on the victim is balanced or effaced by the damages that go to make good the loss. Since these damages are paid by the offender, they operate as an additional punitive sanction.

The theory of justice is open to many objections. As applied to the criminal law, it is now rejected by the weight of opinion: we no longer suppose that every offence must justly be balanced by punishment. As applied to the civil law, the theory that every offence must justly be balanced by compensation neglects the relative financial position of the parties. It would imply that a poor man must make compensation for the smallest fault, even though to do so would ruin him, and even though the person to whom he must make the payment is so wealthy that he did not feel the loss caused by the other's fault. This is certainly the legal rule, but it is not quite obviously the rule of justice. Again, the theory of fault requires an objective test of negligence which must often wear the appearance of fiction. Every person, at least if he has reached years of discretion, is held to an objective standard of care which he may in fact be incapable of attaining. Some people are constitutionally feckless and clumsy, unable to look ahead and with a slow reaction-time. An assessment of fault that overlooks these deficiencies can hardly be regarded as fully consonant with justice. Yet a theory of fault that sought to allow for the constitutional deficiencies of the individual would speedily find itself with no standard at all.

There are also many practical objections to the justice theory. We have lately come to realise how difficult it is to reconstruct the past in a court of law. Most accidents are by their nature almost instantaneous. When an unexpected accident takes place, particularly in fatal cases, there may be no witnesses, or the witnesses may be unreliable in their observation and recollection. A plaintiff in a negligence action may fail although the defendant was negligent, if he cannot prove it. In a 'hit-and-run' accident the plaintiff may not even be able to find a defendant. Proving fault is costly – the income limits to qualify for legal aid and advice are still low and even those who are entitled to aid may be ignorant of their rights or chary of going to court.[19] An injured worker and his representatives have no right of access to the place of work where the accident occurred in order to obtain evidence; and the injured person will have to pay for a medical report. He and his advisers will have to negotiate with insurance companies who are experts in such claims and are backed by safety consultants. The uncertainties of litigation may lead the plaintiff to accept a settlement for considerably less than the amount of damage inflicted on him. It is small wonder that relatively few of those who suffer damage receive compensation through the tort system.[20] Liability for fault can – and often does – actually result in a failure of justice.

The deterrence theory is, at least superficially, more attractive. Just as the punitive theory of the criminal law has been superseded by the deterrence theory in the opinion of the majority of those who have considered the subject, so there is much to be said for the view that the paramount purpose of the law of tort is the prevention of injury and damage. We all know that great harm can follow even from acts of inadvertent negligence, and it cannot adequately be redressed by a monetary award. Any social machinery that operates to prevent such negligence from occurring has a strong argument in its favour. The question therefore is:

19 See above, Chap 3, p 77, and Pearson Report, vol 2, Chap 18.
20 Above, p 77.

does the operation of the law of negligence tend to make people more careful?

Certain difficulties prevent an unqualified affirmative answer. Many people know little of the law and do not realise the wide ambit of the law of tort. Even if they know it, there is apparently a logical difficulty in asserting that the threat implicit in the law is capable of deterring men from inadvertent conduct. If a man does not think of the possibility of causing harm by his acts, he is not capable of being influenced by the threat. A threat can influence only those who realise that it is directed against them.

Take the case of a motorist who drives carelessly according to an objective test, but who is convinced that his driving is in fact perfectly careful. Since he thinks he is driving carefully, his conduct can hardly be affected by a rule which penalises negligent driving. Only after he has once been adjudged guilty of negligence can the rule have a chance to affect his conduct for the future. It is not the general law of negligence that then operates to deter him, but the specific finding by the court in his own particular case.

These difficulties, although real, do not altogether destroy the case for saying that the law of negligence has a deterrent effect. A person who knows the law may be brought anxiously to consider his conduct to see if he can discover any danger in it. He may be led to safeguard himself even against temporary inadvertence. An illustration is provided by an event that occurs to many of us every morning, when the alarm clock rings. No one can guarantee that he will awake spontaneously out of a heavy sleep; but he can make a habit of setting the alarm before he goes to sleep. In the same way, he can repair deficiencies of memory by keeping written records and reminders. If, as he grows older, his eyesight or co-ordination become impaired, he can refrain from driving a car. If he is the occupier of property, he can supplement his own assessment of dangers existing on the property by calling in expert opinion. If he drives a car he can have the brakes checked regularly, and he can wear a seat belt.[1] If he is a doctor he can keep abreast of medical knowledge, not least by reading the annual reports of the Medical Defence Union and the reports of malpractice suits in the standard practitioners' journals.[2]

One can put this another way by saying that conduct that may consist of inadvertent negligence in one respect may be combined with deliberate conduct in another respect. It is a rule of prudence not to point a gun at another, even though it is believed not to be loaded. A person who points a gun at another, believing it to be unloaded, violates the rule of prudence. Should the gun turn out to be loaded, and accidentally be discharged, he will be held to be negligent. So far as the consequence is concerned, namely the injury to the person at whom the gun was pointed, the case is one of inadvertent negligence. Yet the culprit's conduct in pointing the gun was intentional, and his breach of the rule of prudence was therefore (assuming at least that he knew of it) intentional. Where the law of negligence sanctions a rule of prudence, the defiance of the rule of prudence may be intentional, even when the evil that the rule was designed to prevent was unintentional.

The chief difficulty with this attempt to reconcile the deterrence theory with liability for inadvertent negligence is the case of the mentally unsound person or someone else who is not educable. The criminal law has developed special rules for dealing with persons of unsound mind. By way of

1 The criminal law appears to act as a far more effective deterrent than the threat of a 15–25% reduction in damages for failure to wear a seat belt. The Department of Transport estimated that five months after the wearing of front-seat belts was made compulsory in 1983, there was a wearing rate of 94% compared with 40% a year earlier, and road deaths and serious injuries were 20% lower than a year earlier: 50 HC Official Report (6th series) col 5.
2 See eg the remarks of Denning LJ in *Roe v Minister of Health* [1954] 2 QB 66 at 86.

contrast, although there is little direct authority, those suffering from mental illness are said to be responsible in tort for negligence as if they were sane.[3] There is no justice or admonitory effect in condemning a man for failing to come up to a standard that he is mentally incapable of achieving. As an educator, tort law seems to be as arbitrary and unfeeling as Dickens's character, Mr Squeers of Dotheboys Hall.

Several other features of the law of tort are in conflict with the deterrence theory.[4]

(1) The repetition of wrongs is a matter of public concern, yet the State is disinterested in the enforcement of the sanction for tort. Remedies of self-help are allowed,[5] but the police will scarcely lift a finger to aid the plaintiff, apart from providing an accident report.

(2) It is possible to contract out of tortious liability in advance. If the aim of the law was deterrence all such exemption clauses would be void as against public policy. Instead it has been left to Parliament to legislate against certain types of exclusion clauses on an ad hoc basis.[6]

(3) If crime and tort are both deterrent systems why is there no protection against double punishment? A person who is punished in the criminal courts is not immune from a later suit for damages.[7]

(4) Liability to pay damages generally survives the death

3 See *White v White* [1950] P 39 at 59, per Denning LJ.
4 For a full discussion of these, see (1951) 4 CLP at 156–72.
5 See Chap 1 above, p 10.
6 The main examples are Unfair Contract Terms Act 1977, s 2 (avoidance of liability for negligence etc in respect of business liability); Road Traffic Act 1972, s 148(3) (restrictions on liability in respect of use of motor vehicles); Carriage by Air Act 1961, Sch 1, chapter 3, art 23 (liability fixed by Warsaw Convention); Law Reform (Personal Injuries) Act 1948, s 1(3) (provisions in contracts of employment excluding employers' liability); Employers' Liability (Defective Equipment) Act 1969, s 1(2) (liability for supply of defective equipment to employee).
7 For certain qualifications, see Chap 1, p 4.

of the tortfeasor and attaches to his estate. Punishment is not usually inflicted on a wrongdoer's next-of-kin, or bene-ficiaries of his estate, so the civil law is explicable only on a theory of compensation.

(5) Contributory negligence on the part of the plaintiff was, at common law, a complete defence in tort, and now operates to reduce the plaintiff's damages. The wording of the Law Reform (Contributory Negligence) Act 1945 supposes that the apportionment is made on the basis of justice rather than of deterrence. Damage is supposed to be proportionate to the fault. It must be said, however, that in practice the apportionment can operate as a fortuitous 'penalty' depending upon the extent of the loss suffered by the plaintiff. A victim who is held to be only 10% at fault, but whose injuries merit an award of £20,000, will incur ten times greater reduction in compensation than one who is held 80% at fault but whose injuries are assessed at £250.[8] The criminal law would not assess a fine as a proportion of the individual's loss; it would look at the circumstances of the particular offender, including his means.

This discussion of the theories of justice and deterrence wears an appearance of unreality once one realises that many tort actions are in fact fought out between two insurance companies, one subrogated to the rights of the nominal plaintiff (that is to say, exercising his rights after paying him compensation under the policy) and the other standing behind the nominal defendant. A censorious inquiry into the conduct of the two parties who are themselves disinterested in the outcome of the litigation serves neither justice nor deterrence.[9] Before we conclude our evaluation of the underlying philosophy of the law of tort, we must examine the role of insurance and social security.

8 This point is made by 'Justice', *No Fault on the Roads* (London, 1974) para 26.
9 The revival of the deterrence theory in an economic guise is considered in Chap 7, below, p 203.

5 Insurance

This is where the plot thickens. . . . It usually does when insurance is mentioned.

Anthony Shaffer *Sleuth* Act I

The law of tort stretches into every department of conduct, and a man who deviates from its rules may be made liable in crippling damages. It is only natural, therefore, that the practice of insuring against liability has become widespread. The tortfeasor who insures protects his savings from the loss that may follow from some casual act of negligence on his part. The victim is also assisted, because he knows from the start that the tortfeasor will be able to satisfy the judgment.

SOCIAL JUSTIFICATION

But, it may be asked, is not the practice of insurance socially objectionable, in that it may remove the legal sanction for careless conduct? To some extent this is true, but there are countervailing considerations.

Insurance does not wholly remove the financial inducement to take care. A person who has to claim on a motor insurance policy may lose his no-claim bonus,[1] or he may

1 The no-claim bonus is, in effect, a discount on the premium payable when the insurance policy is renewed. It is sometimes said that 'knock-for-knock' agreements between insurance companies (below, p 168) curtail the limited deterrent value of the no-claim discount, but the insurance companies maintain that if a claim is paid *purely* because of a 'knock-for-knock' agreement, the insured's no-claim discount will not be affected.

find that he has to pay a larger premium when he comes to renew his policy, or eventually he may be refused cover altogether.[2] Another incentive to accident prevention is that an insurance company may require to be satisfied, before undertaking a risk, that the assured is running his business in a careful way. The contribution of the insurance companies to accident prevention lies mainly in the field of damage to premises, plant and equipment.[3] Variable premiums, depending on the safety precautions taken by the insured, are more frequently found in this field than in relation to employers' liability and motor vehicle insurance. Some insurance companies employ or commission specialist staff to inspect machinery and premises and to recommend safety precautions as a condition of providing insurance cover.

Without insurance, the law of tort can work harshly. It may result in liability out of proportion to the defendant's fault. Once fault is established, in however slight degree, the defendant becomes liable for all – or almost all – the damage he has caused. Suppose that a bus driver, in a moment of inattention during the twilight, runs into a group of people and kills several of them. If he is prosecuted for the crime of careless or dangerous driving, or manslaughter, his punishment will depend upon the degree of his negligence rather than upon the harm he happens to have done – at least, that is the theory. Hence his punishment may be light in comparison with the harm caused. But if he is sued in tort, the damages depend only on the harm done, and are not reduced merely because the fault was slight. If the defendant was not at fault, he will be free of liability; but a small degree of fault will make him liable for the whole. This is because, when the plaintiff has been injured by the defendant's fault,

2 The Pearson Commission, vol 1, para 989, doubted whether such a penalty 'weighs heavily with a driver in the heat of the moment'.
3 This was the finding of the Committee on Safety and Health at Work, under the Chairmanship of Lord Robens (Cmnd 5034, 1972), paras 439–41.

it is thought just that the defendant should suffer rather than the plaintiff, even though the defendant's fault was small. Justice requires the defendant to compensate the plaintiff, but it does not forbid the defendant to transfer the burden to an insurance company if he is able to do so. Insurance saves the wrongdoer from liability that is out of all proportion to the degree of fault.

INTENTIONAL TORTS AN EXCEPTION

There is one exception to the rule that a person may insure against his liability in tort. A person may not insure against liability for his own intentional torts; such an insurance is void, as being against public policy, because it would tend to diminish the deterrent effect of the law of tort.[4] This reason shows that to some extent the law of tort shares with the criminal law the aim of controlling conduct. Damages for intentional torts are awarded not merely to compensate the plaintiff but to punish the defendant, with the aim of deterring people from wrongful conduct. Hence insurance is not allowed.[5] In the case of negligent torts on the other hand, the deterrent aim of the law is subordinate to the compensation of the plaintiff, and insurance is allowed.

It follows from these principles that at common law there can be no claim under an accident liability policy where there has been a deliberate act of violence by the insured, and

---

4 *Haseldine v Hosken* [1933] 1 KB 822 (solicitor entered into champertous agreement, not realising that to do so was criminal at that time; *held* that his indemnity policy did not cover this intentional criminal act). Cp. (1951) 4 CLP pp 165–8.
5 This is legislative as well as judicial policy: s 11 of the Defamation Act 1952 provides that an agreement for indemnifying any person against any civil liability for libel shall not be unlawful 'unless at the time of publication that person knows that the matter is defamatory and does not reasonably believe there is a good defence to any action brought upon it'.

this is so even if a criminal court has acquitted him on a criminal charge arising out of that violence.

In *Gray v Barr*[6] the defendant had killed the plaintiff's husband with a shotgun. The defendant was acquitted of manslaughter in the criminal trial. Being now sued for damages he brought in his insurance company under a claim for indemnity. The company was allowed to go behind the verdict and prove that the shooting was not an accident but a deliberate act by the defendant which was outside the insurance policy on grounds of public policy.

The rule, as laid down by the English courts,[7] applies as well to deliberate torts committed with a motor vehicle, such as by a lorry driver who in a fit of temper drives into a small car. But, as said before, it does not apply to an unintentional tort that is also a crime. A motor vehicle insurance policy against third-party claims is valid even though the claim is made in respect of driving that is so negligent as to be not only a tort but the crime of manslaughter.[8]

The exception in relation to intentional torts is based on the premise that the courts should not allow rights to arise out of seriously anti-social acts.[9] This is perfectly intelligible

6 [1971] 2 QB 554, [1971] 2 All ER 949. See J. G. Fleming (1971) 34 MLR 176, regarding the issues of public policy raised by the decision in the court of first instance.

7 *Hardy v Motor Insurers' Bureau* [1964] 2 QB 745 at 760, 765, 769. It is to be noted that the rule of public policy debarring an indemnity was limited to cases of 'wilful and culpable crime' (per Lord Denning MR) or 'intentional crime' (per Diplock LJ) by the insured. In the State of Victoria, in *Fire and All Risks Insurance Co Ltd v Powell* [1966] VR 513, the more flexible formulation was adopted that 'the court must decide whether the criminal act was of such an anti-social character that the interests of the public require that the court's aid should be refused' (at 522, 527). See generally, on the forfeiture rule, Paul Matthews in [1983] J Soc Wel L 141 at 141–4.

8 *Tinline v White Cross Insurance Association* [1921] 3 KB 327; *James v British General Insurance Co* [1927] 2 KB 311. Indeed, most comprehensive motor insurance policies provide that the insurer will pay the cost of defending criminal charges such as manslaughter, arising from driving.

9 *Hardy v Motor Insurers' Bureau*, above (per Diplock LJ at 767). The Latin tag *ex turpi causa non oritur actio*, usually applied in the context of contractual illegality, is sometimes used to describe this rule of public policy in the law of tort.

when applied to loss insurance, for example when an insured person who deliberately sets fire to his premises is denied the benefit of a fire policy.[10] But the denial of recovery is capable of working injustice to both the insured and his victim in the case of liability insurance. The more opprobrious the wrong done to the victim the less likely he is to be certain of compensation. From the insured's point of view the punishment against which it is impossible to insure may not fit the crime, since he stands to pay enormous damages if he kills a famous actor but will have to pay only £3,500 or so if he kills a child outright.[11] Moreover, this is a punishment that may be inflicted outside the control of the criminal court – indeed, contrary to the verdict of the criminal court[12] – and without the ordinary safeguards for the defendant attaching to a criminal prosecution. The only satisfactory solution of the problem would be to validate the liability insurance policy and to leave the punishment of the offender to the discretion of the criminal court.

The Forfeiture Act 1982 has attempted to deal with some aspects of the problem but it is incomplete and inadequate.[13] Where a court determines that the forfeiture rule has precluded a person who has unlawfully killed another from acquiring any interest in certain types of property, the court may modify the effect of the rule, but may not cancel that effect altogether. The court must have regard to the conduct of the offender and of the deceased, and so it can be expected

---

10 Another reason for denying recovery in such a case is that there is an implied term in a contract of insurance that the insured person will not intentionally bring about the event insured against. For this reason it seems that an ordinary life policy still does not cover suicide, notwithstanding that the Suicide Act 1961, s 1, abrogated the rule that suicide was a crime. But the policy may expressly cover suicide.

11 The award for bereavement, see above, Chap 3, p 87.

12 As in *Gray v Barr*, above, p 146.

13 See Matthews in [1983] J Soc Wel L 141. The Act was initiated by Private Members, who were mainly concerned with the forfeiture of social security benefits, as in *R v Chief National Insurance Comr, ex p Connor* [1981] QB 758, [1981] 1 All ER 769.

that a mercy killer would benefit from the Act. Unfortunately, the Act is so worded that it would exclude most insurance policies of the kind we have been considering, such as the 'hearth and home' policy in *Gray v Barr*, or the case where A holds an assurance policy on the life of B whom he kills in circumstances of no moral blameworthiness.[14]

An intermediate and exceptional solution has been laid down by legislation relating to compulsory motor vehicle insurance. The third party victim has a statutory right under the Road Traffic Act to recover from the insurer the amount of any judgment (together with interest and costs) that the victim has obtained against the insured motorist. The insurer is bound to pay the victim even though he had a right to avoid or cancel the policy as against the insured, for example because the tort was intentional.[15] But the insurer has a right of reimbursement from the insured.[16] One writer suggests that this is a 'felicitous solution, which accommodates both the paramount need to compensate the injured as well as the wish to punish the injurer';[17] an Australian judge has even said that it can be achieved through judicial *fiat*.[18] In our view, it can be unduly punitive; in any event, the usual logic of judicial reasoning permits only of the insurance policy being completely void or completely valid.

---

14 Section 2(4)(b) refers to 'property which, before the death, was held on trust for any person', and this type of policy would not qualify: see Matthews, op cit, at 151.

15 Road Traffic Act 1972, ss 148, 149. See further below, p 154.

16 Road Traffic Act 1972, s 148(1) proviso. The statutory right to reimbursement applies only to such motor vehicle insurance as is compulsory, but the standard motor insurance policy, which covers non-compulsory matters as well, has a reimbursement clause, as does the standard employers' liability policy.

17 Fleming, op cit pp 179–80.

18 *Fire and All Risks Insurance Co Ltd v Powell* [1966] VR 513 at 527 (per Smith J).

LIMITS OF LIABILITY INSURANCE

Liability insurance is a matter of contract between insurer and insured. The insurer promises to indemnify the insured against all sums that the insured becomes legally liable to pay as damages to third persons. The damages may be limited, for example to those arising from bodily injury (a term usually defined to include death or disease) to any person, or to loss of or damage to property. For most liability risks the insurer will impose financial limits on the indemnity in respect of any one loss and sometimes also on the aggregate in any one year.[19] The limit will vary from say £1 million or less in the case of a home insurance policy to £5 million for the professional indemnity policy of a barrister specialising in taxation, or to £200 million or more in the case of aircraft products liability.[20] There are other ways in which the insurance market can absorb risks: for example the practice of reinsurance under which some part of the risk is passed on to other insurers. But the vision of unlimited liability to limitless plaintiffs haunts insurers. They do not want so-called 'catastrophe' risks, where the cost of possible claims is out of all proportion to the premium income derived from that class of insurance.[1] In such cases it is only government intervention that can save the individual defendant from

19 Financial limits are not usually imposed in the case of employers' liability insurance. However, the reluctance of the insurance companies to accept unlimited liability may be seen from the regulations made under the Employers' Liability (Compulsory Insurance) Act 1969 (SI 1971/1117), reg 3 which provide that the maximum amount for which such insurance *must* be maintained is £2m in respect of claims arising out of any single occurrence.
20 In the case of products liability the limit is usually expressed as an aggregate amount in any one year. Sometimes, however, liability may be limited to 'any one event'. It was a matter of dispute between the Distillers Co (Biochemicals) Ltd and Lloyds underwriters whether this phrase meant any one birth of a child deformed by thalidomide or all such births within a particular year: Times, 9 January 1973.
1 This is the definition of 'catastrophe' used by A. V. Alexander (an insurance broker) in (1972) 12 JSPTL (NS) 105.

ruin and protect the injured plaintiff. An example of this is liability for nuclear incidents. The consequences of a mishap at a nuclear site may be very extensive indeed, and the radiation effects may linger on for millenia. The insurance companies would not accept such an exposure to risk, particularly if site operators were to be made liable without proof of fault. Consequently, legislation limits the liability of the site operator to £20 million,[2] and it is understood that the government itself will accept responsibility for claims in excess of £20 million. This is an exceptional case, however, and the 'excess' of damages over the available insurance cover usually has to be borne by the insured tortfeasor or, if he cannot pay, by the victim.

TYPES OF LIABILITY INSURANCE

Subject to limits of the kind described, the ingenuity of the insurance companies has devised cover for most kinds of potential legal liability. Traditionally, insurers have distinguished between employers' liability insurance (the earliest of the modern kinds of non-marine liability insurance) and 'public' liability insurance, by which insurers mean tort liability. To these, cover for 'products liability' has been added. Although the types of policy vary considerably from company to company, the following are typical examples of those available:

Employers' liability: Bodily injury (including death and disease) to an 'employee' (which may be defined widely to include the self-employed).

Public liability: Bodily injury (including death and disease) and loss to third parties who are not employees, excluding claims, or for libel or breach of copyright, or for products or motor vehicles or property in the custody or control of the

2 Nuclear Installations Act 1965, s 16(1) as amended by Energy Act 1983, s 27.

insured or nuclear incidents or war, rebellion, revolution, insurrection, military or usurped power.

Products liability: Bodily injury (including death and disease) and damage to or loss of property in respect of goods sold supplied repaired altered treated or installed; excluding liability to employees, for damage to insured's own property or that of employees, for nuclear incidents, for war, etc, and for loss of or damage to the goods, replacement costs of the goods or refund of payments received for the goods.

Home insurance: This is primarily loss insurance in respect of building and contents, but a standard extra is liability to third parties in damages for bodily injury (including death and disease) and loss of or damage to property; excluding liability in respect of motor vehicles, business, or ownership or occupation of land other than that covered by the loss insurance. Useful for animal owners and players of cricket, etc, as well as covering potential liability to visitors.

Motor insurance:[3] 'Comprehensive' cover is a combination of loss and liability insurance, covering accidental damage to the insured's vehicle or loss of or damage to the vehicle and certain personal effects therein by fire or theft, and personal accident insurance for the insured and his family arising out of the use of the vehicle, with an indemnity for liability to third parties[4] for driving of the insured vehicle or any other vehicle by the insured, or the driving of the insured vehicle by any person permitted to drive by the insured in respect of damages for death or bodily injury or damage to property.

---

3 The Pearson Commission, vol 1, para 972, estimated that 70% of motorists have policies covering risks other than liability to third parties for death or bodily injury; insurance for the latter is compulsory (see below). There are more elaborate policies in respect of commercial vehicles and for motor traders.

4 Under such a policy it is quite possible for a chauffeur's liability to his employer (the insured) to be covered: *Digby v General Accident Fire and Life Assurance Corpn Ltd* [1943] AC 121, [1942] 2 All ER 319 (Merle Oberon, the actress, recovered damages from her chauffeur; he was allowed indemnity under her policy).

The policy sometimes covers legal fees in respect of defence to criminal charges arising out of driving.

Libel: Usually 90–100% of damages that the insured may become liable to pay in satisfaction of an award of damages, or of a settlement consented to by the insurer. The insured must 'exercise diligence care and restraint' in an endeavour to avoid libel actions.

The insured does not get the benefit of any overlap between different policies covering the same risk. The usual clause in a liability policy which avoids this result reads:

> If an indemnity is or would but for the existence of this insurance be granted by any other insurance the Company shall not provide indemnity except in respect of any excess beyond the amount which is or would but for the existence of this insurance be payable.[5]

COMPULSORY INSURANCE

So successful is insurance as a way of dealing with the impecunious defendant that some steps have been taken to make it obligatory. Insurance against liability in respect of death or bodily injury arising from the use of a motor vehicle on a road has been compulsory since 1930 in the United Kingdom.[6] Since 1 January 1972, insurance has had to be effected by every employer in respect of liability for bodily injury (including death and disease) sustained by his employees.[7] Any solicitor wishing to practise in England and Wales is obliged to purchase professional indemnity insurance under a special scheme arranged by the Law

---

5 This is taken from the Guardian Royal Exchange Group, Liability Policy; see too their Motor Insurance Policy, to similar effect.
6 See now Road Traffic Act 1972, s 145. Since 1972, cover has been required in respect of voluntary passengers.
7 Employers' Liability (Compulsory Insurance) Act 1969.

Society.[8] The paramount aim of compulsory insurance legislation is to ensure that the victim gets his damages,[9] but, as we shall see, there are several loopholes, with the result that the legislation has not been entirely successful.

The practice of compulsory insurance for motor vehicles has not been found to increase the amount of negligent driving. In Massachussetts, which was the first of the United States to introduce compulsory insurance, there was a decrease of traffic fatalities by 51% after the law was introduced, as compared with a decrease of 28.8% in the United States as a whole.[10] Since then Massachussetts has, on occasion, won awards for being a 'safe-driving' State.[11] Indeed it can confidently be argued that *un*insured drivers are likely to be the most uncaring and dangerous road-users.[12]

A distinctive feature of compulsory road traffic insurance is that any person whom the policy purports to insure may enforce the policy against the insurance company.[13] This validates the common type of policy under which the insurance extends to all who may be driving with the consent of the insured. It constitutes an exception to the

---

8 As from 1976, under the powers granted by the Solicitors Act 1974, s 37.
9 Other examples of compulsory insurance are the Riding Establishments Acts 1964 and 1970 (hiring out of horses), and the Dangerous Wild Animals Act 1976 (wild animals). It is the practice of the Civil Aviation Authority to refuse a licence to a commercial aircraft without insurance; and hospital doctors in the National Health Service must either be members of a defence society or subscribe to an approved insurance arrangement.
10 (1943) 21 Can BR 166; see further the studies referred to in Chap 7, p 206, n 2, below, for somewhat different views. There has been no comparable study in the United Kingdom of the effect of either motor vehicle or employers' liability insurance. Comprehensive statistics in Great Britain have been available only since 1934. Accidents and casualties were lower in 1935–8 than in 1934. This was due in part to the Road Traffic Act 1934, which introduced driving tests, a 30 mph speed limit and 'zebra' crossings.
11 Keeton and O'Connell, p 102.
12 Prosser *Torts* (4th edn) §85.
13 *Tattersall v Drysdale* [1935] 2 KB 174, decided under a provision of the 1930 Act now contained in Road Traffic Act 1972, s 148(4).

inconvenient doctrine of English law of 'privity of contract', which generally makes it impossible for one person to take out an insurance policy to protect another person against tort liability. The person who is purported to be insured cannot claim under the insurance (apart from the road traffic exception) unless he supplied consideration for the insurance.[14]

THIRD-PARTY RIGHTS

Road traffic. The original Road Traffic Act 1930 required owners and drivers of motor vehicles to be insured, under penalty for non-compliance, but it did not affect the principle that insurance is a matter of free contract between the parties. The insurance company was entitled to insert any conditions it pleased into the policy, and to repudiate liability either for breach of those conditions or for any other material misrepresentation or non-disclosure leading up to the making of the policy. Some of the resulting dexterity on the part of the companies was stopped by a later statute,[15] the general effect of which, subject to many particular provisions, is that the insurer is deprived of his usual ability to set aside the policy unless he obtains a declaration within three months after the third party institutes proceedings against the insured that he is entitled to avoid the policy on grounds of material misrepresentation, non-disclosure or the like. The effect is to afford limited protection to the victim of a road accident. On obtaining judgment against the insured in

14 *Vandepitte v Preferred Accident Insurance Corpn of New York* [1933] AC 70. The road traffic exception in effect creates a statutory contract between the permitted driver and the insurer; the driver is bound by the conditions of the policy.
15 Road Traffic Act 1934; now Road Traffic Act 1972, s 148(1).

respect of any liability for which insurance is compulsory, he has a statutory right to claim an indemnity for the amount of the judgment, together with interest and costs, from the insurer.[16] In order to obtain this benefit the third party must give notice of his action against the insured person to the insurance company within seven days of its commencement.[17] The insured defendant may have to reimburse his insurance company if the company is made to satisfy a claim that would not have made them liable apart from the Act.[18] Even if the insurance company's defence of misrepresentation or non-disclosure succeeds the third party will be able to claim from the Motor Insurers' Bureau.[19]

Employers' liability. The employee is not as well protected as the road traffic victim by the compulsory insurance legislation.[20] Although the employer must be insured against liability under an approved policy, the employee is not given a statutory right, analogous to that conferred upon road traffic third parties, to claim the amount of an unsatisfied judgment direct from the insurer. If the insurer does satisfy the employee's claim, however, he may exercise any contractual right to claim reimbursement from the policy holder.[1]

Another unfortunate gap in the legislation relates to the terms of the policy. The policy must not contain certain specified conditions relieving the insurer of his contractual

---

16 Road Traffic Act 1972, s 149. One of the effects of s 149(3) is that the insurer cannot rely on a 'basis of the contract' defence against the third party.
17 Ibid, s 149(2)(a).
18 Ibid, s 148(1) proviso.
19 Below, p 158.
20 Even the compulsory insurance under the Road Traffic Act does not extend to liability *to* a person employed by the insured for injury arising out of and in the course of his employment: s 145(4). Such liability is covered by an employers' liability policy.
1 Employers' Liability (Compulsory Insurance) General Regulations, SI 1971/1117, reg 2(2).

liability under the policy,[2] but there can be various other
conditions in the policy between the insurer and employer
(eg where the risk has been increased since the proposal form
was signed) that can be used to defeat the claim by the
employee. It appears that the insurer can also refuse to
indemnify if the employer was 'reckless' and not merely
'negligent' in bringing about the risk.[3]

Even more serious is the fact that insurers can avoid
employers' liability policies, and so prevent payment of
compensation to the injured employee, on grounds of
misrepresentation or non-disclosure of material facts by the
insured employer. In addition, the insurer may be able to
repudiate liability, and so deny the employee his compensation, because of an employer's incorrect answers on the
proposal form even though those answers were not material
to the risk, where a clause in the contract provides that the
answers form the 'basis of the contract'.

Insolvent defendants and insurers. In one exceptional case the
victim of a tort is given by statute a direct right of recourse
under the tortfeasor's insurance policy. This is when the
tortfeasor is insolvent.[4] It applies whenever there is a liability
insurance policy and is not confined to the road traffic or
employers' liability context. It would obviously be unsatisfactory if while the tortfeasor's trustee in bankruptcy could
recover the amount of the insurance in full from the insurance company the injured party were confined to a proof
in the bankruptcy of the tortfeasor, receiving only such

---

2 Ibid, reg 2, prohibits conditions that would preclude liability (i) if something
   was done or omitted to be done after an event giving rise to liability (eg late
   reporting of an accident), or (ii) the policy holder failed to keep specified
   records or provide the insurer with information, or (iii) the policy holder
   failed to take reasonable care to protect his employees, or (iv) the policy
   holder failed to comply with statutory safety requirements.
3 *R S Hartley Ltd v Provincial Insurance Co Ltd* [1957] 1 Lloyd's Rep 121.
4 Third Parties (Rights Against Insurers) Act 1930, s 1.

dividend on his claim as other creditors received. Under the statute the victim of the tort gets the whole of the insurance money and does not have to share it with other creditors of the tortfeasor. The tort victim, however, cannot have better rights against the insurer than the insolvent tortfeasor had, so that if the insurer had grounds for avoiding or cancelling the policy the third party cannot recover.[5]

It sometimes happens that an insurance company itself is unable to meet its liabilities. Recent legislation has established a Policyholders Protection Board to indemnify those whose claims are not met because of the failure of an insurer.[6]

FAILURE TO INSURE

There are criminal sanctions for the failure to comply with the compulsory insurance provisions,[7] but they bring little consolation to the victim of an uninsured motorist or employer. This consideration led the Court of Appeal, in *Monk v Warbey*,[8] to invent a new tort: it is a civil wrong to permit another to drive an uninsured vehicle contrary to the provisions of the Road Traffic Act.

> In *Monk v Warbey*, Warbey violated the statute by lending his car to an impecunious friend who was uninsured. Owing to the negligence of the friend's driver Monk was injured. Monk obtained a barren judgment against the friend and then proceeded against Warbey for damages for breach of statutory duty. The Court of Appeal held

---

5 *Post Office v Norwich Union Fire Insurance Society Ltd* [1967] 2 QB 363, [1967] 1 All ER 577; cp. Road Traffic Act 1972, s 150, which gives road traffic victims better protection.
6 Policyholders Protection Act 1975.
7 While the police enforce the road traffic provisions, the responsibility for enforcing the employers' duty to insure and display a certificate of insurance rests on inspectors of the Department of Employment.
8 [1935] 1 KB 35; discussed in (1960) 23 MLR 233, 247 ff.

Warbey liable to pay the damages Monk could have recovered from the friend had he possessed the means to pay.

This decision suffers from the limitation that the traffic victim can succeed against the owner of the vehicle only if he is unable to recover damages from the negligent driver. However, he will be allowed to take proceedings against the driver and the owner in the same action, and to obtain immediate judgment against the owner provided he can show that the driver is a person of limited means who will be unable to satisfy the judgment against him promptly. He need not show that the driver will not pay at all.[9]

The decision in *Monk v Warbey* is capable of causing hardship, because an uninsured owner has to pay the damages out of his own pocket. The owner is liable even though he did not know that the driver was uninsured.[10]

THE MOTOR INSURERS' BUREAU

The problems of obtaining damages against uninsured drivers and of tracing unidentified (hit-and-run) drivers has led to voluntary arrangements by the insurance companies to compensate traffic victims. In July 1937 a Departmental Committee[11] recommended the creation of a Central Fund made up of contributions levied from all licensed insurers to protect third party victims of road accidents who were unable to recover damages because compulsory insurance had not been effected. Under pressure from the then Ministry of War Transport, the insurance industry set up the Motor Insurers' Bureau in 1946. By an agreement between

---

9 *Martin v Dean* [1971] 2 QB 208, [1971] 3 All ER 279.
10 *Houston v Buchanan* 1940 SC (HL) 17 (HL Sc). On the creation of torts out of penal legislation generally, see above, Chap 4, p 116.
11 Report of the Committee on Compulsory Insurance (the Cassel Committee), Cmd 5528.

the Bureau and the Ministry, subsequently amended and now replaced by an agreement dated 22 November 1972,[12] the Bureau undertakes to pay any unsatisfied judgment in respect of a liability required to be insured under the Road Traffic Act, provided certain conditions are fulfilled. The most important practical point is that notice of the bringing of the proceedings must be given to the Bureau within seven days' of their commencement.

The typical case in which the Bureau pays is where there is an identified uninsured motorist who was legally responsible for the accident. (He may be uninsured either because he had not taken out a policy or because the insurer has lawfully repudiated liability under the policy.) But the Bureau will also pay where an identified motorist was insured but the insurer is unable to meet the claim because it has become insolvent and gone into liquidation. By arrangement with the liquidator, and with the sanction of the court, the Bureau takes over the insurance company's liability.[13]

A separate agreement, also dated 22 November 1972 and a supplemental agreement dated 7 December 1977,[14] between

---

12 For the text, see Hepple and Matthews, p 696. A useful short account of the Bureau's work will be found in D. B. Williams *Hit and Run and Uninsured Driver Personal Injury Claims* (Chichester, 1983).

13 In addition, the Bureau has entered into a so-called 'Domestic' Agreement with its own members which improves upon and supersedes in practice the statutory provisions regarding third-party rights. This occurs when there is an identified insured motorist but the insurer is not legally liable under that policy. We have seen that the insurer cannot avoid liability to the third party by repudiating the policy in cases of misrepresentation or non-disclosure, unless he has taken certain formal steps to obtain a declaration that he is entitled to avoid it. Under the 'Domestic' Agreement members of the Bureau agree, in effect, to act as agents for the Bureau where the insurer is entitled to repudiate liability under the agreement, for example if the vehicle was being used for business instead of domestic purposes. In such cases the third party victim must give the insurer notice within seven days of the commencement of proceedings (Road Traffic Act, s 149, above, p 155), but the Bureau will pay the amount awarded.

14 The supplemental agreement introduced a less formal and more speedy procedure for most claims.

the Bureau and the Secretary of State for Transport provides that the Bureau will make payment where the motorist cannot be traced, provided that the death or injury occurred in circumstances in which the motorist would have been legally liable to the victim, and the untraced person's liability is one which is required to be covered by the Road Traffic Act. The Bureau will not deal with deliberate running-down cases, and applications must be made within three years after the date of the accident. Before 1969, the Bureau sometimes made ex gratia payments to the victims of hit-and-run drivers, but this informal procedure was strongly criticised[15] because it meant that claimants could not get a judicial ruling on the amount of damages. Under the current agreement the Bureau makes investigations into the accident and, if it decides to make a payment, will assess the damages on ordinary common law principles. The applicant may appeal to an arbitrator who is a Queen's Counsel selected from a panel appointed by the Lord Chancellor.

THE GAPS THAT REMAIN

The agreements between the government and the Motor Insurers' Bureau are striking examples of the way in which the autonomous regulation of business and industry can supersede rules of law. Since compulsory motor vehicle insurance must be effected with an insurer who is a member of the Bureau,[16] the statutory provisions on third party rights and the rule in *Monk v Warbey* are not of much practical importance. Yet the claim against the Bureau by

---

15 *Adams v Andrews* [1964] 2 Lloyd's Rep 347; Justice *Trial of Motor Accident Cases* (London, 1966) App 3.

16 Road Traffic Act 1974, s 20. In law, the fact that the MIB will meet the claim is irrelevant to a *Monk v Warbey* action: *Corfield v Groves* [1950] 1 All ER 488.

the accident victim does not rest on any sound *legal* foundation. The obligations of the Bureau are laid down in contracts under seal between itself and the Department. These contracts cannot be enforced by the third party victim because of the doctrine of privity of contract. It is true that the Department as a party to the agreement could obtain an order for specific performance in favour of the third party if the Bureau failed to honour its obligations,[17] and that if the Secretary of State hesitated to sue it might be open to the third party victim to make him a defendant and thus compel performance. But, unlike the statutory obligation of an ordinary insurer under the Road Traffic Act, the Bureau's legal obligation is not *directly* enforceable by the third party himself.

While acknowledging that this is the formal position,[18] the Court of Appeal has allowed the Bureau to make itself a party to an action brought against a defendant in circumstances where the Bureau would become liable under its agreement with the Department and accordingly has an interest in ensuring that all proper defences are raised to the plaintiff's action.[19] This recognises the reality of a situation in which the defendant is a purely nominal party to the proceedings and the real contest is between the injured plaintiff and the Motor Insurers' Bureau. Conversely, the third party victim is able in practice to institute proceedings against the Bureau, simply because the Bureau does not take the privity of contract point. It would not be in the Bureau's

---

17 *Beswick v Beswick* [1968] AC 58, [1967] 2 All ER 1197; *Gurtner v Circuit* [1968] 2 QB 587.

18 One described by Viscount Dilhorne in *Albert v Motor Insurers' Bureau* [1972] AC 301, [1971] 2 All ER 1345 at 1354 as unsatisfactory: 'This House is asked to say that judgment should be given in favour of [the third party] when it is clear that she has no cause of action'.

19 *Gurtner v Circuit* [1968] 2 QB 587, [1968] 1 All ER 328. But where, under the 1969 agreement, the Bureau required a claimant to take proceedings against one of the possible tortfeasors, the Court refused to allow the joinder of the Bureau: *White v London Transport* [1971] 2 QB 721, [1971] 3 All ER 1.

interests to do so since this would be to invite legislation on a matter which the insurance companies prefer to regulate themselves.

The Bureau, when sued or when intervening in proceedings against an insurer, can raise any defences open to the insurer. Thus the Bureau may deny that the plaintiff was injured through the motorist's negligence; or they may show that insurance was not compulsory under the Road Traffic Act[20] (for example, in relation to damage to property); or they may dispute the amount of damages.

There is no institution comparable to the Motor Insurers' Bureau to deal with claims against uninsured or 'fly-by-night' employers. This is, perhaps, less serious than might appear, because an injured worker will usually have received some compensation under the social security system. Nevertheless, so long as it is possible for a plaintiff who proves fault on the part of his employer to recover common law damages in addition to social security benefits, the purpose of the compulsory insurance legislation may be defeated if an Employers' Liability Insurers Bureau is not established.[1] The most serious weaknesses of employers' liability compulsory insurance are these.

(1) It does not extend to all workers but only to 'employees', ie those employed under a contract of service. The growing practice of 'labour-only' sub-contracting, particularly in the construction industry, exposes 'self-employed' workers to the risk of obtaining barren judgments against defaulting employers.

---

20 One major limitation (and source of litigation) before 1 December 1972, was that compulsory insurance did not extend to liability to passengers. This limit has now been removed. An example of a successful defence is where it can be shown that the accident did not occur on a 'road'; *Buchanan v Motor Insurers' Bureau* [1955] 1 All ER 607, [1955] 1 WLR 488; cp. *Randall v Motor Insurers' Bureau* [1969] 1 All ER 21, [1968] 1 WLR 1900.

1 For an elaboration of this point see R. C. Simpson in (1972) 35 MLR 63 and Hasson in (1974) 3 ILJ 79.

(2) The employer does not have to insure in respect of certain employees who are close relatives of his.

(3) The Act and regulations do not require the cover to be comprehensive.[2] Employers may comply technically with the Act but find themselves without insurance in respect of certain of their activities (eg the use of certain kinds of machine, or activities involving the risk of contracting certain diseases).

(4) Defences, such as non-disclosure of information or misrepresentation by the employer when filling in the proposal form, may defeat the employee's claim.[3]

THE EFFECT OF LIABILITY INSURANCE ON THE LAW OF TORT

Judges nowadays assume that the defendant in an action in tort is insured unless the contrary appears.[4] The rule of professional ethics that counsel should refrain from mentioning the fact of insurance to the jury, for fear of encouraging them to make a larger award of damages than would otherwise have been the case, has lost most of its sting because, apart from defamation cases, actions in tort are now nearly always before a single judge sitting alone, and there is no objection to mentioning the fact of insurance to the judge.[5] However, judges have often asserted, what is clear on principle, that the existence of insurance should not affect

---

2 Hasson in (1974) 3 ILJ at 81–2.
3 Ironically, the very situation that gave an impetus to the passing of the Act of 1969 – a fire in Glasgow in 1968 – was one in which the insurers had refused to indemnify the employers on grounds of misrepresentation and non-disclosure. The Act does not make any change in this situation.
4 Per Lord Denning MR in *Post Office v Norwich Union Fire Insurance Society Ltd* [1967] 2 QB 363 at 375, [1967] 1 All ER 577 at 580; Winn Committee Report, para 349.
5 *Harman v Crilly* [1943] 1 KB 168, [1943] 1 All ER 740; but counsel may still be reluctant to do so, as in *Launchbury v Morgans* [1971] 2 QB 245 at 253.

the determination of the issue of negligence.[6] Occasionally, a judge will bolster a decision about the existence or non-existence of a duty of care by referring to the insurance position.[7] But so long as English law retains the principle of liability based upon fault, rather than upon 'risk-distribution', it is, strictly speaking, irrelevant whether or not the defendant is insured. Whether or not English law *should* adopt, as the basis of tort liability, the criterion of superior risk-bearing capacity is debatable.[8] That criterion is not the foundation of the existing law: consequently, the courts are not concerned with the question whether the defendant is insured, or ought as a prudent man to have been insured.

There is one exceptional situation in which the availability of insurance has occasionally been regarded as relevant. This is where the plaintiff seeks to make the defendant vicariously liable for the torts of another. As long ago as 1778, Lord Mansfield[9] justified the liability of a sheriff for the acts of one of his men on the ground that the sheriff could protect himself by a fidelity bond. In 1912 Lord MacNaghten[10] supported the responsibility of a solicitor for the acts of his fraudulent managing clerk on the same ground. But the courts now refuse to extend vicarious liability substantially beyond the established categories by arguments based on insurance, taking the view that they lack sufficient information or an adequate grasp of the social

---

6 'As a general proposition it has not, I think, been questioned for nearly two hundred years that in determining the rights inter se of A and B, the fact that one or other of them is insured is to be disregarded' per Viscount Simonds in *Lister v Romford Ice and Cold Storage Co Ltd* [1957] AC 555 at 576.

7 Eg Lord Denning MR in *SCM (UK) Ltd v Whittall & Son Ltd* [1971] 1 QB 337 at 344; *Spartan Steel and Alloys Ltd v Martin & Co (Contractors) Ltd* [1973] QB 27 at 38; *Nettleship v Weston* [1971] 2 QB 691 at 703.

8 See below, Chap 7, p 201.

9 *Ackworth v Kempe* (1778) 1 Doug KB 40, 99 ER 30.

10 *Lloyd v Grace Smith & Co* [1912] AC 716.

problems involved to make a large legislative decision.[11]

The explicit reference to insurance in the vicarious liability cases is perfectly intelligible in view of the social purposes of vicarious liability. This is a form of enterprise liability, and it is proper to investigate the risk-bearing capacity of the enterprise which it is sought to make responsible. A number of academic writers, however, go further. They assert that the principles of fault liability have themselves been 'invisibly' affected by the existence of liability insurance. The most perceptive of these writers[12] admits that one cannot show that common law rules have been modified directly because of liability insurance. But he claims that liability insurance has produced a climate of opinion in which certain changes in the legal rules have become acceptable. For example, the rule that a learner driver must observe the same standard of care as a fully licensed driver is partially explicable on the ground that the driver does not have to pay the damages himself.[13] Conversely, the rule of non-liability of utility companies for breach of statutory duty to provide sufficient water to extinguish fires may perhaps be explained on the ground that householders and businessmen are more likely to be insured against the risk of fire than the utilities.

---

11 In *Morgans v Launchbury* [1973] AC 127, [1972] 2 All ER 606 Lord Wilberforce said there were four different systems of vicarious liability that might be adopted in cases where it was sought to make a vehicle owner responsible. The choice between them, being a matter of policy, was for Parliament. The House of Lords ignored the fact that a vehicle owner is criminally liable for permitting any other person to use the vehicle on a road without a liability insurance policy: see Jolowicz in [1972A] CLJ 207.

12 Fleming James in (1948) 57 Yale LJ 549 is still the most illuminating of the discussions of this topic.

13 Although, as we have seen, the insurance policy may be subject to an excess clause: above, p 149.

THE EFFECT OF INSURANCE ON THE BRINGING OF ACTIONS

Whatever the 'invisible' effects of liability insurance on the substantive rules, insurance has had a significant impact on the procedural side of the law. Three illustrations will be given.

First, when an insurance company has paid a claim under a policy (whether the insurance be of property or against liability) it is *subrogated* to the rights of the insured against third parties. Subrogation means that the company can stand in the shoes of the insured and sue third parties to the same extent as the insured could have done. The action against third parties is brought by the insurance company in the name of the insured, but it is the insurance company that will get the benefit of the action, just as it is the insurance company that will have to pay the legal costs. As an example of subrogation where the insurance is against liability, take a traffic accident where D_1 and D_2 negligently collide with P. If D_1 and D_2 are concurrent tortfeasors (ie, both were at fault in causing the accident), each is liable in full to P. Suppose that D_1 is insured, and the insurance company settles D_1's liability by paying P his full damages. The insurance company is then, by virtue of the doctrine of subrogation, vested with any right to contribution that D_1 may possess against D_2.[14] The company may sue D_2 in D_1's name for the share of the damages that D_2 ought in justice to pay. This will not necessarily be to the liking of D_1, but if he is insured he must put up with it.[15]

Second, it is invariably an express provision in a contract of insurance against liability that the insurance company shall have full control over the conduct of any proceedings.

14 As to the right to contribution see above, p 132.
15 An action in an employer's name against his employee might antagonise the workforce. For this reason the Court of Appeal held in *Morris v Ford Motor Co Ltd* [1973] QB 792, [1973] 2 ALL ER 1084, by a majority, that in an industrial setting the right to subrogation is excluded.

The insured will not be able to settle any claim against him without the insurance company's consent, and he must give the company all the information and assistance they require. From the insured's point of view it is highly advantageous to have experts conduct the litigation and reach a settlement. The insurer, and the solicitor whom the insurer instructs, have to conduct the negotiations in a manner which they honestly believe to be in the common interests of themselves and their insured. If they do not do so, the insured may have an action for damages for breach of contract against either the insurer or the solicitor (who, strictly speaking, acts for the insured), or both of them. Usually, the only possible injury he is likely to suffer from a settlement of which he personally disapproves is a stain upon his reputation (as where his advisers have admitted, contrary to the facts of the case, that he was negligent, in order to settle the matter[16]). He will not suffer financial loss through an unsatisfactory settlement, unless the insurance company becomes insolvent before satisfying its terms. On the other hand, the plaintiff in the action against the insured may not enjoy the same professional help as the defendant, unless he himself has a personal accident or loss insurance policy and his insurers are acting on his behalf in attempting to recover from the defendant's liability insurers. A Justice Report[17] pointed out that

> the majority of insurance companies are reputable concerns who do not seek in negotiation to take an unjust advantage of their greater knowledge of the law and practice to obtain oppressive settlements. But insurance is a highly competitive business and it is within the

---

16 This happened in *Groom v Crocker* [1939] 1 KB 194, [1938] 3 All ER 394. The Winn Committee Report, para 371, thought this case had led to misunderstanding and hindered settlements, and proposed a clarification of the law to create a presumption that the insurer has authority to make admissions, including admissions of negligence.

17 *Trial of Motor Accident Cases* (London, 1966) p 2.

knowledge of some of us that there are insurers who, given the chance to do so, do extract such settlements.

At present the only settlements that require the approval of the court are those relating to minors.[18]

A third illustration of the impact of insurance is in the arrangements made between certain motor insurance companies. Suppose that P and D are each comprehensively insured by different companies and that D negligently damages P's car. Under the 'knock–for–knock' arrangement between the companies P's company will settle his claim and will not claim from D's company. This saves legal costs, and it works out evenly in the long run, but it means that the civil law of negligence is suspended. The effect of the arrangement is that P may lose his legal entitlement to his no–claim bonus, although in practice his insurance company will usually allow him this bonus if he was not personally at fault.

EVALUATION

At the beginning of this chapter we put forward two justifications for the practice of insurance. Is the practice, as we have described it, compatible with the theories of deterrence and justice?

The primary effect of insurance is to remove the element of individual responsibility for careless conduct. The extent to which insurance companies vary the rates of premium according to the accident record of the insured and undertake safety surveys, and so contribute to accident prevention, is limited by the competitive nature of the

18 The Pearson Commission, vol 2, para 65, found that 86% of tort claims are settled without the issue of a writ, and only 1% reach the courts. See further Chap 3, above, p 77.

insurance market.[19] Insurers who raise rates, or exercise their power to cancel the policy of an insured with a bad accident record, may find that the insured takes his business elsewhere. Similarly, competition restricts the amount that an insurance company can afford to expend on accident prevention. Companies that try to overcome this by combining to fix rates may run foul of the laws against restrictive practices.[20] 'The insurance system', in the words of the New Zealand Woodhouse Commission,[1] 'can offer no central impetus in the important areas of accident prevention and rehabilitation'. The experts employed by the insurance companies cannot hope to achieve the degree of specialisation or the unified administration that are features of the Health and Safety Executive – the administrative agency that enforces safety laws in Great Britain. And, as regards 'experience' rating (making the premium depend on the insured's accident record), there is no positive evidence that this reduces accident rates. If it does have any effect this seems likely to be in respect of large organisations where the reduction in premiums may be sufficient to encourage a safety effort.[2] There are, however, many imponderables, such as the possibility that the insured may be able to pass the increased premium forward to his customers or back to his employees; the difficulty of measuring experience of accidents, particularly when many minor accidents are never reported and 'near misses' are neglected altogether; the

---

19 This was the finding of the Robens Committee on Safety and Health at Work, Cmnd 5034, para 439.
20 See, eg the Report of the Monopolies Commission on the Supply of Fire Insurance (HMSO, 1972) paras 373–85.
1 Woodhouse Report (1967), para 491(3).
2 For a full discussion see P. S. Atiyah in (1975) 4 ILJ 1, 82. In employers' liability insurance, British insurers use a mixture of what Professor Atiyah calls 'classified' rating (based on the risks of each industrial classification such as mining and fishing) and 'experience' rating. 'Penalty' rating (payment of a premium greater than is commensurate with the additional risk) is not known in Britain. See further, Chap 7, below, p 213.

guesswork involved in estimating costs, aggravated by the lump sum system of awarding common law damages; the time lag between accident experience and the calculation of premiums (which may be as much as five or six years); and the reluctance of insurers to penalise an insured who has suffered a single catastrophic loss. If insurance makes any contribution to deterrence, then, this is largely fortuitous. The deterrent purposes of the law could probably be better served by more direct means.

Tort law works on the fiction of a contest between the individual victim in search of justice and the tortfeasor. We have seen that, in reality, there is a search for the best *bargain* that can be achieved – either between insurance companies,[3] where both parties are insured, or between an insurance company and the uninsured plaintiff and his representatives. The results are indefensible from the point of view of justice. A motorist whose use of the vehicle is insured is (as regards the civil law) virtually immune from the personal consequences of his conduct, however negligent he has been, unless he has acted intentionally. But an uninsured pedestrian (and his 'innocent' family) must bear all the losses flowing from his own momentary 'error', where no motorist is at fault. There is an obvious lack of connection between the fault basis of liability and the insurance principle.

---

3 It is not unknown for different departments of the same insurance company, or different subsidiaries of the same holding company, to be locked in litigation behind the nominal plaintiff and defendant, where different types of insurance (eg road traffic and employers' liability) are involved.

6 Social security

He who would do Good to another must do it in
Minute Particulars.

William Blake *Jerusalem*

The evaluation of tort and insurance as compensation systems for personal injury and death is incomplete without some consideration of the way in which social security legislation deals with the needs of those suffering from misfortune. 'Between them,' said the Pearson Commission, '[the tort and social security systems] meet many needs twice over and others not at all.'[1] Social security is by far the most important source of compensation for those suffering personal injuries in the United Kingdom. It has been estimated[2] that each year 1.5 million injuries attract social security payments, while only 215,000 injuries are compensated by tort damages. Together State cash benefits and tort damages account for three-quarters of all compensation for personal injury, the remainder being provided by occupational sick pay; occupational pensions; occupational health services and insurance provided by employers; first-party insurance; and benefits from trade unions, friendly societies and charities.[3] To the cash benefits must be added other forms of State provision such as free medical advice,

---

1 Pearson Report, vol 1, para 271.
2 Pearson Report, vol 1, Table 4, p 13. The aggregate value per year of social security was estimated to be £421m, of tort damages £202m, and other sources such as occupational sick pay and private insurance £204m
3 Pearson Report, vol 1, para 136 and, generally Chap 6 for a description of these other sources.

treatment, hospitalisation and rehabilitation under the National Health Service, and personal social services for the disabled. Overall, it can be said that State cash benefits are the primary source of compensation for the working population (who suffer 60% of all injuries), tort damages are the primary source for those, like housewives and pensioners, who are not part of the workforce (40% of all injuries), while nearly 1.4 million of the 3 million or so injuries and deaths by misfortune each year are not compensated at all.[4]

THE GROWTH OF SOCIAL SECURITY

The term 'social security' is a newcomer to the legal vocabulary. It was first used in the U.S. Federal Social Security Act 1935 and in the New Zealand Social Security Act 1938. In the United Kingdom, the present-day legal connotation, under the Social Security Acts, includes benefits depending upon the payment of certain contributions[5] such as those for unemployment, sickness, invalidism, widowhood, industrial disablement, and retirement, as well as a few non-contributory benefits for the aged, disabled, and mothers and guardians. This excludes child benefits and means-tested family income supplements and supplementary benefits (formerly national assistance). The division is confusing and illogical[6] and in a broad sense 'social security' may be taken to cover all financial benefits which are administered by the Department of Health and Social Security.

4 Pearson Report, vol 1, paras 160–63.
5 These were formerly payable under the national insurance schemes, and now referred to simply as 'contributory benefits'.
6 A. I. Ogus and E. Barendt *The Law of Social Security* (2nd edn, London, 1982) pp 37–8. This excellent textbook provides detailed treatment of the background and present highly complex law.

The law of social security shares with the law of tort the aim of providing compensation, but it does so from a different perspective. While tort stresses the principles of ethical compensation and deterrence – as we have seen, with only limited success – social security emphasises the responsibility of the community for the safety and welfare of its members.

The first steps towards social security were, in part, a response to the inadequacy of the common law as a means of compensating those suffering from work-related injuries. During the greater part of the nineteenth century, a trilogy of defences militated against the worker's action in tort against his employer. First, the worker was deemed to consent to all the obvious dangers of his job (*volenti non fit injuria*); second, his claim could be wholly defeated by a finding that he had been contributorily negligent; and third, the employer was not liable to one employee for the negligence of a fellow-employee (the doctrine of common employment). These defences were judicial inventions. They were eroded by judicial decisions towards the end of the century, when many of the judges came to appreciate the destitution and hardship that they caused to injured employees,[7] and the Employers' Liability Act 1880 partially restricted the scope of the doctrine of common employment. The trade unions and friendly societies, however, continued to press for the complete abolition of the doctrine and for the prohibition of the practice of contracting out of liability which the judiciary had sanctioned following the Act of 1880.[8] The liberal advocates of reform favoured the retention of private law as the instrument of compensation

---

7 The plaintiff in the case which became the foundation of the doctrine of common employment, the poor Mr Priestley, could not pay the costs of his unsuccessful action against his employer, Fowler the butcher (1837), and so spent some years in the debtor's prison.
8 *Griffiths v Earl of Dudley* (1881) 9 QBD 357.

on the grounds that those enterprises causing accidents, especially in dangerous trades, should bear the cost. This solution was embodied in the Workmen's Compensation Act 1897, which broke away from the common law in two major respects. First, by making compensation payable by the employer without proof of fault. Second, by fixing compensation not on an indemnity basis but on the principle of division of loss between employer and employee; this reflected the fear that full compensation on a no-fault basis would be too heavy a burden on enterprise. The employer was free to insure against his liability, but, except in coalmining from 1934, this was not compulsory. The original Act was limited in scope, but it was generalised in 1906 and amended on several subsequent occasions.

The worker had to elect between his tort remedy and his claim under the workmen's compensation scheme. The great majority claimed under the scheme because it had the advantage of allowing them to obtain some compensation for basic economic losses with relative speed. However, the operation of the Acts came under increasing criticism.[9] 'In no time at all,' one experienced practitioner wrote, 'workmen's compensation descended from its lofty ideals of being a no-fault social service into a squalid legal battlefield between trade unions and insurance companies, with lying, cheating and chicanery on all sides and astronomical expenditure on administrative, legal and medical costs.'[10] The authors of the original Act had contemplated that disputes would be settled by friendly and informal arbitration, but both insurance companies and trade unions had an

9 See the massive study by A. Wilson and H. Levy *Workmen's Compensation* (2 vols, Oxford, 1939), especially Chap 3; and the Report by Sir William Beveridge, Social Insurance and Allied Services, Cmd 6404 (1942), paras 77–80; and generally, P. W. J. Bartrip and S. B. Burman *The Wounded Soldiers of Industry: Industrial Compensation Policy, 1833–1897* (Oxford, 1983).

10 O. H. Parsons in (1974) 3 ILJ 129 at 137. Beveridge, para 79, gives estimates of the relatively high percentage of administrative costs involved.

interest in backing litigation through the county courts and up to the Court of Appeal and the House of Lords.[11]

The system failed to give complete security because insurance was generally not compulsory. It failed to guarantee necessary income, in particular because it allowed the worker to settle a claim by payment of a lump sum, which, because of the unequal bargaining position of the parties, was often insufficient. The lump sum was expended to meet pressing temporary needs, and failed to provide a permanent source of income for the long-term disabled; it placed the cost of medical care on the worker or charity or poor relief; and it did little to encourage rehabilitation. 'The pioneer system of social security in Britain,' Sir William Beveridge concluded in 1942 'was based on a wrong principle and has been dominated by a wrong outlook.'[12] The system was replaced in 1946 by social insurance.

The social insurance principle had already been developed outside the area of employment risks, and accorded with the liberal ideals of self-help and individual responsibility. There is a long tradition of mutual insurance. Since ancient times people in the same occupation and social class have come together in friendly societies to arrange burials, benefits in the case of sickness and death, and other financial benefits. The inadequacy of the common law and the fear of the workhouse led to a rapid growth in these societies in the period of industrialisation and later. It has been estimated that by 1875 there were 4 million members of societies in Britain and 6 million by 1905.

However, the societies were seriously inadequate as a form of social protection. The basic principle was the

11 The enormous volume of case law built up in 45 years can be seen in the 37 volumes of Butterworths' Workmen's Compensation cases, and the gigantic practitioners' works, regularly reissued, such as Willis' *Workmen's Compensation* which had reached its 37th edition of 2,106 pages by 1945, with a 101 page supplement in 1946.
12 Beveridge Report, para 80.

payment of a premium or contribution. This had the consequence that in general only those who were higher-paid and in regular employment could belong. The contributions were not always adequate to meet the claims at the time of greatest need, such as epidemics and disasters, and at these times the societies had to raise contribution levels. Even when special funds were established, such as colliery disaster funds in the second half of the nineteenth century, these were insufficient. The commitment of the societies to pay death benefits and retirement pensions came under increasing strain owing to the demographic pressure of an ageing population. At the beginning of the twentieth century over half the working population had no sickness insurance. The solution adopted (following the example of Germany) was compulsory social insurance. The National Insurance Act 1911 compulsorily insured all those between 16 and 70 in manual employment and all in non-manual employment earning below a certain amount. In return any contributor was entitled to enrol on the panel of a doctor who agreed to participate, and to receive from him free medical treatment. The contributor also received sickness benefit which lasted for 26 weeks and could be extended for disablement. The scheme was administered by Approved Societies, including friendly societies and trade unions, controlled by their members. The number of persons covered was gradually increased between 1911 and 1946.

The idea of community responsibility for welfare was partly reflected in the sharing of costs between employers and workers; but the private nature of friendly-society insurance was retained in the discretion of individual societies to pay additional benefits from their surplus funds. The fear, never far from the surface in social insurance schemes, that individual responsibility might be under-mined and idleness encouraged, was met by paying benefit only at survival level and by not providing dependants' allowances. For those who fell outside the scheme (eg because of insufficient contributions) there remained poor relief with special assistance to the old (1908) and the unemployed (1934). In 1942, Beveridge criticised the provision for sickness and invalidism on the grounds that it was insufficiently concerned with improving health, provided too low a level of benefits, and was inadequately administered by the Approved Societies. The scheme initiated in 1946 under the inspiration of the Beveridge Report retained the basic principle of social insurance conferring benefits at a flat-rate subsistence level in respect of the major causes of income loss, combined with a means-tested national insurance benefit (replacing poor relief) for the remainder. The radical changes were that social insurance was made comprehensive, covering groups previously excluded, and that the administration was unified under a department of State.

DEVELOPMENTS SINCE BEVERIDGE

The basic philosophy of the Beveridge scheme was that the State should establish a national minimum level of subsistence on the basis of 'normal needs', while leaving 'room and encouragement for voluntary action by each individual to provide more than that minimum for himself and his family'.[13] The scheme failed to meet this objective. Beveridge had believed that a comprehensive national insurance framework would lead to a gradual reduction of means-tested benefits, in particular national assistance (renamed supplementary benefit in 1966). However, successive governments kept the level of flat-rate insurance benefits below the subsistence level, so that the number of those relying on supplementary benefits has steadily

13 Beveridge Report, para 9.

increased from 1 million in 1948 to 4 million in 1982. The means-tested benefit, rather than contributory social insurance, provides the minimum level of income for the poorest section of injured and disabled persons. Moreover, the Beveridge scheme failed to make adequate provision for the long-term disabled. This has led governments, in response to a variety of pressure groups, to make ad hoc provision for specific sections of the disabled so as to reduce their dependence on supplementary benefits.[14]

Another controversial aspect of Beveridge's policy has been his principle of flat-rate 'subsistence' benefits. There is a difference in social philosophy between those who believe that social security should operate as a means for redistributing resources from the rich to the poor and those who see it as being akin to the tort system in compensating losses of earnings and support so as to maintain an existing structure of income and wealth. For adherents of the redistributive philosophy, 'needs' must be defined in terms of relative deprivation from the overall level of earnings, and benefits should be conferred upon deprived groups such as the sick and disabled without either means tests or income differentials. For supporters of the compensation approach, benefits should be related to earnings, as a reward for individual initiative or, from a slightly different perspective, as part of the 'social wage' which reflects existing earnings differentials established by the process of collective bargaining between employers and trade unions. Earnings-related benefits reduce the need for private insurance.

The earnings-related principle was introduced in 1966 for short-term sickness and unemployment benefits, and this was later extended to some other benefits including invalidity pensions. This departure from the Beveridge scheme brought the British social security system closer to

14 See below, p 183.

that on the Continent.[15] However, there was a radical reversal in 1982 when earnings-related supplements were abolished in respect of short-term benefits such as sickness benefit. This was designed to save public expenditure and to facilitate bringing the relevant benefits into taxation. The underlying issue between redistributive flat-rate benefits and income insurance remains unresolved.

The financing of benefits has also departed from the Beveridge scheme. There has been a marked shift from the insurance concept to the use of progressive taxation as a source of revenue. Although insurance was central to the liberal idea of 'self-help', Beveridge himself pointed out that the analogy between private and social insurance is a false one. Private insurance premiums are related to the degree of risk depending upon individual circumstances (eg health, age, occupation), while social insurance contributions are generally not risk-related. Moreover, apart from earnings-related pensions, social insurance benefits, unlike private insurance, are not closely related to the contributions paid. The belief that social insurance is a form of self-provision overlooks the fact that only a small part of the cost is met by the individual's contributions, and full benefits can be obtained after a few months contributions.[16]

Beveridge was committed to the insurance principle and rejected taxation based upon the ability to pay as a means of financing benefits; but his system of flat-rate contributions failed to generate an adequate level of benefits. As a result, there has been a shift to a system of earnings-related contributions; the liability to contributions has been

---

15 The principle of income insurance rather than flat-rate support has also been adopted in the New Zealand Accident Compensation Scheme, under which earnings-related benefits are payable (after the first week for which the employer is responsible). The New Zealand scheme is unique in basing this on loss of earning capacity, on the analogy of the common law tort system. See further Chap 7.

16 Pearson Report, vol 1, para 175.

extended; and a special levy has been imposed upon employers. Contributions are now analogous to a form of ear-marked taxation. Reliance on general taxation as a source of revenue has also increased with the growth of non-contributory benefits, such as supplementary benefit.

The balance between private and public provision of welfare, the redistributive and compensatory approaches to benefits, and the crucial question of cost, involve political choices. We shall return to these issues in the next chapter. We must now describe some specific features of benefits payable to those suffering personal injuries, and then consider the problem of overlapping sources of compensation.

INDUSTRIAL INJURIES

The substance of the law on industrial injuries benefits remained largely the same from 1946 to 1982, when the first of a number of proposed steps to restructure the scheme in favour of the long-term disabled was taken. The traditional policy, originating with the Workmen's Compensation Acts and perpetuated by the Beveridge scheme, has been to give preferential treatment to those injured at work. Although Beveridge believed that the ideal solution was a 'completely unified scheme for disability without demarcation by the cause of disability',[17] he saw reasons for special treatment of work-related injuries: a special scheme for workers had existed for 45 years; some industries were particularly dangerous; and workers might be injured while under orders. The principle of industrial preference was embodied in the post-war legislation which replaced workmen's compensation. In order to obtain the high-rate benefits, there must be a personal injury caused by an

17 Beveridge Report, para 80.

accident arising out of and in the course of employment. Certain prescribed industrial diseases are also covered.

The Pearson Commission thought that the arguments for the preference 'carry a good deal less weight now'.[18] The scheme is not limited to dangerous trades, and in any event it seems illogical in a social security system to relate the amount of compensation to the degree of hazard. The argument that the worker is 'under orders' and so deserves more is unconvincing. The student who slips and is injured on the defective floor of his college premises incurs the risk no more voluntarily than the worker who slips on the factory floor. The decisive argument has, however, proved to be an economic one. It was estimated that in 1980 the administration of the industrial injuries scheme absorbed 13.3% of benefit expenditure compared with only 4.2% for the general contributory social security scheme.[19] Moreover, as a result of inflation, in terms of 1982–3 rates, industrial injury benefit was only 12% higher than state sickness benefit, compared with 75% in 1947. The government accepted these comments and in 1981 committed itself to a number of important changes, removing short-term benefits from the scope of the scheme and improving the position of the long-term disabled.[20]

The first step was taken in the Social Security and Housing Benefits Act 1982. This abolished, from April 1983, short-term industrial injury benefit. Those off work for short periods, whatever the cause of their injury or disease, must rely on statutory sick pay (SSP) which the employer is obliged to pay for the first eight weeks' absence in each tax

---

18 Pearson Report, vol 1, para 290; and for a general review, Richard Lewis in (1980) 43 MLR 514 at 525–9.
19 *Industrial Injuries Compensation*, DHSS Green Paper, 1980; see generally Richard Lewis in [1980] J Soc Wel L 330.
20 *Reform of the Industrial Injuries Scheme* Cmnd 8402; proposals have also been made in respect of industrial diseases in *Industrial Disease: a Review of the Schedule and the Question of Individual Proof* Cmnd 8393.

year, at a prescribed minimum level.[1] Thereafter, state sickness benefit is payable, but if the injury is due to a work-related accident or prescribed industrial disease the claimant need not satisfy any contribution conditions. Thirteen weeks' after the accident, disablement benefit may be payable. This is a weekly pension (or lump sum where there is less than 20% disablement) for the loss of mental or physical faculty resulting from the work-related accident or industrial disease. There is a fixed tariff: for example, absolute deafness represents 100% disablement; loss of one eye, the other being normal, 40%; and amputation of the tip of a middle finger without loss of bone, 4%. In this we have a striking fulfilment of Holmes' predication that the law would return to the Anglo-Saxon expedient of settling claims by pre-appointed *bót*.[2] The benefit is payable according to the degree of disablement, the rates being fixed according to assumed rather than actual needs. However, to some extent there is also compensation for the loss of earnings in the form of a special hardship allowance (which the government proposes to replace with a more appropriately called 'reduced earnings allowance')[3] payable if the claimant is unable to return to his regular job and cannot work at a job of similar standard. Disablement benefit can also be increased by certain other allowances, such as for constant attendance (in case of 100% disablement), exceptionally severe disablement, and hospital treatment.

So we see that the industrial preference, which makes it necessary to establish the cause of the accident or disease, remains significant in two respects: (1) to obtain state sickness benefit, after eight weeks' absence, when the normal

1 See below, p 185.
2 In (1897) 10 Harv LR at 1467. In the laws of Ethelbert (AD 600) 12 shillings had to be paid for striking off an ear, 50 shillings for an eye, 4 shillings for a middle finger. *Bót* means 'betterment' and represents the sum paid to buy back the peace the offender has breached.
3 *Reform of the Industrial Injuries Scheme* para 39.

contribution requirements have not been satisfied; and (2) in order to receive disablement benefit and the associated allowances 13 weeks after the accident.

SICKNESS AND DISABILITY

The Beveridge scheme, as implemented in post-war legislation, improved sickness benefit and made provision for dependants' allowances. Benefit was payable for an unlimited period but the distinction between short-term and long-term benefits was retained in the form of more stringent contribution conditions after a year's entitlement to benefit.[4] In 1971, an invalidity benefit was introduced for those incapable of work for more than six months. This supplemented the standard flat-rate benefit by an allowance graded according to the age at which the claimant became incapable of work. It was based not on the idea of replacing lost earnings but on the assumed greater financial commitments of younger persons and their inability, due to misfortune, to save money for retirement. The invalidity benefit is available with fewer contribution conditions than the standard benefit, and dependants are treated more generously.

A feature of the present British system is that it does not provide, in the case of ordinary sickness and disability, for comprehensive income maintenance according to the degree of disablement. The emphasis has been on identifying specific needs and meeting them with non-contributory benefits. For example, an attendance allowance (introduced in 1970) provides for those severely disabled persons who

---

4 Between 1966 and 1982 another distinction was that earnings-related supplement was payable for only the first 26 weeks of incapacity, but this supplement has been abolished: see above, p 178.

require frequent attention,[5] and this has been complemented (since 1975) by a non-contributory invalid care allowance for those who are unable to work because they have to stay at home to care for a severely disabled relative. A non-contributory invalidity pension (introduced in 1975) is to be replaced in 1984 by a new benefit called severe disablement allowance for those continuously incapable of work and disabled to the extent of 80% for more than 28 weeks, and also for those disabled for 28 weeks on or before their twentieth birthday. Mobility allowance (since 1975) is payable to severely disabled persons unable or virtually unable to walk.

The importance of pressure groups in securing provision for the needy may be illustrated by the Vaccine Damage Payments Act 1979 which provides for payment of a lump sum (currently £10,000) to anyone who suffers severe disablement as a result of vaccination against certain diseases. This legislation followed extensive campaigns on behalf of this group of the disabled. The resulting scheme is a narrowly defined one, restricted to children who are 80% brain damaged. Another illustration is the Family Fund, set up in 1973 on a non-statutory basis as a result of the public debate on the thalidomide victims. The Fund, administered by an independent charitable body but financed from general taxation, complements the provision of services and benefits to families having the care of a child with a severe congenital disability. An example of a scheme introduced specifically because of the deficiencies of the tort system is the Pneumoconiosis etc (Workers' Compensation) Act 1979, which grants lump sum payments to workers suffering from certain dust-related diseases who cannot claim tort

---

5 This is payable (since 1973) at a higher rate where the attention is required both day and night.

damages because their former employers are no longer in business.

These sporadic responses to specific needs of different groups of long-term disabled persons may be contrasted with the recent trends towards withdrawing State support from those incapable of work owing to illness or injury for short periods. The major source of compensation for this group between 1946 and 1983 was sickness benefit for which both employed and self-employed persons, paying the requisite contributions, were eligible. The value of the benefit to high earners was considerably reduced by the withdrawal of earnings-related supplement in 1982, and benefits have been uprated below the rate of inflation. Since April 1983 sickness benefit has been partly replaced for employees by statutory sick pay (SSP), which employers are obliged to pay, up to prescribed minimum levels, for the first eight weeks' absence (after three waiting days) in any one tax year. During this period there is no entitlement to state sickness benefit.[6] The main justification put forward[7] was the reduction of administrative expenditure, by placing responsibility in private hands. However, it is doubtful whether the savings will be substantial because during the legislative process the government abandoned the original objective of offloading the costs of initial sickness on to employers without compensating them in full. The Social Security and Housing Benefits Act 1982 leaves the State with ultimate financial responsibility because employers can recoup the SSP they pay by deducting it from their social security contributions.[8]

6 The unemployed and self-employed, who have paid the requisite contributions, continue to be eligible for sickness benefit.
7 Green Paper *Income During Initial Sickness: a New Strategy* Cmnd 7864 (1980). Full details will be found in the DHSS booklet *Employer's Guide to Statutory Sick Pay* (NI 227).
8 See generally, Richard Lewis in (1982) 11 ILJ 245 especially at 253.

Another objective of SSP is to prevent the over-compensation of those employees who previously received both state sickness benefit and occupational sick pay. The extent of this overcompensation is frequently exaggerated: although about 80% of employees receive pay from their employers during some period of sickness absence, only about half of these receive payments which, when added to their State benefits, amount to their full wage.[9] The 1982 Act prevents the overlap, but does so only for the first eight weeks' absence; and employers remain free to pay above the minimum levels prescribed. There are three rates (depending on earnings), and, unlike State sickness benefit, SSP is subject to taxation and there are no increases for dependants. Those with large families, those on low pay, and those in small firms without occupational sick pay schemes which pay above the minimum levels, are likely to suffer a significant drop in income.[10] Those still incapable of work after eight weeks' absence may claim State sickness benefit.

OVERLAP WITH TORT DAMAGES

Compensation may be payable from two or more sources in respect of the same injury. A survey for the Pearson Commission indicated that about three-quarters of the recipients of tort damages also receive social security

9 Lewis, op cit at 251, who also points out the patchy character of occupational sick pay schemes, and the fact (revealed by a DHSS survey) that 11% of men and 19% of women covered could claim sickness benefit on top of full basic earnings.
10 Lewis, op cit at 250–52. Those absent for repeated short periods are also worse off under SSP than sickness benefit. Neither can be claimed unless there are four or more days' incapacity. Two or more periods of absence can be linked only if separated by less than two weeks in the case of SSP, compared with an eight weeks' gap allowed in the case of sickness benefit (before 1980 this was 13 weeks).

benefits,[11] and 2% receive compensation from four or more sources, the common combination being occupational sick pay, social security benefits, private insurance and tort damages.[12]

This prompts the question whether tort damages should be reduced by other benefits received by the plaintiff, or alternatively whether those benefits should be reduced by tort damages. One possible approach would be to allow the plaintiff to keep the tort damages and the other sources of compensation. This is the current practice in relation to gifts (eg the proceeds of a disaster fund), as well as benefits received under private insurance policies, occupational pensions, and benefits under permanent health insurance schemes, none of which are deductible from tort damages.[13] The earliest rationale of this approach was retributive: the tortfeasor 'deserved' to pay and should not be allowed to benefit from the benevolence of another or from private arrangements for which the plaintiff had paid.[14] Later notions of causation were invoked: it was said that the benefit fell to be disregarded if there was insufficient causal connection between the tort and the benefit conferred by the third party. So the 'cause' was said to be the donor's benevolence and not the tort. In the case of a gift or benefit intended to replace something to which a financial value cannot readily be ascribed (eg grief or a loss of amenity) there is no real danger of 'double compensation' because there is no precise monetary assessment of what is being 'compensated',[15] but where the gift or private insurance benefits

11 Pearson Report, vol 2, para 52; see generally, P. J. Davies in [1982] J Soc Wel L 152.
12 The introduction of SSP will reduce the overlap between sick pay and social security; see above.
13 The Pearson Report, vol 1, paras 516, 523, 529, 530, recommended no change in respect of these benefits.
14 Per Tindal CJ in *Yates v Whyte* (1838) 4 Bing NC 272 at 283, 132 ER 793 at 797; see too Lord Reid in *Parry v Cleaver* [1970] AC 1 at 14.
15 Atiyah *Accidents, Compensation and the Law* (3rd edn, London, 1980) pp 456–7.

replaces lost earnings or medical expenses the objection usually raised from the welfare standpoint is that the same need should not be met twice over.

While this objection has not prevailed in respect of private provision it has been particularly influential in the case of social security benefits since these are based on the concept of welfare. A logical solution would be to deny social security benefits to a person who is adequately compensated by tort damages in respect of a quantifiable loss. However, at present social security benefits (apart from supplementary benefits) are paid without regard to the claimant's other resources such as tort damages. This reflects the contributory basis of social insurance, as well as the administrative problems which would arise if tort damages had to be taken into account when assessing contributory benefits. For these reasons the favoured approach has been to deduct certain social security benefits from tort damages. The Law Reform (Personal Injuries) Act 1948, s 2(1) enacted a compromise solution.[16] In assessing damages for loss of income due to personal injury, the court must take into account one-half of the value of certain social security benefits[17] for five years from the time when the cause of action accrued. SSP is apparently not deductible, but most other payments by an employer under the contract of employment are liable to be deducted from tort damages.[18] No deduction is made from a

---

16 The majority of a Departmental Committee on Alternative Remedies, Cmd 6860 (1946), had proposed that tort damages should be reduced by other compensation, or alternatively the compensation should be reduced by tort damages. A minority wanted social security benefits to be disregarded altogether in assessing common law damages.

17 The current list is industrial disablement benefit, sickness benefit, invalidity benefit and non-contributory invalidity pension.

18 Eg continued payment of wages: *Turner v Ministry of Defence* (1969) 113 Sol Jo 585. One way around this has been for the employer to specify that the payment is a loan repayable to him in the event of a successful claim for tort damages: *Browning v War Office* [1963] 1 QB 750, [1962] 3 All ER 1089.

damages award under the Fatal Accidents Act 1976 for any social security payments.[19] The question of deduction of other social security benefits has been left to judicial decision. The current practice is to deduct unemployment benefit[20] and supplementary benefit[1] but not attendance and mobility allowances[2] nor State retirement pensions.[3]

The Pearson Commission sought to rationalise the rules by recommending that the full value of social security benefits should be deducted from tort damages. Each category of social security benefit, for loss of earnings, expenses and non-pecuniary loss, would be deducted in assessing the corresponding portion of the tort award.[4] This would allow for 'full co-ordination' of the compensation provided by tort and social security.[5] It would reduce the function of tort to that of supplementing the no-fault compensation already provided by the State, and many small claims would not be worth pursuing through the tort system at all.[6] In 1981 the government announced its intention to implement this recommendation.[7] A proposal[8] that any saving attributable to maintenance at public expense in a hospital, nursing home or other institution should be set off against tort damages has already been followed.[9] On the other hand, in assessing the reasonableness of medical expenses the court must disregard the possibility of using the National Health Service,[10] so a claim may be made for

---

19 Fatal Accidents Act 1976, s 4, as amended. See above, p 86.
20 *Nabi v British Leyland (UK) Ltd* [1980] 1 All ER 667, [1980] 1 WLR 529.
 1 *Lincoln v Hayman* [1982] 2 All ER 819, [1982] 1 WLR 488.
 2 *Bowker v Rose* (1978) 122 Sol Jo 147.
 3 *Parry v Cleaver* [1970] AC 1 at 15.
 4 Pearson Report, vol 1, paras 484, 487, 488.
 5 Pearson Report, vol 1, para 475.
 6 Pearson Report, vol 1, para 279.
 7 *Reform of the Industrial Injuries Scheme* Chap 8.
 8 Pearson Report, vol 1, para 512.
 9 Administration of Justice Act 1982, s 5.
10 Law Reform (Personal Injuries) Act 1948, s 2(4).

private medical treatment or nursing. There is apparently no intention to implement a proposal by the Pearson Commission that private medical expenses should be recoverable only if it was reasonable on medical grounds to incur these.[11]

Another solution to the problem of overlapping benefits which reconciles the retributive and compensatory approaches to damages, is to limit the injured person to an indemnity for his actual loss while ensuring that the tortfeasor pays the full measure of damages. This can be achieved in several ways. One is to allow the collateral source of compensation a right of recoupment from the tortfeasor. This is done in the case of property and fire insurance by subrogating the insurer to the rights of the insured against the tortfeasor to the extent that the insurer has made payment. Under personal accident and life policies, however, there are generally no rights of subrogation.[12] Nor does the National Health Service or the Department of Health and Social Security have the right to claim reimbursement from tortfeasors.[13] An alternative method would be to require the victim compensated by tort damages to reimburse the benefactor but this has not generally been the practice in Britain.

The picture which emerges is of a complex variety of sources of compensation for personal injury and death, each pursuing conflicting aims, and with no overall theory or strategy, resulting in overcompensation of some and under-compensation or no compensation at all for others. The law relating to compensation for misfortunes is ripe for reform.

---

11 Pearson Report, vol 1, para 342.
12 See generally above, Chap 5, p 166.
13 In many other countries tortfeasors are compelled to reimburse the collateral source: eg under Australian and Canadian Workers' Compensation statutes, the employer or his insurer has an independent right of indemnity: see Fleming *XI International Encyclopaedia of Comparative Law* Chap 11.

7 Theory and the future

All theory, dear friend, is grey, but the golden tree of actual life springs ever green.

Goethe *Gretchen am Spinnrad*

PATHS OF REFORM

The fundamental question facing reformers is the balance between tort and other sources of compensation, in particular social security. No modern society relies exclusively on tort; and one country with a common law background has abolished the tort action for personal injury and death, replacing it with a comprehensive no-fault accident compensation scheme.

The New Zealand Accident Compensation Act, in operation since 1974 and amended on various occasions, provides no-fault benefits for accidental injury and death.[1] These are paid out of three public funds: one for earners, another for victims of motor vehicle accidents, and a third for those not covered by the first two funds (eg housewives

---

1 The scheme follows the main recommendations of the Royal Commission of Inquiry on Compensation for Personal Injury in New Zealand (the Woodhouse Report) (1967). The background is described in detail by G. W. R. Palmer *Compensation for Incapacity: a study of law and social change in New Zealand and Australia* (Wellington, 1979), and there is a valuable commentary on the operation of the scheme by Terence G. Ison *Accident Compensation. A Commentary on the New Zealand Scheme* (London, 1980); see too, Pearson Report, vol 3, Chap 10, pp 183–205; and D. R. Harris in (1974) 37 MLR 361.

injured at home).[2] Before the scheme was introduced the main sources of compensation, apart from tort, were workers' compensation (at relatively low rates) and social security payable only to those who could satisfy a means test. The new earners' scheme compares favourably with the former sources of compensation, but non-earners who would previously have been lucky enough to prove fault in a tort action (eg a housewife intending to return to the labour market) are less generously treated.

The aim has been to give something to all accident victims by rationalising the various sources of compensation and utilising the savings made by the abolition of tort which was costly to administer. The scheme provides income insurance in the form of weekly benefits (after the first week for which the employer is responsible) at a rate of 80% of pre-accident earnings (subject to a maximum amount), together with a relatively small lump sum for impairment of bodily function and another lump sum for loss of amenities or capacity for enjoying life including disfigurement, and for pain and suffering.

The main shortcomings of the New Zealand scheme are the limitation, on grounds of cost, to 'accidents' and certain occupational diseases and those resulting from medical misadventure;[3] some inadequacies in the administration of the scheme;[4] and the method of financing.[5] Despite these criticisms, the general verdict is that it has been a success;[6] and there has been no move to reverse it.

An even more radical proposal was made in Australia in

2 See below, p 209, regarding the financing of these funds.
3 See below, p 209.
4 Administration is in the hands of an Accident Compensation Corporation with appeals to an Appeals Authority and thence (with leave) to the Supreme Court. Ison, op cit pp 81, 94, is critical of the absence of hearings before initial claims decisions, while F. Sutcliffe in (1977) 7 NZULR 305 at 324 criticises the absence of a clear standard of proof.
5 See below, p 209.
6 See in particular, Ison, op cit p 187.

1974 by a Committee of Inquiry[7] which advocated a national scheme of compensation for all incapacity, whether caused by sickness, disease or congenital defect. This scheme would replace tort. A National Compensation Bill embodying these proposals lapsed on the change of government in 1975 and is unlikely to be revived. Instead, largely for reasons of cost and the tremendous opposition from groups with a stake in the present compensation systems, the path of reform in Australia seems likely to be gradualist, with a stage by stage introduction of no-fault schemes for particular types of misfortune.[8]

In the United States, dissatisfaction with the tort system has led to a refashioning of compensation for motor accidents, using private rather than State insurance.[9] The no-fault plans for compensating traffic victims vary considerably in detail but their common feature is that they provide a system of first-party insurance, regardless of fault, for basic economic loss. The injured occupants of a car, or pedestrians struck by it, claim against the car's insurer. One type, the 'add on' plan, merely adds no-fault benefits to

---

7 *Compensation and Rehabilitation in Australia.* Report of the National Committee of Inquiry (the Woodhouse–Meares Report) (1974); see Palmer, op cit and Pearson Report, vol 3, Chap 9, pp 153–81.

8 In Victoria and Tasmania limited no-fault road accident compensation schemes, funded from third-party insurance premiums and administered by a State agency, have operated since 1974, but common law rights remain intact with provisions to avoid overlap. In the Northern Territory tort claims for pecuniary loss arising from injury or death in motor accidents were abolished in 1979, in return for no-fault benefits, and there is an election whether to waive damages for pain and suffering in return for a limited lump sum payment. In New South Wales, the Law Reform Commission in a Working Paper *A Transport Accident Scheme for New South Wales* (1983), has proposed a no-fault scheme for motor, rail and ferry accidents in that State, accompanied by the abolition of common law claims in respect of those accidents.

9 The main inspiration came from the blueprint by R. E. Keeton and J. O'Connell *Basic Protection for the Traffic Victim* (Boston, 1965); see Pearson Report, vol 3, pp 56–72 and annex 2 for details. Workmen's Compensation is provided under State and territorial laws broadly similar to the British system before 1948, but in some States as the sole remedy.

existing motor insurance policies, leaving intact the right to sue in tort.[10] This no-fault insurance, found in nine American States, is usually sufficient to meet basic economic losses in the case of minor injuries, and so discourages tort actions with a corresponding reduction in the cost of liability insurance. 'Add on' plans are of little help to those with severe injuries. This led some 16 States, between 1971 and 1976, to adopt 'mixed' plans which go further by partially abolishing tort liability in return for no-fault benefits. Tort claims are allowed only above a certain threshold expressed in financial limits (eg $500 medical expenses and $5,000 non-economic losses) sometimes coupled with requirements that the victim must have died or suffered permanent injury or, in some States, that he must have been incapable of working for more than six months. The effect is that tort is retained only for serious cases. The consequent savings in the cost of liability insurance premiums have generally been greater than the extra costs of providing no-fault benefits. Accordingly the schemes have proved attractive to insurance companies in a period of declining profitability of motor insurance business.

The main advantages of these no-fault schemes over the fault-based tort system are that they ensure that nearly all traffic victims receive compensation for basic economic losses; they bring about a saving in insurance premiums; and they achieve rapid compensation through a system of periodical payments. Studies of the operation of some of the schemes[11] suggest that the number of tort trials has been

10 'Add on' plans were pioneered in the Canadian province of Saskatchewan (1946) followed 25 years later by Ontario and then other provinces: see Linden *Canadian Tort Law* (Toronto, 1977) pp 529–43. Some Canadian schemes are administered by government agencies; these were the model for Victorian and Tasmanian schemes, above.

11 A. I. Widiss et al *No-Fault Automobile Insurance in Action: the experiences in Massachussets, Florida, Delaware and Michigan* (New York, 1977). Cp. E. M. Landes in (1981) 11 J Leg Stud 253, for a defence of tort claims in motor accidents.

greatly reduced. However, the continued, albeit attenuated, operation of tort law and the retention of the fault principle as the basis for arbitration in the settling-up process between insurers means that the savings are relatively limited.

It had been widely expected that in the United Kingdom the Royal Commission on Civil Liability and Compensation for Personal Injury (under the chairmanship of Lord Pearson), appointed in 1973, would propose a rationalisation of the many different statutory and common law compensation schemes.[12] Instead, after deliberating for five years, the Commission made recommendations that, although amounting to 188 in number, were disappointingly modest in purpose. It took the view[13] that its terms of reference precluded it from proposing universal compensation. Neither the United States' no-fault plans nor the New Zealand scheme were regarded as transplantable to the United Kingdom, with its comprehensive National Health Service and extensive social security benefits.[14] Instead, the Commission's strategy was to examine the case for extending particular categories of no-fault provision. It concluded that a considerable shift of emphasis from the tort to the social security system was desirable.[15] This included an improvement of the industrial injuries system, the introduction of a no-fault road accident scheme administered by the Department of Health and Social Security,

---

12 D. R. Harris in *Accident Compensation after Pearson* (eds D. K. Allen, C. J. Bourn, J. H. Holyoak) (London, 1979) at pp 85–9, lists over 30 such categories of compensation, to which the Pearson proposals would have added a further seven.

13 Pearson Report, vol 1, para 239. This was unnecessarily restrictive: see A. I. Ogus, P. Corfield and D. R. Harris in (1978) 7 ILJ 143 at 144.

14 Pearson Report, vol 1, paras 232–6. Cp. R. Hasson in (1979) 6 Brit J Law and Soc 119, and M. Franklin in (1975) 27 Stanford LR 653 who point to the more important criterion of accident rates, in respect of which New Zealand does not appear to differ significantly from other countries.

15 Pearson Report, vol 1, para 1722.

and a special benefit for severely handicapped children. But the Commission favoured the retention of tort liability, even for those covered by no-fault (social security) schemes, and proposed the extension of strict tort liability for certain new categories.[16] Many of the recommendations were aimed at removing the overlap between different sources of compensation, but nothing was proposed that would have reduced the complexity of the law relating to compensation.

Developments since the Report make it increasingly unlikely that tort will 'wither away' as improvements are made in the social security system. On the contrary, the privatisation of short-term sickness benefit, as well as the fall in the real value of social security benefits, may increase the attractiveness of tort actions for making good basic economic losses. The new bereavement award and other minor improvements in the assessment of tort damages[17] also point to the relative permanency of the law of tort in this field. There appears to be no present intention to implement the main recommendations of the Pearson Commission, let alone to undertake more drastic reforms.

This hiatus in law reform has led to a revival of interest in the theoretical debate about the rationale of tort law. The threat of collectivist solutions has led in the United States to what one scholar aptly describes as a 'desperate scholarly rearguard action to preserve a traditional system of individualism in a changing world'.[18] In Britain too there is still a powerful strand of opinion believing that there will always be a role for tort, even in securing compensation for personal injuries, because it embodies 'the socially valuable principle that, where a person negligently or intentionally causes injuries to another, amends should be made for the

---

16 See below, p 201.
17 By the Administration of Justice Act 1982, Pt I. See above, pp 80 ff.
18 I. England in (1980) 9 J Leg Stud 27 at 68. Cp. G. Calabresi in (1978) 56 Texas LR 519.

consequences of his fault',[19] and because tort induces a 'sense of responsibility for the effect of one's actions on others' which is 'an essential element in a civilised community'.[20] This makes it desirable to consider some of the principal theoretical issues and their practical implications.

CORRECTIVE AND DISTRIBUTIVE JUSTICE

In the debate about the future of tort law one hears echoes of the philosophical arguments between the Kantians and the Utilitarians. The one opinion, which views the principal goal of tort law as 'corrective justice', concentrates on restoring or maintaining a balance between the wrongful injurer and the victim for moral reasons.[1] The other focuses on whether a rule of liability or non–liability enhances overall social welfare. In the 1950s and 1960s, torts scholars who believed that the law of negligence has never con-formed fully to the requirements of a moral system, emphasised the distributional function of tort rules coupled with the practice of insurance in spreading the costs of accidents. In the 1970s the utilitarian approach took on a distinctly economic flavour. Calabresi[2] and other lawyer-economists regard the principal function of tort law as being to reduce the costs of accidents. Calabresi divided this goal into three sub–goals: first, the reduction of the number and severity of accidents; second, the reduction of the costs to society (usually in the form of compensation) resulting from

---

19 Pearson Report, vol 1, para 1716 (the long-term view of some of the Commissioners).
20 Pearson Report, vol 1, para 1717; and see J. A. Jolowicz in *Accident Compensation after Pearson* 35 at 36–7.
1 For a full discussion see P. Cane in (1982) 2 Oxf J Leg Stud 30 at 32 who characterises conduct-based fault liability as corrective rather than distributive.
2 G. Calabresi *The Costs of Accidents: a Legal and Economic Analysis* (New Haven, 1970) pp 26–136.

accidents; and third the reduction of the costs of administering the treatment of accidents. The economic approaches seek ways of reducing accident costs by deterring 'accident-prone' activities, either by specific prohibition or regulation of those activities enforced by penalties, or by making those activities expensive and thereby less attractive to those who can avoid them.

The underlying assumption of the economic approaches to tort law, that individual rights should be determined according to the collective goal of maximising social welfare, has been challenged by those whose starting point is that the tort system exists 'to protect individual liberty and private property' by 'rectifying changes in entitlements brought about by impermissible means'.[3] For the American writer Epstein,[4] corrective justice is and should be the basis of tort law: 'rendering to each person whatever redress is required because of the violation of his rights by another'.[5] According to Epstein, individuals should be free to choose self-interested courses of action, even though this conflicts with social good. He rejects cost and utility as grounds for liability in tort because they restrict individual freedom. However, he recognises that 'the liberty of one person ends when he causes harm to another'.[6] This leads him to advocate a theory of strict liability. His method is to construct an idealised model of tort analogous to the old writ system. If B causes A harm, then B is presumptively liable. 'Cause' is defined in a few primitive forms. Proof of

3 R. Epstein in (1975) 4 J Leg Stud at 441; see generally on 'rights-based' conceptions of justice, P. Cane in (1982) 2 Oxf J Leg Stud 30.

4 R. Epstein in (1973) 2 J Leg Stud 151, (1974) 3 J Leg Stud 165 (both reprinted in *A Theory of Strict Liability* (San Francisco, 1980)); (1975) 4 J Leg Stud 391; but see the modifications of his views in (1979) 8 J Leg Stud 49 and (1982) 96 Harv LR 1717; see too Frederick L. Sharp in (1976) U Tor L 84 (arguing that corrective justice supports the decision in *Rylands v Fletcher*).

5 (1979) 8 J Leg Stud at 50, 99.

6 (1973) 2 J Leg Stud at 203–4.

causation is made out by showing that B used force directly on A, or frightened A, or compelled another to use force or frighten him, or created a dangerous condition that resulted in harm to A. B can then assert a limited number of defences which show a contribution by A to his own injury (causation, assumption of risk) or that A trespassed on B's property (since the protection of property overrides A's liberty). On the other hand, defences such as necessity, compulsion, insanity and infancy or mistake are insufficient because they represent efforts by B to shift the cost of his own problems on to the shoulders of A. The apparent purpose of this formalistic system is to minimise the judicial discretion involved in balancing conflicting social values. Judgments are expected to be more precise and predictable.

Although Epstein rejects fault as a standard of liability, his notion of causation itself implies a moral judgment of blameworthiness. For example his paradigm of the creation of a dangerous condition involves three categories that require an evaluation of things which are 'dangerous' in themselves or because of their position or because they are 'defective'.[7] Many examples can be found in the law of negligence[8] and under the rule in *Rylands v Fletcher*,[9] to show that this involves the very kind of 'balancing' which Epstein wishes to avoid; and it is significant that in his writings on nuisance law, Epstein has conceded that the rules of liability have to be a compromise between corrective justice and utility.[10] Moreover, it can be said that his presumption of liability is not without parallels in the tort of negligence, for example when the notion res ipsa loquitur is applied to

---

7 *A Theory of Strict Liability* at 36.
8 Eg the old category of things dangerous per se current before the decision in *Donoghue v Stevenson*: see *Salmond and Heuston on the Law of Torts* (18th edn, London, 1981) pp 286–8.
9 See above, Chap 4, p 128.
10 (1979) 8 J Leg Stud 49; cp. R. Posner (1981) 10 J Leg Stud 187 who suggests that corrective justice must be a component part of economic theory.

damage caused by a thing under the defendant's control.[11] The attempt to apply this as an *exclusive* theory of liability ignores important ways of causing economic loss (eg by statements) and would exclude many cases of indirectly caused economic loss which are actionable at present. The most serious objection to the theory is that Epstein ignores the actual world of loss distribution, through private and social insurance, of which tort law is only a part.

Another attempt to resuscitate ideas of corrective justice is that by Fletcher who finds the ultimate rationale of tort liability in the idea that 'all individuals in society have the right to roughly the same degree of security from risk'.[12] From this he deduces that the general standard of liability should be the principle of 'reciprocity' of risks between the parties. The party subjecting the other to a disproportionate share of risk must compensate him. Certain creators of non-reciprocal risks are excused, for example if they were compelled to create the risk or did so through unavoidable ignorance.[13] 'Reciprocity' is said to require 'a single conclusion based on perceptions of similarities, of excessiveness, and of directness'.[14] An objection to this is that it is even more ambiguous than the negligence standard and certainly involves a finding as to the social value of different activities in order to decide what are reciprocal risks. The very examples Fletcher cites illustrate the difficulties. Are driving a car and riding a bicycle in the road reciprocal risks, and are the owning of a cat and a dog sufficiently reciprocal to excuse the dog owner from responsibility if the dog kills the cat?[15]

---

11 See above, Chap 4, p 115.
12 (1972) 85 Harv LR 537 at 550.
13 Ibid, at 553.
14 Ibid, at 573.
15 See the comment by G. Edward White *Tort Law in America. An Intellectual History* (New York, 1980) p 225: 'his example embodies a judgment based on the perceived comparative worth of dogs and cats in society'.

Fletcher's main concern is to prevent the tort system being used as a means of distributing accident losses.[16] As with Epstein, the theory turns a blind eye to the deep penetration that private and social insurance have made into the operation of tort law.

In Britain, too, there is a school of thought which advocates strict liability based on the creation of risks. But unlike the strict liability schemes of Epstein and Fletcher, an essential aspect of this proposal is that the traditional refusal of the courts to consider the factor of insurance should be reversed.[17] The courts would be required to pose the question in each case, 'Whose risk was it that this damage might occur?' in place of the present, 'Whose fault was it that this damage did occur?' and they would not have to assume that the defendant has to find the damages from his own pocket.[18] This approach recognises that the law of tort operates in a distributional way, and seeks to harness liability rules as a means of allocating the cost of risk-bearing. This is based on the view that it is fair that those who reap the benefits of an activity such a motoring should bear the costs.[19] A householder might be expected to carry the risk of falling down his own stairs; but if he is injured by an explosion of gas, it is argued that the cost of compensating him should be borne by other consumers of gas in the district, and so the Gas Board should be strictly liable.[20]

The Pearson Commission gave occasional hints of agreeing with this approach. For example, when recommending the strict liability of manufacturers for defective

---

16 (1972) 85 Harv LR at 547, n 40: 'what is at stake is keeping the institution of taxation distinct from the institution of tort litigation'.

17 J. A. Jolowicz in [1968] CLJ 50; and in *Accident Compensation after Pearson* at 41–42; cp. R. E. Keeton *Venturing to do Justice* (Cambridge, Mass, 1969) Chap 9.

18 Jolowicz in [1968] CLJ at 60.

19 P. Cane in (1982) 2 Oxf J Leg Stud at 47.

20 Jolowicz [1968] CLJ at 61.

products they took account of the fact that manufacturers were protected against potential liability and could be expected to pass on through prices the cost of insurance. 'We think it justifiable and sensible,' said the Commission, 'that consumers as a whole should pay for the cost of insuring against injuries caused by a product from which they benefit just as they pay for its other costs.'[1] Two other recommendations for strict liability – in respect of volunteers for medical research[2] and victims of vaccine damage[3] – were also explicitly based on the cost of risk-bearing. The Commission also proposed that strict liability be imposed upon the controllers of things or operations which are of an 'unusually hazardous nature' or which are 'likely, if they go wrong, to cause serious and extensive casualties'.[4] This is not dissimilar to the rule in *Rylands v Fletcher*, without the restrictions stated by Blackburn J.[5] However, the Commission rejected the idea of a general principle of liability for hazardous activities and, instead, recommended that there should be a statutory list of dangerous activities to which strict liability would attach.[6]

1　Pearson Report, vol 1, para 1233. The assumption that insurance is always readily available for products liability is dubious. For example, in the immediate aftermath of the decision in *Junior Books Ltd v Veitchi Co Ltd* [1983] 1 AC 520, [1982] 3 All ER 201, above, Chap 4, p 108, it was reported that manufacturers were having difficulties in obtaining insurance against liability for economic loss, and so would have to pass the cost of compensation directly to consumers.

2　Pearson Report, vol 1, para 1341.

3　Pearson Report, vol 1, para 1413. This was to be in addition to the proposed no-fault scheme; but only the latter has been implemented by the Vaccine Damage Payments Act 1979 (see above Chap 6, p 184).

4　Pearson Report, vol 1, para 1643. The Commission's proposals for strict liability in respect of accidents caused by commercial aircraft operators (vol 1, para 1129), and those caused by the movement of rolling stock on railways (vol 1, para 1186) also appear to be based on the hazardous operations principle.

5　See above, Chap 4, p 128; and Jolowicz *Accident Compensation after Pearson* at 48.

6　Pearson Report, vol 1, para 1651.

The absence of a coherent theory of strict liability is also reflected in the Commission's refusal to countenance the extension of strict liability to a number of other areas where this could be justified on the risk-bearing approach, such as road accidents,[7] medical injuries,[8] and occupiers' liability,[9] and the Commission's failure to propose a rationalisation of the existing categories in which there is strict liability.[10]

ECONOMIC EFFICIENCY

The economic analysis of tort law[11] has also so far failed to produce any convincing justification either for strict liability or for negligence as the foundation of liability. It is frequently argued that liability should be determined in a way which will lead to the most efficient allocation of resources. Optimum efficiency, in theory, is that achieved by a perfect market system.[12] An incentive to keep activities safe would be provided by placing the cost of accidents on the activities and persons who cause them –

---

7 Pearson Report, vol 1, paras 1060–8.
8 Pearson Report, vol 1, paras 1337–8.
9 Pearson Report, vol 1, |para 1567.
10 Pearson Report, vol 1, para 1670; see above, Chap 4, pp 116 ff.
11 There are several different views on the efficiency of the tort system. The literature is vast and rapidly expanding in Britain as well as North America. The following introductions are recommended: Roger Bowles *Law and the Economy* (Oxford, 1982) Chaps 2 and 7; Atiyah *Accidents, Compensation and the Law* (3rd edn, London, 1980) Chap 24; and C. Veljanovski in *The Economic Approach to Law* (eds P. Burrows and C. Veljanovski) (London, 1981) Chaps 5–7.
12 R. Dworkin in (1980) 9 J Leg Stud 191 points out that when lawyer-economists ask whether a rule of law is 'efficient' they generally do so in the sense of 'wealth-maximisation', ie goods and resources are in the hands of those who value them most, and someone values a good more if he is willing and able to pay more in money (or the equivalent of money) to have it, cp. F. I. Michelman in (1979) U Chi LR at 313–14, and R. S. Markovits in (1980) 8 Hofstra LR 811, and (1983) 11 Hofstra LR 667.

for example, by making power lawn-mower manufacturers liable for all damages caused by malfunctions of their mowers. In theory mower prices would rise and sales fall; some families would be induced to shift to manual mowers, the total amount of power mowing would be reduced, and the level of accidents would abate. Moreover, manufacturers might become choosy about customers, raising prices to non-institutional buyers or perhaps simply to obvious [incompetents]. . . . Finally, they would have an incentive to redesign mowers to provide safety features. A variety of market forces would be set in motion to lower the total loss through accidents.[13]

Calabresi argues that the costs of accidents should be placed on those acts or activities which could avoid accident costs most cheaply. Once the cheapest cost avoider is identified that person would be strictly liable.[14] Although he has suggested some guidelines,[15] the identification would not always be easy. For example, would a blanket decision to make manufacturers of mowers strictly liable lessen the incentive on users to use mowers safely?[16]

The importance of the theory of 'market deterrence' is frequently exaggerated. It does not mean that all policy decisions should be guided by the goal of optimising the use of resources. Calabresi himself emphasises that the direct prohibition or control by public authority of certain behaviour may often be preferable, and that there are other important goals in accident compensation systems such as justice,[17] cutting administrative costs and cushioning the

---

13 Leonard Ross in (1971) 84 Harv LR 1322, reviewing Calabresi, op cit.
14 G. Calabresi and J. T. Hirschoff in (1972) 81 Yale LJ 1055; Calabresi in (1975) 84 Yale LJ 656.
15 *The Costs of Accidents* at 140–2; for an attempt to apply Calabresi's thesis see *Union Oil Co v Oppen* 501 F 2d 558 (9th Cir, 1974), criticised by R. Posner in (1979) 46 U Ch LR at 297–301.
16 R. Posner in (1973) 2 J Leg Stud 205 at 214.
17 Calabresi would accord a higher priority to 'justice' than to a cost-reduction criterion which was morally unacceptable: (1980) 8 Hofstra LR 553; R. Posner in (1981) 10 J Leg Stud 187 regards corrective justice as a component of his economic theory of tort law (see below, p 206, n 1).

impact of accidents on individuals by income redistribution. The argument of 'market deterrence' states only one desideratum. Experience shows that the protection of the consumer and the policing of safety regulations need an active government inspectorate backed by legal powers. Leaving enforcement to sporadic actions for damages by aggrieved individuals is not enough.

Moreover, the 'market deterrence' approach rests upon a number of questionable assumptions. One of these is that the aim and purpose of each individual is to get as much of a Good Thing for himself as possible, and that it is only necessary for everyone to pursue his own profit, under conditions of perfect competition, for the good of all to be attained.[18] But does the market behaviour of individuals reveal their preferences and how can we determine those preferences without making social value judgments?[19] It seems absurd to say that a rational person places a money value on his life when he chooses a less safe means of transport because it is cheaper by a sufficient amount than another available way of travelling.[20] We are also asked to make the unrealistic assumption that incomes are equally distributed. It is obvious that a stronger incentive will be required to induce a person to pay a given price if he is poor than if he is rich. The rich man in doubt whether to buy a 'safe' car, costing £10,000, in preference to a less safe one, costing £5,000, is weighing smaller preferences than a poor man who will have to forego many other wants if he chooses

18 Joan Robinson *Economic Philosophy* (Harmondsworth, 1964) p 53.
19 Ibid, p 50; see too R. Dworkin in (1980) 9 J Leg Stud 191, and A. Leff in (1974) 60 Virginia LR 451. For purposes of analysis we have to assume that individual preferences do not change over time!
20 This leads economists to define 'value of life' in terms of 'the aggregate willingness of those at risk to pay for a safer environment' or 'the value of saving a statistical life': cp. C. G. Veljanovski *The New Law-and-Economics Research Review* (SSRC, 1982) p 72.

the safer car. But most economic analysis of law proceeds on the assumption that distribution has been dealt with by tax or subsidies, and then shows as a matter of logic how a free market leads to maximum satisfaction. An extreme example is the so-called 'descriptive' or 'positive' economic theory of Posner that the common law standard of negligence creates incentives to avoid accidents in the cheapest possible way.[1] This is no more than an unsubstantiated speculation. Little evidence exists about the actual costs of accidents and the impact of liability rules on accident rates.[2]

Once the unrealistic assumptions of the efficiency model are recognised, it becomes impossible to draw any firm conclusion as to whether negligence or strict liability is more 'efficient'.

SOCIAL WELFARE

This discussion has done no more than to give the flavour of the current theoretical debate, but enough has been said to indicate that there is no convincing reason for tinkering with tort rules in order to produce decisions which are more acceptable either in terms of individual responsibility or economic efficiency.[3] The strongest objection to the law of tort, in relation to personal injury and death, comes from the

1 R. Posner *Economic Analysis of Law* (2nd edn, Boston, 1977); (1972) 1 J Leg Stud 29; (1975) 53 Texas LR 757; (1979) 46 U Chi LR 281; and William A. Landes and R. Posner in (1981) 15 Georgia LR 851.
2 Among the few and inconclusive studies are those by R. W. Grayson in (1973) 40 Insurance Counsel Journal 117; James R. Chelius in (1976) 5 J Leg Stud 293; E. Landes in (1982) 25 J Law and Econ 49; and (1982) 11 J Leg Stud 253. On the practical and logical problems of testing such theories, see Joan Robinson, op cit at 50–51, and C. G. Veljanovski (1980) 7 Brit J Law and Soc 158 at 180–7.
3 For a critique of the sweeping claims made for the different social effects of negligence and strict liability see Epstein in (1982) 95 Harv LR 1717; cp. R. Abel (1981) 8 Brit J Law and Soc 199.

philosophy of social welfare.[4] In the words of the Australian Woodhouse-Meares Report –

> The principle of community responsibility carries with it the natural corollary of comprehensive entitlement. Once society as a whole has accepted the need to support those of its members who are burdened by injury or illness they could not, in fairness, be . . . supported by differing levels of compensation, depending merely upon the fortuitous cause of the incapacity.[5]

The law of tort draws arbitrary lines between different *causes* of misfortune. It is concerned exclusively with injury or damage for which some individual human agent is responsible; and, as we have seen, fault must generally be attributed to that person. This excludes most diseases, since these are typically due to 'natural' causes. A child who is born disabled as a result of injuries suffered by his mother whilst he was *en ventre sa mère* may claim damages from the negligent injurer;[6] but a child born with a congenital disability may, at best, claim only social security benefits, and a mother who has had an 'unwanted' but normal child due to the negligent performance of a sterilisation operation cannot claim damages from the wrongdoer for the cost of the upbringing of that child.[7]

Once social responsibility for disease and disability is admitted, there seems to be no logical reason for making distinctions of this kind, or generally, between accidents – used here in the sense of untoward events – and

4 See above, Chap 6, p 172; and for an egalitarian approach to the control and sharing of risks, see R. Abel in (1982) 41 Maryland LR 699.
5 Paras 3 and 6.
6 See the Congenital Disabilities (Civil Liability) Act 1976 (in respect of births after 22 July 1976). The Act does not, however, permit a claim by a child for 'wrongful entry into life', eg that the doctors negligently failed to advise on abortion: s 1(2)(b); this is also the common law rule: *McKay v Essex Area Health Authority* [1982] QB 1166, [1982] 2 All ER 771.
7 *Udale v Bloomsbury Area Health Authority* [1983] 2 All ER 522, [1983] 1 WLR 1098.

diseases. The practical implication of this approach would be the introduction of a universal disability income, seen by one school of thought on the Pearson Commission as a 'desirable social objective'.[8] We are very far from this at present, even in social security law. The historical legacy of the industrial preference,[9] and the plethora of special schemes for groups of disabled persons,[10] means that current British practice is not equitable and a coherent strategy is lacking.

The creation of special no-fault road accident schemes in some countries extends the accident/illness distinction. One justification is said to be that since some groups (eg the industrially disabled) already enjoy preference, there can be no objection to an extension of this preference. Another argument is the scale of motor vehicle injuries, and the likelihood of severe injuries and prolonged disability from this cause. One could support these arguments if the introduction of a no-fault scheme for accidents was part of a long-term strategy towards comprehensive compensation. There is a danger that a piecemeal approach may result in the creation of vested rights to preferential treatment, as with the industrial injuries scheme. This may make it more difficult and expensive in the long run to introduce a comprehensive disability income at the improved level of benefits.[11] However, expediency might dictate a stage-by-stage approach, if no other line of advance is open.

---

8 Pearson Report, vol 1, paras 264, 1713.
9 See above, Chap 6, p 180.
10 See above, Chap 6, p 183.
11 The Pearson Commission estimated that there would be 185,000 beneficiaries of their proposed no-fault scheme, and these would retain their rights to sue in tort. Road accident victims are already preferentially treated because one in four of those injured on the roads receive tort compensation compared to one in ten of the industrially disabled and one in 67 of those injured elsewhere: Pearson Report, vol 1, para 78; vol 2, para 675. See generally, D. R. Harris *Accident Compensation after Pearson* at 85–95; and Richard Lewis in (1981) 10 Journal of Social Policy 161. See too, F. A. Trinidade in (1980) 46 LQR 581.

One must conclude that the present practice of the social security system, as well as the proposals for a no-fault road accident scheme, do not face up to the full implications of accepting social responsibility for misfortune. Just as the law of tort, as it operates in the world of private and social insurance, does not achieve the objective of individual responsibility,[12] so the social security system only partially meets the aim of social solidarity. At the same time, there is no empirical evidence to support the view that the abolition of tort liability for work accidents in several countries, and for all accidents in New Zealand, has made people any less responsible to their fellows. On the contrary, much of the energies once devoted to proving individual fault, can now be channelled towards the far more important tasks of rehabilitation of the disabled, and the prevention of accidents.

REDISTRIBUTING THE COSTS OF ACCIDENTS

A common argument for the piecemeal approach to reform – such as the exclusion of most diseases from the New Zealand scheme – is the cost factor. No one doubts that there is a limit on the total amount, including administrative costs, that the non-injured population are willing to transfer to the sick and disabled. Restrictions on public expenditure and on the use of public manpower make it extremely unlikely that governments will support additional Exchequer expenditure on compensation.[13]

---

12 See above, Chaps 4, p 135, and 5, p 168.
13 Pearson Report, vol 1, para 240. The Commission estimated (paras 1710–11) that the cost of extending the kind of scheme they proposed for road injuries to all kinds of accident would be £250m per annum (25% increase in tort and social security compensation) in addition to the extra £41m their proposals would cost. The extension to illness would cost an extra £2,000m per annum (80% increase in tort and social security compensation). These estimates were based on the continuation of tort as an 'add-on' to social security payments.

The key issue then, is whether the present total expenditure could be more effectively distributed. For example, it might be possible to concentrate on long-term benefits for all types of injury and disability at the expense of short-term incapacity.

The biggest savings of all could be made by the abolition of tort claims for personal injury and death. If all these savings were made available for the improvement of the social security system there would, according to the Pearson Commission's estimates, be enough to extend the industrial injuries scheme to all accidental injuries.[14] Compared to the social security system tort is an extremely costly way to distribute compensation. The Pearson Commission[15] found that the operating costs of the tort system amounted to about 85% of the total value of compensation payments. By contrast, the cost of administering social security benefits was about 11% of the value of compensation payments.[16] So a transfer from tort to social security would result in more money being available for accident victims.[17]

An objection to the abolition of tort liability is that the law of tort is better equipped than social security 'to compensate the widest possible range of the particular losses suffered by a given individual'.[18] This is, of course, distorted by the present practice of lump sum compensation

---

14 Pearson Report, vol 1, paras 1673–1708, and Atiyah *Accident Compensation after Pearson* at 242 and n 12. The total average tort payments 1971–6 were £202m per year, and it cost £175m per year to collect and distribute that sum.
15 Pearson Report, vol 1, paras 83, 121.
16 Pearson Report, vol 1, para 121 and vol 2, Chap 29.
17 A more limited approach would be to eliminate tort damages for non-pecuniary loss. This was estimated by the Pearson Commission to amount to £130m per year or more than half of all compensation. But it is not clear how far this would reduce administrative costs: vol 1, para 81. Parliament has, in fact, taken a step in the reverse direction by introducing damages for bereavement: see Chap 3, p 87.
18 Pearson Report, vol 1, para 1716.

for loss of earnings, which is bound to under- or over-compensate individuals.[19] Moreover, the awards for non-pecuniary loss, particularly for small claims, tend to over-compensate the victim. The New Zealand scheme has attempted a compromise between the common law and social security approaches by retaining small lump sum awards for loss or impairment of bodily function and for loss of amenities etc. This has been criticised[20] on the grounds that the assessment of the lump sums, requiring the exercise of administrative discretion, adds to costs and may act as a disincentive to rehabilitation because they are not assessed until the claimant has made the maximum possible physical recovery and his medical condition is stable. Against this, it can be argued that for many disabled persons a lump sum of this kind may have both material and therapeutic benefits. In the British industrial injuries system disablement benefit[1] compensates non-pecuniary loss but does so in a more objective way, excluding items like pain and suffering and using a fixed schedule of degrees of disablement. Although this has been criticised for distorting in favour of visible anatomical losses,[2] there is general satisfaction with this method in Britain, and it could be extended to a general scheme of compensation for misfortune.

If tort law were to be abolished, wholly or partially, the issue would have to be faced as to who should finance no-fault compensation. Some systems of financing have little or no redistributive effects, while others redistribute from higher to lower earners, or vice versa. An example of the first kind is first-party insurance for motor accidents like that adopted in the United States. The premiums are fixed in relation to the

---

19 See above, Chap 3, p 79.
20 Ison, op cit p 164.
 1 See above, Chap 6, p 182.
 2 Woodhouse–Meares Report, vol 1, para 400, advocating a new approach based on an American Medical Association report, which is more tailor-made to the needs of the individual claimants.

risk that the insured person and his passengers will be injured
or killed, taking account both of the risk of a claim arising
and of the level of benefits to be paid. Under this system
there is no subsidisation of the higher or lower earner.[3] An
example of the second kind is financing through general
taxation, such as the New Zealand supplementary scheme
for non-earners, which is redistributional from higher to
lower earners. A flat-rate system of social security benefits
also tends to redistribute downwards. A redistribution from
lower to higher earners would be likely to occur under the
proposed method of financing a no-fault road injuries
scheme in Britain by a levy on petrol (1p per gallon was
suggested).[4] This would mean that the costs would be
allocated according to the motorist's annual mileage and the
petrol consumption of his vehicle. Since this levy would not
be earnings-related and does not match the level of benefits
with the level of contributions, the average and higher
earner (who would get the maximum benefits under the
scheme) would be subsidised by the lower earner using a
motor vehicle for the average annual mileage –

> For instance, a low earner with a large, old car and a high mileage
> would be subsidising others, while the earner entitled to the
> maximum no-fault benefits who drives a small car for a low annual
> mileage would be subsidised.[5]

The disadvantages of this kind of redistribution might,
however, be outweighed by the relative cheapness and
administrative advantages of a petrol levy. This consideration led the majority of the Pearson Commission to reject
the alternative proposal of a percentage levy on motor
insurance premiums which, while using the expertise of

---

3 D. R. Harris *Accident Compensation after Pearson* at 109.
4 Pearson Report, vol 1, para 1054, subject to the important dissent of the
   economist member of the Commission, paras 1093–1102.
5 D. R. Harris *Accident Compensation after Pearson* at 108.

private insurers in fixing premiums according to the characteristics of the driver and vehicle, would be expensive to operate in relation to the amount raised.[6]

The other major consideration in determining the method of financing no-fault social security schemes is whether charges should be made according to the risk that an activity may cause an accident and the expected amount of compensation. For example, it is typical of third-party insurance for motor vehicles that premiums are fixed in relation to these factors. In the field of social insurance for industrial injuries it has for long been argued that the contributions by each industry should be related to the risks which those industries create, for example by variable premium rating according to the industry's accident record.[7] This would avoid the subsidisation of high-risk industries by low-risk ones, and would encourage incentives to avoid accident costs by taking safety precautions and the like.[8] But in Britain the majority of the Pearson Commission believed that the administrative costs of collecting variable premiums would be too great in relation to the relatively small effect on safety.[9] In Australia, the Woodhouse-Meares Report also rejected variable premium rating on the ground that 'in the end the community pays anyway'[10] and a similar view was taken by those who

---

6 The Commission rejected the New Zealand method of financing the Motor Vehicle Compensation Fund through a levy on every motor vehicle, collected as part of the motor vehicle licence fee, because the element of risk relation was too tenuous and a distinction is made only between broad categories of vehicle: Pearson Report, vol 1, para 1052.

7 For detailed consideration see P. S. Atiyah in (1975) 4 ILJ 1, 82.

8 See for a detailed consideration Jenny Phillips in (1976) 5 ILJ 148; and generally, G. Calabresi *The Costs of Accidents*.

9 Pearson Report, vol 1, para 904, again subject to the dissent of the economist member, paras 940–50.

10 Vol 1, paras 438–40, 495–7. In New Zealand provisions to surcharge employers with bad accident records are contained in the Accident Compensation Act.

established the industrial injuries scheme in Britain.[11] This rests on the view that no industry works in isolation from any other: the products of dangerous industries are used in many other industries and so an element of cross-subsidisation is justified.

THE REGULATORY APPROACH

Even if financial incentives, such as variable premium rates, were adopted in a comprehensive scheme for compensation for misfortune, this could never be more than a supplement to the specific regulation of accident-creating activities through criminal sanctions or the administrative enforcement of legislative standards.

One of the most important examples of regulation is the Health and Safety at Work etc Act 1974, which radically expanded the scope as well as the enforcement of legislation designed to protect workpeople. For the first time, the Act extended to the public at large the protection afforded by statutory duties owed by those carrying out work activities. The Health and Safety Executive has extensive powers of inspection and inquiry, and the Executive's inspectors have powers, not generally available before 1974, to require action to remedy a contravention of health and safety rules, or to stop a process that causes risk of serious personal injury until matters are put right.[12]

The control of pollution and the protection of the environment are tasks beyond the limited scope of tort

---

11 Report of the Minister of Reconstruction: Workmen's Compensation, Cmd 6551 (1944) para 314; and see the Beveridge Report, paras 88–92.

12 See generally, Charles D. Drake and Frank B. Wright *Law of Health and Safety at Work: The New Approach* (London, 1983).

remedies such as nuisance and the rule in *Rylands v Fletcher*.[13] We now have statutory authorities to control water pollution, and local authorities have extensive powers to prevent atmospheric pollution and to abate noise, under the Control of Pollution Act 1974 and other legislation. Licensing systems are widely used as a means of control, for example to prevent nuclear pollution,[14] and to control the disposal of waste.[15]

In the sphere of trade and business, as well, the law of tort has been largely by-passed. The negligence action against manufacturers of defective products can hardly match the powers of the Director of Fair Trading, and the powers of inspectors to enforce the Trade Descriptions Act are a more effective lever against certain misleading statements than actions in tort or contract. The common law rules against combinations proved to be woefully inadequate and have been overtaken by the investigations of the Monopolies and Mergers Commission and the procedures of the Restrictive Practices Court. The tort of passing-off is of less significance since a register of trade marks was created. The general picture is one of regulation by governmental agencies supplementing or even supplanting the spasmodic action of the law of tort, on the principle that prevention is better than punishment, control better than compensation.

---

13 See generally on the rationale for government intervention in this field, Genevra Richardson with Anthony Ogus and Paul Burrows *Policing Pollution* (Oxford, 1982); and for the social history, John P. S. McLaren in (1983) 3 Oxf J Leg Stud 155.

14 Nuclear Installations Acts 1965 and 1969 as amended.

15 Control of Pollution Act 1974, Part I. Local authorities and others may also claim statutory compensation, eg for oil pollution under the terms of statutory instruments implementing the International Convention on Civil Liability for Oil Pollution Damage.

RESIDUAL ROLE OF THE LAW OF TORT

It must be said, however, that regulatory agencies themselves suffer from a number of weaknesses. They tend to concentrate on a few serious accidents rather than on the daily risks of injury;[16] they are nearly always inadequately funded; they tend to become enmeshed in bureaucratic procedures which are slow and cumbersome; not infrequently they fail to use their powers in respect of known risks;[17] and the sanctions imposed by the criminal courts are feeble.

An action in tort sometimes serves the valuable function of applying pressure on those in power to remedy a wrong. A recent example is the actions brought on behalf of the victims of the drug thalidomide. These actions dramatically brought to light the difficulties of proving negligence against the manufacturers of the drug and the (then) disputed question whether a person could sue for damage done to him before his birth.[18] *The Sunday Times* took a keen interest, and public pressure was aroused, so that the manufacturers – who had settled the claims of 62 victims for about £1m in 1968 – were eventually compelled to make payments totalling over £20m for 410 children. The legal difficulties raised led the Lord Chancellor to ask the Law Commission to consider the question of ante-natal injuries and their proposals culminated in the Congenital Disabilities (Civil Liability) Act 1976. Attention was focused on the plight of other children with congenital disabilities and, in addition to substantial subventions of taxpayer's money, a

---

16 See K. Carson *The Other Price of Britain's Oil* (Edinburgh, 1982) especially Chaps 2 and 3.

17 For a detailed catalogue of deficiencies, see Abel in (1982) 42 Maryland LR at 699–701; see too Calabresi *A Common Law for the Age of Statutes* (1982) p 47.

18 The background and legal issues are discussed by Harvey Teff and Colin Munro *Thalidomide: the Legal Aftermath* (London, 1977).

Minister for the Disabled was appointed in 1974 and the regulations governing the production and advertising of drugs were tightened.[19] It is by no means certain that the same results would have occurred without a tort action to highlight the legal problems. Another example is the litigation brought against the Central Asbestos Co Ltd by employees who had contracted the painful and fatal disease of asbestosis while working in the company's premises between 1953 and 1967. Despite grave breaches of the Asbestos Regulations the factories' inspectors did little to enforce the law.[20] After surmounting many legal obstacles the employees recovered damages, and, through their actions, in the words of the Robens report, 'stimulated public concern about the insidious and potentially deadly nature of the long-terms risks to which certain groups of workers may be exposed.'[1]

Relatively few tort actions are capable of achieving this kind of publicity, and they are an expensive and indirect way of putting pressure on public authorities. Alternatives can sometimes be found through the development of a combination of private and public enforcement of legislative standards in certain areas. Examples are the Sex Discrimination Act 1975 and the Race Relations Act 1976. These give a right of action to individuals in respect of the statutory torts

---

19 Concern over the issue was also one of the factors leading to the government's decision to set up the Pearson Commission. An incidental result of the litigation was a change in the law of contempt of court following *The Sunday Times*'s successful action in the European Court of Human Rights against the injunction prohibiting publication of an article on the subject during the protracted civil proceedings.

20 See Hepple and Matthews, Chap 1, for a more detailed account.

1 Report on Safety and Health at Work, Cmnd 5034 (1972), para 18. A. M. Linden *Canadian Tort Law* (Toronto, 1977) p 20 and (1973) 51 Can BR 155, refers to the propaganda value of tort actions as the 'ombudsman' function of tort.

of sex discrimination and racial discrimination[2] and also allow the Commission for Racial Equality and the Equal Opportunities Commission to assist and represent complainants in appropriate cases, and itself to bring certain proceedings. This combination of the right of individual access to the courts with strategic functions assigned to a Commission responsible for enforcing the law in the public interest is an ambitious attempt to combine the virtues of tort and administrative law. The extension of public law remedies (such as mandamus) to enable individuals to compel public authorities to carry out their duties is another way in which a function imperfectly fulfilled by tort in the past could be given a new dimension.[3]

Developments along these lines will reduce the importance of the law of tort and will in part replace it. But it is likely that the law of tort will retain residual importance for a long time to come. There is no likelihood of intentional torts to the person being affected: particularly battery, wrongful interference and false imprisonment. A civil action for assault and battery at present provides a far better remedy than a criminal prosecution for assault, because the police are slow to interfere where serious injury is not caused, and magistrates also take a lenient view, whereas a civil action can give the complainant substantial, even exemplary, damages.[4] These torts to the person also serve the important public function of helping to control police powers, because the enforcement of the civil law is in no way in the hands of the police. In the field of interference with property, English

---

2 The proceedings in the county court 'may be made . . . in like manner as any other claim in tort' (Sex Discrimination Act 1975, s 66(1); Race Relations Act 1976, s 57(1)) and the damages may include compensation for injury to feelings (ibid, s 66(4) and s 57(4) respectively). In the employment field proceedings are brought in the industrial tribunals.

3 Unfortunately, it has to be said that the law has moved in the opposite direction: see above Chap 1, pp 9–10.

4 See Chap 3, p 75, n 7.

law uses the tort of trespass to test questions of disputed possession and the tort of conversion to protect the possessor of goods against their misappropriation. The tort of negligence is likely to continue to be utilised in cases of damage to property, although the practice of insuring one's own property is widespread.[5] Again, the existence of administrative powers for the suppression of nuisances does not always mean that those powers will be effectively used, and the ability of the aggrieved citizen to bring proceedings himself is a valuable recourse. An example is the celebrated success of an anglers' society in gaining an injunction against manufacturers to cease polluting the River Derwent.[6]

Nor is there any reason to see the demise of tort as a regulator of economic activity, for example in giving a remedy for negligent statements causing loss. There are grounds to believe that the blurring of the lines between contract and tort in situations where one person acts in reliance upon the words or conduct of another will continue and that this will accompany an increased willingness of the courts to extend the categories of wrongful harm.[7] The economic torts (such as inducing breach of contract and interference with business by unlawful means) have assumed increasing importance in the field of industrial conflict. Interests in reputation are protected by the flourishing tort of defamation, and Parliament seems to be moving slowly towards the creation of new statutory torts to protect privacy.[8]

---

5 The case for abolishing the tort action for damage to motor vehicles is made out by Atiyah *Accidents, Compensation and the Law* (3rd edn) pp 627–8.

6 *Pride of Derby and Derbyshire Angling Association Ltd v British Celanese Ltd* [1953] Ch 149, [1953] 1 All ER 179.

7 See in particular *Junior Books Ltd v Veitchi Co Ltd* [1983] 1 AC 520, [1982] 3 All ER 201, and above, Chap 4, p 108. The current lively debate about how the law of obligations should be divided up is reflected in the literature referred to in Chap 1, p 18, n 1.

8 Eg Data Protection Bill 1984 (compensation for damage suffered as result of loss, destruction or disclosure of personal data).

So, while we may see important advantages in superseding much of the law of tort, which may totally eliminate the tort action in accident cases, this will not represent the end of a body of law with a long tradition.

Appendix. Further reading

GENERAL TEXTBOOKS

It is nearly always advisable to consult more than one of the standard texts, and it is essential to use the most up-to-date edition. The established texts are J. G. Fleming *The Law of Torts* (while taking Australia as its point of departure this book deals with other common law jurisdictions, especially England, and has the merit of concentrating on the 'philosophy' of tort law); *Salmond and Heuston on the Law of Torts*, currently edited by R. F. V. Heuston and R. S. Chambers; Harry Street *The Law of Torts*; and *Winfield and Jolowicz on Tort*, currently edited by W. V. H. Rogers. P. S. Atiyah *Accidents, Compensation and the Law*, is a critical survey of the law relating to compensation for personal injuries and death, paying particular attention to the social, economic and political context.

CASEBOOKS

Tony Weir *Casebook on Tort*, contains not only a selection of cases and statutes but also a series of fascinating notes and searching questions. B. A. Hepple and M. H. Matthews *Tort: Cases and Materials*, contains cases, statutes and contextual materials such as specimen insurance policies, committee reports and guides to other compensation systems.

SPECIALIST BOOKS

Among those useful on particular topics are P. S. Atiyah *Vicarious Liability in the Law of Torts*; R. A. Buckley *The Law of Nuisance*; A. M. Dugdale and F. Stanton *Professional Negligence*; J. D. Heydon *Economic Torts*; F. H. Lawson *Remedies of English Law*; M. A. Millner *Negligence in Modern Law*; John Munkman *Employer's Liability at Common Law*, and the same author's *Damages for Personal Injuries and Death*; P. M. North *Occupiers' Liability*, and the same author's *Modern Law of Animals*; A. I. Ogus *The Law of Damages*; Anthony Speaight and Gregory Stone *The Law of Defective Premises*; Harry Street *Principles of the Law of Damages*; Glanville Williams *Joint Torts and Contributory Negligence*, and the same author's *Liability for Animals*.

PRACTITIONERS' GENERAL REFERENCE WORKS

Lawyers dealing with practical problems are served by Clerk and Lindsell's *Law of Torts*, by specialist editors; *McGregor on Damages* (formerly Mayne and McGregor); Kemp and Kemp *The Quantum of Damages; Charlesworth on Negligence* currently edited by R. A. Percy; and *Gatley on Libel and Slander*, currently edited by Philip Lewis.

COMPARATIVE

The student is introduced to the general conceptions of civil responsibility in Continental legal systems by F. H. Lawson and B. S. Markisenis *Tortious Liability for Unintentional Harm in the Common Law and the Civil Law* vol 1, text, and vol 2, materials. An invaluable source is Vol XI (Torts) of the *International Encyclopedia of Comparative Law* (ed A. Tunc), and, for readers of French, the general survey by André Tunc *La Responsabilité Civile*.

Australia. In addition to Fleming's textbook (above), there is an excellent casebook by H. Luntz, A. D. Hambly and R. Hayes *Torts: Cases and Commentary*. H. Luntz *Assessment of Damages for Personal Injury and Death*, is also useful.

Canada. A. M. Linden *Canadian Tort Law*, and K. D. Cooper-Stephenson and I. B. Saunders *Personal Injury Damages in Canada*, have interesting comparative insights.

New Zealand. A number of studies of the New Zealand Accident Compensation Scheme are referred to in footnotes to Chap 7.

United States. In addition to the works referred to in footnotes to Chap 7, attention is drawn to: Harper and James *Law of Torts* (2 vols); J. O'Connell *The Lawsuit Lottery: Injuries, Insurance and Injustice*, and the same author's *Ending Insult to Injury*; J. O'Connell and R. C. Henderson *Tort Law, No Fault and Beyond* (teaching materials on compensation for accidents and ailments in modern society); and W. L. Prosser's *Handbook of the Law of Torts*.

PERIODICAL LITERATURE

Reference is made in the footnotes to a number of periodical articles, and other references will be found in the books referred to. One can keep up to date through *Current Law*, the *Index to Legal Periodicals*, and the *Index to Foreign Legal Periodicals*, available in any good law library.

Index

Accidents
  allocation of costs, 203–204
  fatal. *See* FATAL ACCIDENTS
  inevitable, 93–94
  redistributing costs of, 209–214
Act
  God, of, 131
  stranger, of, 118, 131
  voluntary, 91
  See also INTENTION, NEGLIGENCE,
    OMISSION
Action, forms of
  abolition of, 32–38, 52, 54
  case, upon the, 40, 45–49, 60 *et seq.*,
    95
  influence on legal categories of,
    38–39
  limitation of, 19–20
  nominal damages and, 57–66
  old rules, 31–32
  See also TRESPASS
Aircraft
  insurance of, 149
Anglo-Saxon Law, 182
Animals
  dogs, 12–13, 130
  extra-judicial remedies, 11–13
  insurance, 151
  strict liability for, 93, 129, 135
Assault
  tort of, 4, 13, 38, 49–50, 74, 218

Australia
  Compensation and Rehabilitation,
    Committee of Inquiry into,
    192–193
  National Compensation Bill, 193

Bereavement
  damages for, 85, 87

Care. *See* DUTY OF CARE
Carriage, 14
Causation, 180, 181, 182, 207
Compensation
  criminal injuries, for, 4–6
  damages as, 7, 28
  double, 187
  ethical, 82–85
  exemplary damages and, 73–78
  future losses, for, 79
  personal injury, 78–85
  statutory, 24–26
  theory of, 28, 30, 135–142, 191 *et seq.*
  See also DAMAGES, JUSTICE, PERSONAL
    INJURY, SOCIAL SECURITY
Confidence
  breach of, 21–22
Conspiracy
  tort of, 60, 72
Contract
  damages for breach of, 60

225

Contract—*cont.*
  excluding liability, 141
  inducement of breach of, 60, 72, 92
  interference with, 72
  limitation of actions, 19–20
  privity of, 154
  quasi-contract. *See* QUASI CONTRACT
  tort compared with, 13–20, 27–30, 46
Contributory negligence, 50, 142
Conversion
  tort of, 2, 11, 24, 25–26, 46, 60, 93
  See also DETINUE
Crime
  aim of law, 136–137
  insurance and, 146
  legislation, 116–123
  tort, overlap with, 2–6, 77
Criminal injuries compensation
  orders, 6
  scheme, 5–6

Damage
  general, 65–66, 66–68, 88, 95
  glossary, 88
  meaning, 56, 88
  non-pecuniary, 79, 85, 88
  pecuniary, 79 *et seq.*, 88
  special, 36–37, 66–68, 88
Damages
  aggravated, 75–76, 88
  bereavement, for, 85, 87
  compensation, as, 7, 28
  compensatory, 15
  contemptuous, 58–59, 88
  contract or tort, in, 15–19
  death, in case of, 86–88
  defamation, 61, 74
  exemplary, 73–78
  expectation interest in, 15, 27, 89
  glossary, 88–89
  injunction, in lieu of, 21, 70–73
  lump sum award, 79–80, 89, 170, 175
  mental shock, for, 41–42

Damages—*cont.*
  nominal, 57–66, 67*n*, 73, 88
  periodical payments, 81–82
  restitutionary, 15
  social security benefits, overlap with, 186–190
  substantial, 88
  See also PERSONAL INJURY
Death. *See* FATAL ACCIDENTS
Deceit
  tort of, 46, 60, 76, 92
Declaration
  action for, 58
  status, of, 29–30
Defamation
  damages, 61, 74, 78
  insurance, 145*n*, 152, 163
  libel, 30, 58–59, 78
  negligent, 95
  slander, 78
Defence
  "private", 12
  See also CONTRIBUTORY NEGLIGENCE
Deterrence
  insurance, effect of, 143–144, 168–170
  market, 204–206
  statutory torts as, 121–122
  theory of, 29, 138–142
  vicarious liability and, 134
Detinue
  tort of, 46
  See also CONVERSION
Discrimination
  racial, 65–66, 218
  sex, 218
Distress damage feasant, 11, 129
Dogs, 12–13, 130
Duty of care
  economic loss, 107–111
  generally, 96–101, 124–127, 164
  nervous shock, 104–107
  principle and policy, 101–111
  sufficient relationship of proximity or neighbourhood, 102–103

Employer's liability
common employment, 173
exclusion of, 141n
insurance, 144, 149, 150, 153,
155–156, 162–163, 164, 166n
statutory duties, 116–123
workmen's compensation scheme,
174
See also VICARIOUS LIABILITY
Environment
protection of, 214
Equitable wrongs
remedies for, 7, 8
tort compared with, 20–22, 23

False imprisonment
tort of, 38, 46–48, 58, 74
Fatal accidents
compensation for, 86–88
survival of causes of action, 141–142
tort, effect on claims in, 86–88
Fault
burden of proof of, 53–55, 137
duty of care. *See* DUTY OF CARE
evaluation of principle, 135–142,
168–170
forms of, 91–94
generally, 90–91
principle and policy, 101–111
theory of, 39, 79, 90 *et seq.*, 144–145
trespass. *See* TRESPASS
See also NEGLIGENCE, INTENTION,
STRICT LIABILITY
Fire
insurance, 147, 165
Forms of action. *See* ACTION, FORMS
OF

Habeus corpus
writ of, 8
Home
insurance, 149, 151, 165

Industrial injuries
benefits, 180–183

Injunction
damages inadequate, if, 69
damages in lieu of, 21,70
general, 8, 21, 68–73
interlocutory, 68, 72
labour, 72–73
mandatory, 68
perpetual, 68
prohibitory, 68
quia timet, 69, 70, 113n
relator action for, 8–9
types of, 68
Injuria
damnum sine, 56
damno, sine, 56, 64
Injury. *See* PERSONAL INJURY
Innkeeper
duty of, 14, 65–66
Insurance
actions, effect upon, 166–168
administration of, 81
aircraft, 149
animals, against liability for, 151
cancellation of, 148, 154, 155–156,
157, 159n
compulsory, 152–154, 157–163, 176
crime and, 146
defamation, against, 145n, 152, 163
employers' liability, 144, 149, 150,
153, 155–156, 162–163, 164,
166n
failure to obtain, 157–158
fire, 147, 165
home, 149, 151, 165
insolvency, effect on, 156–157, 167
justification for, 143–145, 168–170
"knock-for-knock" agreements,
143n, 168
liability,
limits on 149–150
types of, 150–152
libel, 145n, 152
motor vehicle, 144, 146, 148,
152–163
no-claim bonus, 143, 168
no-fault, 193–194

Insurance—*cont.*
nuclear incidents, 150, 151
overlapping, 152
policyholders' protection, 157
premiums, 144, 169, 176
products, 150, 151
professional indemnity, 149
public liability, 150–151
settlements, 138, 167–168
solicitor, of, 152–153, 164
subrogation, 166
third party rights in, 148, 154–157,
    159*n*, 160–161
tort, effect on, 142, 152–154,
    163–165
tort, intentional, exception for,
    145–148, 160
vicarious liability, 164–165
See also MOTOR INSURERS' BUREAU
Intention
insurance, none allowed, 145–148
meaning, 91–94, 140
nuisance, in, 124*n*
trespass, in, 40, 49–53
Interests
protected in tort, 38–39
Intimidation
tort of, 72

Joinder
actions, of, 37
Justice
corrective and distributive, 197–203
theory of, 90, 133, 136–137, 145,
    168–170

Legal aid and advice
availability of, 138
Libel
generally, 30, 58–59, 78
insurance, 145*n*, 152
Limitation of actions, 19–20, 40, 64
Lump-sum awards, 79–80, 89, 170,
    175

Malicious prosecution
tort of, 46–47, 60, 92
Mandamus
order of, 8
Motor Insurers' Bureau, 155,
    158–163
See also INSURANCE

Negligence
conflict of values, as, 111–113
contributory, 142, 173
duty of care, 96–101
insurance, effect upon, 163–165
limitation period, 40
meaning, 92–94, 140
operation of, 135–142
reasonable person in, 114–115
statutory duties compared with,
    116–123
tort, as independent, 39, 46, 48–49,
    49–53, 95–96
See further COMPENSATION, DAMAGES,
    FAULT, INSURANCE
Nervous shock
duty of care, 104–107
intentional infliction of, 41–42
New Zealand
accident compensation in, 191–192
social security, 172
Nuisance
abatement of, 10–11, 60
damages for, 60
general, 38, 39, 46
injunction for, 71–72
intentional, 124*n*
limitation period, 40
negligent, 113, 123–127
special sensitivity in, 113

Omissions
liability for, 14, 96

Penalty
action for, 9
Personal injury
amenity, loss of, 83–84

Personal injury—*cont.*
asbestosis, 217
burden of proof in action for, 54, 138
damages for, in general, 78–85
earnings loss, 79, 80
industrial injuries, 180–183
injury, meaning, 56
life, loss of expectation of, 82
pneumoconiosis, 184–185
strict liability for, 132
thalidomide, 149*n*, 184, 216–217
vaccine damage, 184
See also DAMAGES, INSURANCE, SOCIAL SECURITY
Pleadings
forms of action, 39–42
statement of claim, 35–37, 67
writ, 33–35
Pollution
control of, 214
Public law
remedies, 9–10
Punishment. *See* DETERRENCE

Quasi-contract
statutory claims compared with, 25–26
tort compared with, 22–24, 28

Racial discrimination, 65–66, 218
Reasonableness. *See* NEGLIGENCE
Recklessness
meaning, 92
Regulation
examples of, 214–215
Remedies
equitable, 7, 8, 20–22
extra-judicial, 10–13, 26, 128–129, 141
public law, 9–10
See also DAMAGES, EQUITABLE WRONGS, INJUNCTION
Res ipsa loquitur, 54*n*, 115, 123
Restitution. *See* QUASI-CONTRACT

Risk
reciprocity of, 200
theory of, 164
Road traffic
insurance, 144, 146, 148, 152–163
no-fault insurance for, 193–194
strict liability, 51, 135
vicarious liability, 134*n*, 165
See also NEGLIGENCE, INSURANCE, MOTOR INSURERS' BUREAU
Rylands v Fletcher
liability under, 46, 51, 93, 128 *et seq.*, 135, 199

Scots law, 30
Sex discrimination, 218
Slander, 78
Social insurance. *See* SOCIAL SECURITY
Social security
contributions, 179–180
damages, as supplement to, 81
death benefit, 176
developments since Beveridge, 177–180
disability, 183–186
disablement benefit, 182
earnings-related benefits, 178–179
financing of benefits, 179
generally, 171–172
growth of, 172–177
industrial injuries, 180–183
invalidity benefit, 183
meaning, 172
means-tested benefits, 177–178
normal needs, 177, 178
sickness and disability, 183–186
sickness benefit, 182
statutory sick pay, 181–182, 185–186
subsistence benefits, 178
theory of, 134–135
tort damages, overlap with, 186–190
Social welfare, 206–209
Solicitor
insurance, 152–153, 164

Specific restitution, 8
Statute
    action for breach of, 116–123,
        157–158, 165
    compensation, claim for, 20–22
    interpretation of, 116–123
Statutory compensation
    claims for, 24–26
Strict liability
    evaluation, 135
    hazards, for, 127–132
    meaning, 93
    nuisance, in, 123–127
    statute, under, 116–123
    theory of, 198 *et seq.*
    trespass, in, 52
    See also VICARIOUS LIABILITY

Tort
    aims of, 27–30
    classification of, 31, 38–39
    contract, compared with, 13–20
    crime, compared with, 2–6
    economic efficiency, 203–206
    equitable wrongs, compared with,
        20–22
    limitation of actions, 19–20
    meaning, 1–2
    public law remedies distinguished
        from actions in, 9–10
    quasi-contract, compared with,
        22–24
    reform of 191 *et seq.*
    regulatory approach, 214–215
    residual role of, 216–220
    restitution compared with, 22–24
    scope and function, 1 *et seq.*
    statutory compensation, compared
        with, 24–26
    summary of definition of, 27
    waiver of, 24

Trade disputes
    injunctions in, 72–73
Treason
    as a tort, 3*n*
Trespass
    action for, 32, 37, 39, 41, 42–44
    actionable *per se*, 57–58
    burden of proof, 53–55
    common, 45
    continuing, 44, 57
    damage, 50
    de minimis rule, 59
    fault, 49–53
    inevitable accident, 50
    intention in, 40, 49–53
    land, to, 43
    special, 45
    strict liability, 52
    See also ACTION, FORMS OF,
        PERSONAL INJURY
Trust. *See* EQUITABLE WRONGS

United States
    Massachusetts, compulsory insur-
        ance in, 153
    no-fault insurance, 81, 193–194

Vicarious liability
    deterrence theory, 134
    insurance, 164–165
    justification for, 133–135
    meaning, 132–133
    road traffic, 134*n*, 165
Volenti non fit injuria, 173
Vote
    right to, 61,62

Wilfulness. *See* INTENTION